Accolades

"Linda Maloney's book is an uplifting, inspiring, and sometimes sobe[...]y women who fly and raise children. I highly recommend this book for parents, teachers, you[...] aviation and military history. It is a personal, as well as historical, account of women aviato[...] military missions.

Military Fly Moms would have been a wonderful read for me as a teen. It certainly is now. More young women need to understand that flying opportunities are open to them and that 'Yes, you can be a mom and have a challenging and rewarding job!' Young women can pursue the dream of flying without excluding the possibility of having children someday. My career took me to the stars—four times—and three of these flights were as a mom!"

—*Eileen Collins, Colonel, U.S. Air Force, Retired;*
former NASA astronaut and first female commander of the Space Shuttle

"*Military Fly Moms* is a book that's long overdue. It does a wonderful job of showing a side of America's women military aviators that has always existed but is seldom discussed or seen, particularly in such an honest and beautiful light. This is a book that will spark conversations, tears, and laughter—a must-have! There's a place for this book on many tables."

—*Claudia McKnight, Commander, U.S. Coast Guard, Retired;*
President, Women Military Aviators

"In *Military Fly Moms*, Linda Maloney captures in magnificent fashion the personal and professional commitment of many of the women who fly for our armed forces. Their contributions to our national security are significant; their sacrifices make for a great read."

—*Timothy J. Keating, Admiral, U.S. Navy, Retired*

"How do you capture the essence of these amazing women who straddle lives in two fundamentally different worlds: motherhood and military flying? *Military Fly Moms* not only gives a taste of the adventure, accomplishments, and surprises these female pilots face in their professional lives, but also a rare glimpse into how they each balance their personal dreams, triumphs, and sacrifices while blazing paths in a complex world that was not initially designed for them. A must-read for any woman daring to pursue the path less traveled."

—*Susan Healy Feland, founder and president of AcademyWomen*

"*Military Fly Moms* is an awe-inspiring exploration into the lives of ground-breaking women military aviators whose most challenging and rewarding job outside the cockpit is motherhood. Representing all five branches of our armed services, these flyers stood proudly on the shoulders of the Women Airforce Service Pilots of World War II. Many of them pioneers in their own right, these airwomen discuss their love of flying and proudly serving their country, while also tackling the challenges of raising children in a military family. Linda Maloney has generously given a voice to her fellow *military fly moms*, who are role models, each and every one."

—*Amy Goodpaster Strebe, author of* Flying for Her Country:
The American and Soviet Women Military Pilots of World War II

"There are pioneers whose stories must be told. Linda Maloney has done us a great service by telling the stories of military flying moms. How far they've come—from being mistaken for stewardesses in their uniforms to some of their sons and daughters thinking that only women can fly airplanes! This truly inspiring book is a must—especially for youngsters making decisions about their own boundaries."

—Carol A. Mutter, Lieutenant General,
U.S. Marine Corps, Retired

"*Military Fly Moms* is a must-read for all aviation enthusiasts, males and females alike! This is a captivating behind-the-scenes look at the journey of the often undervalued but nonetheless vital role of women past and present in military aviation, specifically those who also chose to be mothers while doing so.

This collection of aviators is extraordinary. Follow those who received little encouragement, encountered many barriers, and yet still successfully balanced flying and family. A magnificent tribute!"

—Carey Dunai Lohrenz, Lieutenant,
U.S. Navy; first female F-14A combat pilot

"Linda has compiled a powerful visual representation of the contributions that women have made in military aviation while still remaining true to themselves as moms. As a founder of an organization to use women in aviation as role models to young girls, I believe that Linda's book provides a resource to encourage their interest and to let them know that having an aviation career and having a family are not mutually exclusive. Thank you, Linda, for highlighting these women and their accomplishments."

—Lynda Meeks, founder and
executive director of Girls With Wings, Inc.

"Of all the advancements made in the 20th century, nothing was more important to the viability of women making a career in the U.S. armed forces than the ability to combine military service with parenthood—just as men did. This was the result of hard-fought policy and statutory battles in the courts, Congress, and the Pentagon. By 1976, all the military departments revised their policies so that pregnant women, including aviators, were no longer automatically discharged. Retired Naval Flight Officer Linda Maloney, one of the first women to serve in combat duty as part of a carrier air wing, has collected the personal stories of many female military aviators who have served on the frontlines as well as the home front. Their service narratives are an important contribution to our national defense, their children, and to the corpus of American military social history."

—Rosemary B. Mariner, Captain, U.S. Navy, Retired;
first female commanding officer of a Navy squadron

"Not only are the descriptions of the difficulties of raising a family while on active duty extremely interesting, but [so are] the many experiences, sometimes dangerous, these military women faced. Their children's reactions all make for a worthwhile read."

—Bernice "Bee" Falk Haydu, WASP
(Women Airforce Service Pilot) in World War II; PT-17 pilot

"This inspirational, educational book is filled with fascinating, factual stories about some of America's most outstanding and courageous women military aviators. I'm proud of each of them."

—Deanie Bishop Parrish, WASP
(Women Airforce Service Pilot) in World War II; B-26 pilot

Military Fly Moms

Sharing Memories, Building Legacies, Inspiring Hope

Compiled and Edited by

LINDA MALONEY

Tannenbaum Publishing Company,
Dowell, Maryland

Published by
Tannenbaum Publishing Company
P.O. Box 117
Dowell, Maryland
20629

First Printing, 2012

Copyright © 2011 by Linda Maloney
All rights reserved

LCCN: 2011932567

ISBN 13: 9780978736972
ISBN 10: 0978736974

Printed and bound in the United States of America

Photographs within were provided by the individual woman profiled in the book, except where attributed to a different photographer.

To order more copies, visit www.tannenbaumpublishing.com or www.lindaheidmaloney.com.

Table of Contents

Barb Rainey with her husband and daughters

Dedication

To the memory of Lieutenant Commander Barbara Allen Rainey,
fellow mom and aviator, and to the family who loves and misses her.

THE FIRST WOMAN TO COMPLETE NAVY FLIGHT TRAINING AND BE DESIGNATED A NAVAL AVIATOR ON FEBRUARY 22, 1974, WAS LIEUTENANT JUNIOR GRADE BARBARA ALLEN. A GRADUATE OF THE NAVY OFFICER CANDIDATE SCHOOL IN NEWPORT, RHODE ISLAND, SHE WAS COMMISSIONED IN DECEMBER 1970. SHE FOLLOWED IN THE footsteps of her Marine Corps aviator brother, Bill Allen, by applying for U.S. Naval Flight Training School.

Shortly after earning her wings, she married fellow aviator John Rainey, and they had their first child, Cynthia, four years later. Barb decided to leave active duty in 1977, but remained active in the Navy Reserve flying the C–118 (DC–6) at Naval Air Station (NAS) Dallas, Texas. After her second daughter, Katie, was born, she returned to active duty in 1981 as a flight instructor, due to a shortage of military pilots.

Assigned to one of the Navy's training squadrons at NAS Whiting Field, Florida, she instructed student pilots in the T–34C *Mentor*. Nine months later, on July 13, 1982, Barb was killed in an aircraft accident, along with a student pilot, during a training flight.

Tragically, she left her husband, John, and two young daughters behind. Buried in Arlington National Cemetery, Barb's headstone is inscribed:

"First woman Naval aviator.
Loving wife and mother."

John Rainey wrote his daughters a letter early in the morning following Barb's accident:

0400 14 July 1982
Dear Cynthia and Katie,

I am writing this to you this morning to tell you a few things about your mother because, in future years, you might not be able to remember her too clearly. Your mother was a super lady. She was the most determined, hardest working person I have ever met. She would set a goal for herself and push and persevere until she accomplished it. Your mom was a great athlete. She excelled in sports in high school and college. Cynthia, you once asked "but how are you as a grownup?" about your mom's athletic prowess. She was good enough as a grownup to beat your dad at golf every time we played. Most importantly, your mom was the kindest, most thoughtful, most loving person we will ever know. Your mom was a famous person. She was the first woman designated by the Navy as a naval aviator. She was justifiably proud of that accomplishment. But she loved all of us so much that she gave up all of the opportunities commensurate with that fame to be Mrs. John C. Rainey and the mother of Cynthia and Katie Rainey. Your mom was as proud, no, more proud, of those last two titles as any she ever achieved.

The Lord took your mom from us yesterday because, as you used to tell us, Cynthia, she had a clean and pure heart. Katie, you won't remember much about your mother, but when you get older, I want both of you to never forget this—your mom was a super lady, a famous lady, and she loved all of us very, very much.

Military Fly Moms

Acknowledgements

THANK YOU TO MY HUSBAND, DAN, WHO MOTIVATED ME TO TELL MY STORY, WHICH LED TO SHARING A BIGGER story. He has been my biggest encourager and sounding board over the years, throughout this amazing journey.

To my two precious, sweet boys—Ethan and Aron. I hope to pass down one of the most important legacies in life—the love of a mom. Being a mom some days is the hardest thing I've done in life but there is nothing else that I'd rather be doing.

To my gem of a stepdaughter, Courtney; her husband, Bill; and my wonderful granddaughters, Erin and Abby. They all have taught me the true meaning of family!

To my parents who instilled a belief in me that I could achieve anything. I am grateful for their constant encouragement and always knowing they were proud of my military service.

To all the women of *Military Fly Moms*, an amazing group of sister aviators and moms. This book could not have been written without their willingness to tell their stories, and share their experiences and legacies. I am honored they trusted me, as one of their own, to share a part of their lives to encourage and inspire others.

To my publisher (and friend), Connie Reeves, Tannenbaum Publishing Company (www.tannenbaumpublishing.com), for her willingness to publish *Military Fly Moms*. Her support, friendship, and mentorship over the years has been a wonderful gift.

To the Rainey family for their generous spirit in sharing their personal stories and photographs about Barb Rainey. I am very honored to dedicate this book to Barb and her family.

To my BFFs who have encouraged me over the years to keep going on this project and have been as excited as I have been to get *Military Fly Moms* into print...especially to Alisa (Albers), Nancy (Morris), Karen (Swanson), Robin (Girard), and Jen (Nothelfer).

To Alisa Albers, Timeless Treasures Photography (www.timelesstreasuresphotos.com), for her usual incredible Maloney family photos for the book and website!

To Tammy Barley (www.tammybarley.com), for her editing expertise. I appreciate her insight and assistance from the beginning days of this project.

To Peg Martin (http://studiopegdesign.com) for the website design of www.lindaheidmaloney.com, I couldn't have done it without her expertise...she does amazing work!

To Val Kester for assisting me along the way with her thorough research.

To Douglas Tschetter, Riven Design (rivendesign.com), for an amazing job on photoshopping hundreds of photographs.

To the military mentors, both men and women, who took an interest in my career and provided invaluable guidance and counsel. Special thank you to ACCS Dixon, my first chief in the Navy when I was a young 18-year-old enlisted air traffic controller, for encouraging me to apply for the BOOST officer program; to Col. Jane Scott, USMC, Ret., my University of Idaho NROTC commanding officer, who told me not to give up when I didn't initially receive an aviation billet; and also to CAPT Don Foulk, USN, Ret.; CAPT James Powell, USN, Ret.; and CAPT Rosemary Mariner, USN, Ret.

—Linda Maloney

Foreword

ON MARCH 10, 2010, THE WOMEN WHO SERVED IN WORLD WAR II AS WOMEN AIRFORCE SERVICE PILOTS (WASP) WERE HONORED WITH THE Congressional Gold Medal, an award equivalent to the Presidential Medal of Freedom. This great honor was long overdue for these brave and honorable women. Thanks to these pioneers and the ground they plowed ahead of me, I was given the opportunity to serve our country and fly for the military. Along with Barbara Allen Rainey, I also was a member of the first class of Navy women trained to fly. Through the years, I've met and shared experiences with many of the WASP, hearing firsthand stories about their flying experiences and the special bonds they formed with the other World War II–era pilots. Throughout my thirty-year career, I was grateful for their service and mentorship, and I in return have mentored many young women coming up through the aviation ranks.

Although it was many years ago, I still remember the officer who informed me that I was accepted for Navy pilot training. She told me I would be a Navy pioneer. Rather than be jealous of an opportunity that she never had, she was very proud of me. She also cautioned me to tread lightly, as the Navy does not often reward pioneers. Wise advice it was! I survived those first few years as a pilot heeding those words. I kept my head down and did not focus on the publicity that constantly surrounded the first women Navy pilots, but rather on being the best pilot, Navy officer, and squadron mate that I could be.

I was also the first female military pilot to have a baby while on active duty. The Navy leadership wasn't quite sure how to handle this situation. My commanding officer assumed that I would leave the Navy, but I was determined that I could have my career and be a mom, too. Together,

the Navy and I plowed this new ground. I am grateful to a very enlightened flight surgeon who made a politically risky decision and allowed me to fly until I believed it was imprudent for my health and the baby's health. My husband and I managed to juggle the responsibilities of parenthood and the Navy, although at times it was downright hard. I look back at those times and wonder how we did it.

My daughters grew up with a mom who wore a flight suit to work every day and they thought that was perfectly normal. They got airplane rides on "Take Your Daughter to Work Day." They finally figured out that my career was nontraditional when they started writing and giving reports about their parents' jobs. I am proud that I was a role model to my girls and imbued in them the conviction that the sky is definitely not the limit!

After reading the inspirational stories in *Military Fly Moms*, it was clear to me that pursuing one's dream and being a mom can be a great combination. As I read through the stories, I laughed as well as cried, and identified with each of the women's struggles and triumphs. I am sure you will find them as inspirational as I did. It warms my heart that there is now a generation of children growing up believing there are no boundaries to what they can accomplish.

I salute Linda Maloney for undertaking this project, particularly while juggling being a mom to two young boys *and* holding down a job. Her book contains unforgettable stories of courageous military women who will serve as inspirations to all, while also capturing the legacy of military fly moms for future generations of women who will fly in our boots. Enjoy!

—CAPT Jane Skiles O'Dea, USN, Ret

Introduction: The Aviator-Moms' Legacy

ASSIGNED TO VAQ-33 IN 1989, I FLEW AS A NAVAL FLIGHT OFFICER IN THE BACK SEAT OF AN EA-7L AND HANDLED ALL THE RADIOS, WEAPONS, and communications equipment. Our squadron provided electronic countermeasures training for fleet combat aircraft and ships. The EA-7L provided real-time simulations of enemy radars and missiles. Of course, I was thrilled to be flying in a Navy squadron, but I wanted to fly in combat, not a support squadron. Unfortunately, the Women's Armed Forces Integration Act of 1948, which provided new opportunities for women to serve in the military, also included numerous restrictions, including a prohibition against women being assigned to aircraft engaged in combat missions and aboard most Navy ships, commonly known as the combat exclusion law.

A year after flying the EA-7L, I requested a transition to the two-seater EA-6A, a vintage combat A-6 *Intruder* aircraft, also utilized in an electronic training role with an expanded role for the naval flight officer. A few months after training in the EA-6A, I went on a weekend cross-country flight with a woman pilot in my squadron—Lieutenant Kara Hultgreen. A couple of hours after leaving Key West, we stopped for fuel at a North Carolina Marine Corps base. I climbed down the aircraft steps toward the Marine Corps ground crew, comprised of all men. Every one of them stared when I removed my helmet and my long hair tumbled out.

Because there were few women flying military aircraft at the time, I was accustomed to long stares and unusual questions. One man asked, "You don't fly this aircraft, do you?" I said, "No, but she does," motioning toward Kara as she climbed down her side of the aircraft and took off her helmet. We laughed about our "unmanned flight," went about our business of getting the jet refueled and serviced, and, shortly thereafter, climbed back in, waved goodbye to the ground crew, and continued on our flight.

For years, I attracted that same reaction and was frequently asked about all aspects of being a woman in the military and what it was like to fly. Not only did the 1986 movie *Top Gun* inspire a generation of young men to follow in the contrails of "Maverick" and "Goose," many young girls also imagined themselves dogfighting and soaring high above the clouds in supersonic aircraft.

In 1943, during World War II, the first group of young women pilots became pioneers, heroines, and role models as members of the Women Airforce Service Pilots, more commonly known as the WASP. These young women would serve their nation in time of war to replace manpower with womanpower so the men could serve in combat areas. These elite women proved themselves to be a vital part of American history as well as the history of women in military aviation. However, WASP were not considered military pilots until 1977, when Congress declared that they were indeed veterans of World War II.

No other women served as military pilots again until October 1972, when Secretary of the Navy John Warner announced that his service would open flight training to women. In November 1973, six Navy women started flight school and earned their gold wings the following year, becoming the first women naval aviators. The Army began training female helicopter pilots in 1974, and, in 1976, the Air Force admitted women to its pilot program.

However, the combat exclusion law forbade women to fly combat missions, and interpretations of the law varied among the different military services. Combat flying missions were usually regarded as those that could seek, engage, or destroy the enemy, or that exposed one to hostile fire. Some women flew combat aircraft but were assigned to support squadrons, while a few actually flew combat missions. During Operation *Desert Storm*, the first Gulf War, an Army helicopter pilot—Major Marie Therese Rossi—became the first American female military pilot killed while flying in a combat zone. (Marina Raskova, Soviet pilot, was killed in combat in 1943.)

Finally, after years of lobbying and testifying by women military aviators, the combat exclusion law was repealed. On April 29, 1993, Secretary of Defense Les Aspin ordered the military to drop restrictions that prevented women from flying combat missions. Chief of Naval Operations Admiral Frank B. Kelso II was the first to act, though women were still excluded from permanent assignment on aircraft carriers. By April 1994, more than sixty female Navy pilots received orders to combat squadrons, and, soon after, were assigned to combat ships, including aircraft carriers. A historic change occurred in the military, allowing women to serve in all combat aviation specialties and assignments, except special forces.

A year after the law's repeal, my longtime wish was finally granted. I was assigned to a fleet combat squadron as a naval flight officer in the EA-6B *Prowler*, a four-seater jammer jet, and subsequently deployed on the aircraft carrier USS *Abraham Lincoln*, which was heading to Iraq in April 1995. My good friend, Kara, from my previous squadron, had also been assigned to an operational combat squadron on the *Lincoln*, flying the F-14 *Tomcat*, along with several other women—many who were friends from my previous two squadrons. Before departing for the Persian Gulf, we spent several short detachments on the aircraft carrier, affectionately known as "the boat," becoming carrier-qualified and conducting training flights.

During an October 1994 detachment on the *Lincoln*, as the squadron duty officer for the day, I was in the ready room, coordinating the *Prowler* flight schedule, answering the phone, and documenting the squadron pilots' carrier qualifications. (Whenever an aircraft carrier prepares to deploy, the pilots must complete carrier landing qualifications (CQ), flying a series of passes (approaches) and landings on the boat. As the aircraft touches down on the deck, the pilot makes an arrested landing—the aircraft's tailhook located on the underside of the jet catches a wire, causing the aircraft to stop.)

Via the ready-room television, I could see all the aircraft conducting their approaches. When my aviator girlfriends (the term *aviator* means pilot, navigator, naval flight officer, weapon systems operator, and other persons who contribute to aircraft flight) approached the carrier in their F/A-18 *Hornets* and F-14 *Tomcats*, I paid particular attention; our excitement and pride at being assigned to combat squadrons remained extremely high. As I documented one carrier landing, I saw Kara approaching the *Lincoln* in her F-14. Within seconds, I knew something was dreadfully wrong.

Horrified, I watched her aircraft lose altitude and start rolling to the left. The landing signal officer screamed, "Power, power, power!" and then yelled for the crew to eject. Kara and her back-seater, the radar intercept officer (RIO), ejected.

I waited anxiously for the carrier's loudspeaker to announce that both aviators were safe. The call came that one of the carrier's helicopters had picked up the RIO, but Kara was missing.

I watched in shock, unable to believe what was happening, and half-expected to see the boat's helicopter land on the deck with Kara in tow. About two hours later, a few women aviators met in one of our staterooms, looking at each other in disbelief, fearing the worst. We kept hoping Kara would be found, until it was obvious she had not survived. Several weeks later, divers discovered her body on the ocean floor, still strapped in her ejection seat.

A few days after the accident, I gave the eulogy at Kara's memorial service on the *Lincoln*. For months, an umbrella of sadness clouded the exhilaration we women aviators had initially felt about our combat assignments. Now, years later, I think of Kara and chuckle at memories of her quick wit and competitive nature and wonder how her career would have progressed had she not died.

My career lasted for twenty years, until 2004, when I retired from military service. As I packed away my flight gear in the basement just a few months after having my first son, I thought about the legacy, as a mom who'd enjoyed a very unique career, that I would pass down to him. I dreamed of him one day proudly telling his friends, "My mom flew jets in the Navy, and she even ejected out of one over the Atlantic Ocean!" I didn't want my aviation experience to be a far-off memory, and I wanted him to have a piece of it even though he didn't experience it with me. I envisioned him piloting a make-believe airplane—aka a kitchen chair—wearing my helmet and one of my flight suits, asking me what it was like to fly low and fast through mountains or to tell him again what a "kick in the pants" it was to be catapulted from 0 to 110 knots in less than three seconds off an aircraft carrier, and then, in the same breath, ask me to make his favorite chocolate chip cookies.

I was part of a unique and intrepid group of military women aviators. I wondered about the path that led other women to the military and to aviation. What inspired them? Were they born with a desire for adventure? Or did they just want something different for themselves, a nontraditional job, something out of the norm? Maybe a teacher or parent inspired them to dream big, take a chance, or go down a different path. Perhaps some grew up around the military or aviation and desired to serve. Did some know from a very young age that the sky was their home and where they were meant to be?

How have these other women balanced family and a military career? I wondered. What types of career, family, and life decisions have to be made to make it all work? What stories would they tell their children?

I interviewed more than one hundred of my fellow sister aviators—all moms—from every military service, asking each to tell me her story—her path to the military and flying, combat experiences, her joys in being a mom, how she balances family and career, the advice and encouragement she would give to other women seeking a military or aviation career, and the legacy she wants to pass down to her children and future generations.

Every woman I interviewed stressed repeatedly that balancing family and a military career was not easy. Many came to the conclusion that things don't always have to be perfect—in fact, frequently they can't be, especially when juggling demanding jobs, flying schedules, and family priorities.

When I asked, "Why stay in the military?" they gave resoundingly similar answers. "I can't think of any job I'd want other than the one I have. Being an aviator and an officer is part of who I am. It's not just a job. I serve because I love my country, and I want my family to live in a country that is free."

As much as these women love their careers and are proud of their military service, they love and cherish being moms even more. Susan Maitre, one of the Coast Guard aviatrix moms says, "I love being a mom, because it reminds me every day what really matters, and what doesn't. The bottom line is very simple: Between the grins and giggles and hugs and kisses, I realize that my husband and I are molding these sweet creatures into [having] remarkable lives of their own."

The following pages are filled with tales of little girls who grew up looking to the skies and dreaming of soaring overhead; of young women hesitantly realizing they could become pilots as well as flight attendants; of young moms juggling flying schedules at odd hours but making time to read bedtime stories to their little ones; of women struggling to decide whether to stay in the military because too many deployments are impacting the family; and of experienced career women military pilots mentoring younger men and women, sharing their own experiences, sprinkled with some "been there, done that" wisdom.

Each woman's perspective is uniquely different, but together they weave a beautiful tapestry that tells a bigger story and passes on a lasting legacy to inspire future generations to reach for their dreams.

Military Fly Moms is a shared legacy among all the women highlighted in the following pages. I salute them and am honored they spent countless hours sharing their experiences, hopes, and dreams so that I may share them with you.

. . . .
They are our daughters, sisters, neighbors, friends, and, yes, even moms.
. . . .

—Linda Maloney

The Repeal of the Combat Exclusion Law

IN 1972, THE NAVY ANNOUNCED IT WOULD OPEN ITS FLYING PROGRAMS TO WOMEN, FOLLOWED SHORTLY BY THE ARMY AND THEN, IN 1976, THE Air Force. Congress continued to keep military women from direct combat, even though the Department of Defense submitted a proposal repealing the combat exclusion law in May 1979. The Women's Armed Services Integration Act of 1948 excluded women from military vessels and aircraft that might engage in combat. Women aviators were limited to transport and auxiliary fixed-wing aircraft and support helicopters, all in noncombat roles.

In late 1976, Lieutenant Joellen Drag Oslund—the first female Navy helicopter pilot— joined a class action lawsuit in U.S. District Court with five other Navy women, *Owens vs. Brown*, challenging the constitutionality of Title 10 United States Code 6015's language restricting women from serving on vessels other than hospital ships and transports. Joellen, assigned to a helicopter squadron, wasn't allowed to even hover above the deck of a ship anchored in port. (The Code of Laws of the United States of America (U.S.C.) is a compilation and codification of the general and permanent federal laws of the United States. Title 10 of the United States Code outlines the role of the armed forces.)

The changing nature of warfare, however, blurred the lines between combat missions and support over the next several years. When President Ronald Reagan sent troops to Grenada in 1983, women pilots flew infantry and cargo to the island. In 1986, during retaliatory bombing raids on Libya, women pilots flew tanker aircraft supporting the mission. The next year, the Secretary of Defense established a Task Force on Women in the Military to review the roles of women and military policy.

During the Persian Gulf War from 1990 to 1991, approximately 35,000 to 40,000 military women deployed to Southwest Asia. Women pilots flew Army helicopters and Air Force reconnaissance, transport, and tanker aircraft. Major Marie Rossi, an Army helicopter pilot, was killed in action. As a result of their highly visible service in the war, women won partial repeal of the combat exclusion law in 1991 with the passage of the National Defense Authorization Act. Section 531 of the legislation repealed the statutory limitations on the assignment of women to combat aircraft. It took nearly a year and a half, however, before the services acted upon the congressional direction. On April 28, 1993, Secretary of Defense Les Aspin directed the military services to integrate women aviators into its combat forces.

Victoria (Uptegraft) Cain

UH-60 *Black Hawk*

IT'S FAMILY TRADITION TO SERVE IN THE MILITARY—MY PARENTS AND BOTH OF MY GRANDFATHERS SERVED. I GREW UP JUST OUTSIDE THE KENTUCKY National Guard post where it was routine to see *Black Hawk* helicopters fly over our house. One day, one flew right over my head so low that I felt I could have reached out and touched its belly. As its roar, vibration, and wind current rippled through me, I wondered how the beast could fly. In that moment, I had a fleeting notion of one day being a helicopter pilot, maneuvering through the limitless, open sky. I remember, though, that it seemed unattainable to me, and I didn't think about it again for years.

I attended college, majoring in both biology and nursing, until the student loan office informed me I had used up my available loans and grants. The Army agreed to pay off my student loans, so in 1997 I enlisted. The next time I was inundated with the roar, vibration, and wind current of a helicopter overhead, I was a private first class serving as an Army medic, and my battalion was training on the ground for a deployment to Bosnia. The day my first sergeant okayed me to join an area reconnaissance mission—I immediately jumped into the back seat of the *Black Hawk*, then trembled, enthralled as the pilot pulled in power and we took off—was the day I knew for certain I wanted to fly.

A short time later, we deployed to Bosnia. As a medic, I assisted with flight physicals, which gave me the opportunity to talk with pilots and get helicopter rides. The pilots noticed my interest and excitement (as if I could hide it) and encouraged me to apply for flight school. I submitted my application the following year. In the meantime, I took daily walks to the flight line and watched preflights and run-ups. I was so excited about the possibility of becoming an aviator. Once, during a battalion training exercise

when I heard a flight of three *Black Hawks* nearby, I immediately yelled for everyone to stop. Surely, everyone else would be eager to admire them, too! Instead, the unit members just looked at me in confusion.

Finally, in 2000, my dream of attending flight school became reality. I was accepted the very first time I applied! I attended the Army Warrant Officer Candidate School and then flight school, both at Fort Rucker, Alabama. The first time I tried to hover in the *Bell 206* training helicopter, I was all over the place, but when I stepped out of that aircraft and walked into the training room full of students, I exclaimed, "I AM AN AVIATOR!" Everyone laughed at me, but it was such a great feeling, one of accomplishment. I was actually doing what I thought I could never do. I received my wings in March 2002, and, thankfully, got my first choice—UH-60 *Black Hawk*.

I joined an air assault battalion at Fort Campbell, Kentucky. The training and atmosphere in the battalion were very rigid. I don't think I saw daylight for three months due to the battalion's philosophy: "If you can fly at night under night-vision goggles, then you can most assuredly perform during the day." We ardently trained to achieve "time on target"—to arrive at a landing zone to drop off troops or equipment within three seconds of our scheduled arrival time.

We deployed to Iraq in 2003 and I flew more than 450 combat hours. All the missions were challenging and many times dangerous. One evening, my copilot and I were scheduled to fly a night combat mission from Mosul, Iraq. Since we were ahead of schedule, we decided to take off early. In the air, we tuned our radios to the ground frequency and immediately heard a request

Victoria and daughter, Kayleigh (4 years old), 2009.

for a medical evacuation of an injured soldier. We flew to the nearby evacuation site to assist.

It was very chaotic—coordinating the radio transmissions, conducting landing checks, and looking for a safe place to land. After touching down, our sister ship (helicopter) provided aerial security and took over the radio calls.

One of our crew chiefs ran over to the injured soldier while the other provided ground security amid a grenade attack. The crew chiefs quickly loaded the injured soldier onto the helicopter, then we lifted off and transported the patient to the local field hospital.

The entire incident took a total of three minutes. Thankfully, our combined efforts saved the life of the Army soldier, David Hurt. He had been exiting his vehicle when some children lobbed grenades at him. He lost a lot of blood and one of his legs, but the doctors said he

would have died if we had not rescued him so quickly. My crew and I visited him in the hospital the next day, glad to know he was going to make it.

I had met my husband, Brandon, at Fort Campbell and we dated a short time before we both deployed to Iraq in February 2003. Most of our courtship took place in a combat zone via e-mail and satellite phone—ahh, military romance. We returned to Fort Campbell in March 2004 and married three months later. After four months of marriage, we felt ready to have a child. As soon as I found out I was pregnant, I had to quit flying because of Army flying restrictions, though I still could fly the helicopter simulator as long as I could get in and out of the seat.

Our daughter, Kayleigh, was born in July 2005. I took two months off after her birth, and then started a flying job at a medical-evacuation unit. I never gave it much thought before, but nowadays I became extremely cautious and concerned that I make it home safely. Of course, I always wanted to ensure a safe flight, but since my daughter was anxiously waiting for me to come home, I was ever more determined to return home to her.

It became increasingly difficult to remain dual-military parents. Kayleigh tolerated my husband's eight-month deployment to Afghanistan well since he was able to call or e-mail daily. However, before he returned home, I was granted a compassionate reassignment because of my father's illness, which moved us five hours away. While I was very grateful for the relocation, the separation of our family strongly impacted Kayleigh, and since it is a given that there will be more deployments, I've decided it's time to leave active duty and finish my time in the Army National Guard in order to provide a more stable environment for our family.

Mom to Mom:

The most rewarding thing about being a mom is the unconditional love from and for a child. I love experiencing life through my daughter's precious little innocent eyes.

Being a full-time mom, wife, and Army aviator has been both difficult and rewarding, especially during a time of war. My hope is to serve in the military for twenty years and, once I retire, to fly for a civilian aeromedical-evacuation team and continue my education. I hope to instill in my daughter confidence and courage, so that she will follow her dreams no matter their magnitude.

The world has no limits, only people do.

Rank:	Army Chief Warrant Officer 3
Years Served:	13
Current Military Status:	Active Duty
Number of Children:	1

Connie Reeves

UH-1 *Huey*

ABOUT A YEAR BEFORE I GRADUATED FROM THE UNIVERSITY OF TEXAS AT AUSTIN, MY DAD—A RETIRED AIR FORCE CHIEF MASTER SERGEANT, with whom our family had been stationed all over the world—suggested I apply to the military. The Army offered the best deal, so, in April 1976, a few months after college graduation, I joined the Army as a second lieutenant. I'd intended to stay in for two years, earn GI Bill benefits, and get out. However, the Army enticed me with innumerable opportunities, including the chance to travel. During my initial Army training to become a military intelligence officer, I became friends with an Army pilot and caught the flying bug. Shortly after I received my private pilot's license, I applied to flight school.

I arrived at Fort Rucker, Alabama, in 1979, to become a helicopter pilot—an Army aviator. Pilot training was the hardest thing I'd ever done up to that point, but I loved hanging out at the flight line and wearing a flight suit and combat boots. When my first flight instructor told me I was his first female student, I realized, along with seeing only one other woman in the class, that I was a novelty. I graduated as an honor graduate, one of the top five in my class.

Following flight school, I was transferred to Frankfurt, West Germany, to fly the UH-1 *Huey* helicopter, where I found myself to be the senior woman and one of four female officers (two commissioned and two warrant) in my company. Being one of few women in the command was challenging, to say the least.

Before I started flight school, I had met a handsome, dashing, charming man who swept me off my feet—Cliff Lewis. Cliff was a military intelligence officer and an Army captain. He combined the best attributes of everyone I had ever dated, and we each thought the other would make a wonderful mate. We were married in May 1979

and transferred to Germany together. Life was *full* of new adventures!

In those days, women couldn't use birth control pills while on flight status—a bit of a quandary for a married woman. When we decided to throw caution to the wind, we found we were expecting our first child almost immediately. We were incredibly excited. I believe I was the first female Army aviator to become pregnant on active duty. My son, Derek, was born in 1982. Thankfully, I found a wonderful woman to watch our son, and I returned to work. The Army gave me six weeks of maternity leave, which certainly wasn't enough time.

After Derek was born, we were totally wrapped up in him, as are all young parents with their firstborn. We took him everywhere—the zoo, the park, to brunch, on walks in his baby carriage, even to Spain and London. We played and read and sang to him, and were totally in love with this new creature. He gurgled and laughed and delighted us with his enjoyment of life. Our lives felt absolutely complete!

A week after my convalescent leave was over, my battalion headed to the field for three days. Aside from doing my job, I spent those days keeping my milk flowing. I had laid up a supply of breast milk before the field exercise for both my husband and the daycare provider to give my baby, but had to go into the port-a-potty or the GP-medium tent to express milk (while sitting on my cot in full view of any male who came into the men's side as only a blanket over a low-slung rope separated their section from the women's). On the day of departure, when the tent and port-a-potty were removed, I walked a long distance into the woods thinned by winter, sat down on my helmet, and began the arduous process of

5

1LT Connie Reeves preparing for graduation formation flyby, May 1980, Fort Rucker, Alabama.

unbuttoning and unzipping and removing chemical warfare outfit, field jacket, fatigue shirt, gas mask, .38 revolver, thermal underwear, T-shirt, and bra, just to remove the pressure and keep the milk going. What lengths I had to go to be able to keep breastfeeding my child! Just a few short months later, the battalion went to the field for ten days and, as much as I tried, I wasn't successful this time. Nevertheless, I was pleased that I was able to breastfeed my son for five months.

Unexpectedly, I became pregnant with our daughter, Jessica, eighteen months later. This time, the Army had reduced its maternity leave to four weeks, immediately after which we moved back to the United States. I attended the Army's first aviation advanced course at Fort Rucker, Alabama, and Cliff was assigned to the Defense Intelligence Agency in Washington, D.C. He took the kids with him because we didn't know what my school requirements would be but believed his work schedule would be more stable.

It was a difficult time as Jessica was only three months old when we separated the family. I missed my kids more than I can describe. During my five months at Fort Rucker, I talked with my husband and kids every day. I read children's stories and sang songs on tapes, which my husband played for them at bedtime so they could hear Mommy's voice each night. I flew home every few weeks and cooked a number of meals, freezing them so my husband wouldn't have to cook.

Upon graduation, I transferred to Davison Army Airfield at Fort Belvoir, Virginia, and our family was back together again. I was assigned as an operations officer, primarily arranging VIP flights.

When the Army decided to limit some aviation command positions to men, I left aviation and returned to military intelligence. While teaching at the Defense Intelligence College, I was selected to attend a master's program in European history at George Washington

University and then the Defense Language Institute in Monterey, California, to learn German. Cliff, Derek, and Jessica remained in Virginia for those seven months; I managed to fly back every six weeks or so, and even flew our then-six-year-old son out to visit me for a week. This was the most painful family separation for me. Our next joint assignment was back to Germany, to Stuttgart. Our family would be reunited and we were off on a new adventure!

This tour was the highlight of my military career, serving as the Western European political/military intelligence analyst for one year and branch chief for two years, including during *Desert Storm*. I briefed four-star generals, ambassadors, visiting delegations from other countries, and many others. It was my job to tell them all, including the highest American military leaders in Europe, what European country capabilities were and what their leaders were thinking. During this time, Cliff was sent to *Desert Storm* for seven months, a time of anxiety for us all, but he returned home safe and sound. I learned what it was like during this period to be a single parent and carry out my military duties.

After our tour in Germany, I was selected for Command and General Staff College for a year at Fort Leavenworth, Kansas, and Cliff returned to the D.C. area. Since neither of us wanted to be without the kids, Cliff suggested that Derek live with him and Jessica with me. After my year at Fort Leavenworth was finished, Jessica and I moved back with Cliff and Derek, reuniting our family once again. Cliff retired and started a real estate appraisal business, and I worked at the Pentagon for the next two years before retiring in 1994.

My main goal in life has always been to make a contribution. One of the things I am proudest of is being part of the second generation of women military aviators, who convinced Congress in the early 1990s to repeal the combat exclusion law so that women can now fly combat aircraft in combat.

After retiring from the Army, I began my career as a writer while volunteering for numerous organizations and our children's school activities. I've written two books for the Army, the definitive history of the Air Force Nurse Corps, several chapters on military nurses that are in anthologies, articles in journals and magazines, two novels (*Hawthorne's Cottage* and *The Elimination Game*), and started Tannenbaum Publishing Company. I know many people believe that raising good children is contribution enough, but I have always wanted to do more.

I am delighted that my children—now adults—are intelligent, loving, decent, and productive human beings who can take care of themselves. When I was diagnosed with ovarian cancer in 2007, my son, Derek, took over Cliff's appraisal business so Cliff could take care of me. Derek now owns the business since Cliff has retired. In addition, Derek is a homeowner, has a home renovation business, is a general contractor, and loves what he does. He is one of the most successful people in his peer group and a leader among his friends.

Our daughter, Jessica, has the same wanderlust as Cliff and I. Following her graduation from college, she received a prestigious Fulbright fellowship and taught English to German high school students for a year, and, in her free time, traveled all over Europe. She recently earned a master's degree in German and European Studies from Georgetown University. In 2011, she left for another year in Germany, on yet another prestigious fellowship, to study renewable energy.

As a cancer survivor, I am now keenly aware of and feel an obligation to raise awareness about cancer and funds for cancer research, particularly ovarian cancer. I have received the opportunity to acquire

Mom to Mom:

The most rewarding thing about being a mom has been watching my children grow through life, from helpless infants to won't-sit-still toddlers, to high school kids finding their identity, to responsible young adults who laugh and love and contribute to the world, who have become people I admire and respect, whom I love to spend time with, and who now give advice to me and their dad perhaps more than they receive it!

more understanding and compassion about the difficulties we all face in life. I have lived a very full, active, interesting, and enjoyable existence and plan to continue to contribute through my writings and my new status as a cancer survivor. I am also keenly looking forward to being a grandmother and seeing my children as parents! I think that will be my greatest legacy.

Rank:	Army Lieutenant Colonel
Years Served:	18
Current Military Status:	Retired
Number of Children:	2

No, it wasn't easy, but it was all worthwhile.

Tami (Beutel) Reynolds

OH58A+ *Kiowa*

AS THE YOUNGEST OF FOUR CHILDREN, I ALWAYS WANTED TO DO IT ALL! IN SIXTH GRADE, I ATTENDED MY OLDER BROTHER'S ARMY BASIC training graduation, amazed when I saw the soldiers run through the confidence course. With bayonets affixed, they ran full force through the artillery simulators, attacking their enemies with vigor. I sensed the unique bond among him and his fellow soldiers, and I wanted that for myself.

During my high school junior year, I attended a career fair and talked with the Army National Guard recruiter. What he told me changed the course of my life—he said I could join the New Jersey Army National Guard and start drilling immediately. In addition to getting paid for drills, I also would qualify for the GI Bill and tuition assistance, which would pay for college down the road. I immediately knew this was the program for me!

For the next two years, I drilled once a month with the local Guard aviation unit and fell in love with aviation. After high school graduation in 1996 and then Army flight operations specialist training, I returned home to New Jersey and worked as often as I could at the local Guard unit, even though I was only required to work a couple of days per month. I loved putting on my uniform and walking through the halls, breathing in the old, musty armory smells.

As I walked across the hangar floor to get to my office, the AH-1F *Cobras* (attack helicopters) sat lined up and poised for action. Call it crazy, but I was drawn to those aircraft. I saw how much the pilots enjoyed their jobs, and I wanted that for myself. If they could fly them, why couldn't I?

A couple of great mentors in my Guard unit—God bless those who encourage others—encouraged me to apply for the Army Warrant Officer Flight Training

program, and I still remember the day I received the call that I had been selected. From my first flight during pilot training, I loved it and knew this was the career for me!

I met my future husband, Gene, day one of flight school. He said he was smitten with me from first glance. Unfortunately, he would graduate a few months ahead of me and transfer to Fort Bragg, North Carolina. I still planned to return home to my New Jersey Guard unit, once I graduated, and fly the AH-1 *Cobra*. However, love got in the way—we became engaged and hoped it would work out. After my flight school graduation, I returned to New Jersey, discussed the situation with my Guard commanders, and asked for a transfer to a North Carolina Guard unit.

Gene and I married, and I moved to North Carolina. However, my flying career went on hold for several months because I was pregnant with our first child and thus grounded for the duration of my pregnancy. Being pregnant completely changed my priorities and my normal risk-taking personality. I was always the girl who tried anything new, but once I found out I was pregnant, I immediately transitioned to mommy mode.

Six weeks after having my son, Christian, I started training to fly the OH-58A+ *Kiowa* and then participated in the North Carolina Guard's drug interdiction program. We conducted aerial interdiction missions searching for illegal drugs. We also went to elementary schools to talk to kids about the dangers of drugs and how to make wise choices.

I loved the unit and the mission, and felt I had found my niche as both a pilot and a teacher. But after Christian arrived, I never wanted to leave him. He completely

9

Tami taking her daughter, Abby, to school on Tami's first day in the Washington Army National Guard, September, 2006, Tacoma, Washington.

changed my world. Having his sister, Abigayle, fifteen months later, changed my world even more. Now I had a little woman to teach and protect. From day one, I knew I had my hands full, and today I call my mom often to say "thank you!" because I now appreciate all she did as a mom, and also to say "I'm sorry" because Abby is just like me, but times ten!

In 2003, Gene transferred to Fort Campbell, Kentucky. I joined the National Guard unit in Smyrna, Tennessee, to fly the *Kiowa* and again fly drug interdiction missions. The commute was an hour and a half from my home, but the unit was wonderful and I enjoyed the tight, close-knit camaraderie.

Immediately after Hurricane Katrina devastated Mississippi and Louisiana in 2005, our unit was alerted and activated for disaster relief operations. We started our preparations for deployment to Mississippi in order to provide aid and relief to the people living in the affected areas. Because so much of the infrastructure was gone, our unit took everything we needed to function for a few weeks, including our own food, water, shelter, and, most importantly, fuel for everything—aircraft, generators, and cooking.

After we arrived at Stennis International Airport, the Mississippi Army National Guard was already on station and assisted us in getting set up and briefed on the situation. Fortunately, our *Kiowa* helicopter was small enough to land in tight spots with little worry of causing more damage to the area by our rotor wash. Over the next two weeks, we flew all over the Pass Christian and Gulfport coastal areas searching for people and dropping off food, ice, medicine, and baby essentials. We flew whenever and wherever we were needed during all hours of the day or night. We flew humanitarian missions as well as law-enforcement operations to help combat the unjustified lawlessness during that time. Even seemingly simple tasks, such as flying to the nearest Red Cross station to fill a prescription or retrieve baby formula for a family in need, seemed like a miracle for recipients. It didn't matter how small the favor was, the reaction was always the same—gratitude. Helping these families and supporting the hurricane relief efforts remains a highlight of my career.

Gene received orders again in 2005, this time to Fort Lewis in Washington. I dreaded leaving our home and my Guard unit, but I joined the Washington National Guard, Counter Drug Unit, and also got involved in the unit's homeland security mission of conducting border patrols, deploying several times in 2006 to fly border patrol missions.

Thankfully, my husband didn't deploy at the same time. However, we spent the next year playing tag—we were never home for long at the same time.

We try to expose our children to all the good things in life. With all the different and varied, wonderful opportunities available, I hope to open as many doors as possible for them. Joining the Guard was the first open door for me, and the start of my career. I am so thankful that my parents were willing to sign the enlistment form fourteen years ago.

My daughter says that she wants to do everything I do. This motivates me to be a good example to her. My

Mom to Mom:

The most rewarding thing about being a mom are the times when you have a teaching moment and you take it...when your child asks those crazy questions that you know are going to be difficult but you seize the opportunity and teach a life lesson that no one else can but you.

son thinks every mom flies. When he meets a new friend, he will say, "My mom flies helicopters. What does your mom fly?"

Gene separated from the Army in August 2010, and we decided to sell everything and spend our time together. As we embarked on this most recent journey, we had such a unique opportunity to teach our kids what is truly important in life. My kids told people, "We would rather have time together than have lots of stuff." It was so amazing to hear children say that, when many grown people think material things in life bring happiness. So, as we packed our lives up into 560 square feet and headed off into the great unknown, we did so with smiles and knew we were teaching our children that true wealth cannot and will not be measured by the things we collect, but by the acts we do.

We have spent the last year in Mexico on our sailboat enjoying time together as a family and working together with the local community. I am not currently active with a National Guard unit but plan to join back up in another year or so and finish my twenty years. I am also looking into a new career that will allow me to continue to influence and impact the lives of young people.

The only difference between an adventure and an ordeal is attitude.

Rank:	Army Chief Warrant Officer 2
Years Served:	14
Current Military Status:	Separated
Number of Children:	2

Karen (Williams) White

UH-1H *Huey,* RC-12 & C-12 *Huron*

THERE ARE DEFINING MOMENTS WHEN THE COURSE OF OUR LIVES CHANGE, EITHER SUBTLY OR DRAMATICALLY. ONE SUCH MOMENT FOR ME was in high school, when my father discussed future career opportunities with me and told me that he knew I could do anything I put my mind to. This was the biggest validation of his faith and belief in me that I had ever received.

The next defining moment in my life occurred during college when I was given a ride in the back of a C-172. The pilot was my age, and he had just gotten his private pilot's license. After that flight, I went to the Army recruiter and asked him about the Army aviation program.

Since I didn't yet have my college degree, he told me that I could enlist first and then apply to become a warrant officer. So that's what I did. I first attended the Army training at Fort Rucker, Alabama, to become an air traffic control tower operator. Fort Rucker just happened to be the home of Army aviation, and one of the training officers helped me complete an application to the Army's warrant officer flight school program

After only a month at my new duty station, Fort Campbell, Kentucky, my orders came through for flight school. However, it took a year to get a flight school slot, and I finally earned my wings in 1979.

My first flying tour was at Fort Lewis, Washington, where I flew the UH-1H *Huey* helicopter. Our mission was combat lift—transporting soldiers, fuel, and supplies. However, after the Mount St. Helens volcano erupted in 1980, I flew medical-evacuation flights and I also transported photographers, scientists, and local officials to view the destruction. Mount St. Helens had been steaming for months, and there was a "no fly zone" put in place prior to the eruption to ensure an adequate safety perimeter was established. After the volcano erupted, the physical appearance of the area completely changed—everything was coated with a monochromatic grey color of mud and ash. All the trees fell like matchsticks and the affected area was completely stripped of foliage.

Interestingly, our squadron's helicopter engines started running much cooler because the ash was so abrasive that it actually cleaned the carbon buildup inside the engines. We had to remove all engine filters and lubricate the tail rotors and heads after each flight to try to reduce the amount of wear and tear from the ash.

After this tour, I deployed to Ansbach, West Germany, where I got the opportunity to fly with night-vision goggles (NVG). Flying with NVGs was in its infancy at this time and we even flew in formation with other helicopters while on NVGs, flying low level, going as low as fifty feet. We'd fly as close to the ground as we could to mask ourselves behind trees and hills. It wasn't unusual to be flying low over the German countryside, and have a BMW or Mercedes blow past us on a nearby road, going 140 kilometers per hour. This was the most fun way imaginable to see Germany and other parts of Europe up close and personal.

I met my husband, Frank, during this tour. He was also a pilot—flying *Cobras* and *Hueys.* We spent time together with other fellow aviators, became friends, and toured Germany during off-duty time. Frank, who had been to Germany before, became our appointed tour guide.

Our friendship grew, and eventually we started dating. After Frank and I became engaged, we transferred to Texas, but to two different Army bases exactly 357 miles apart. The reason I know this is that we spent a lot of weekends wearing out the highway pavement traveling

Karen and her family at her son's (Trevor) Army commissioning
ceremony, May 2009.

back and forth to see each other. My career continued to blossom and I received a direct commission as an Army officer since I now had my college degree. I had always wanted to fly fixed-wing aircraft, so I was thrilled to be selected for a fixed-wing transition, and learned to fly the RC-12D (a *King Air* with multiple antennas).

By now, Frank and I were married and we transferred together back to Germany, where I would fly the RC-12, conducting intelligence missions. We were also expecting our first child. Morning sickness was an all-day event, and soon we discovered that we were expecting twins. A few months after we arrived in Stuttgart, Germany, Trevor and David were born.

I also commanded my first company there, the head-quarters and service company of the military intelligence battalion. A few days before taking command, I went from the flight line directly over to the new office to meet with the outgoing commander. After introducing me around,

he pointed to a place on my shoulder and said, "There's the mark of a parent! I have a matching one." Looking at my shoulder, I noticed the telltale sign of baby burp-up decorating my flight suit.

After Germany, I was assigned to a mostly non-flying job at Fort Belvoir, Virginia, working on the staff of the Army's Intelligence and Security Command. It was tech-nically not a flying job, but my boss let me fly with one of our subordinate units to stay current. While there, I was selected for command—of the largest fixed-wing VIP detachment in the Army. The command flew the C-12 aircraft in a charter-like operation. This tour was one of the highlights of my career.

When my twins were seven years old, I was flying C-12s at Fort Belvoir, and my husband was flying the *Learjet* 35 and Gulfstream aircraft at Andrews Air Force Base, Maryland. We gave a party at our house, and one of my coworkers asked my son if he was going to fly airplanes when he grew up. He answered, "Turboprops are for *girls* (with all the scathing inflection that anyone with girl-cooties deserves); I'm going to fly *jets*!"

Our third son, Michael, entered the world when our twins were seven. In first grade, Michael was diagnosed with an autism spectrum disorder. I can truthfully say that having an autistic child is a much larger challenge than any other I have faced in my life—breaking into the all-male universe of macho helicopter pilots in the 1970s was nothing compared to the challenges we have faced in advocating for our son to get the support he needs. My hope for Michael is that someday he'll employ his considerable talents and his gifts in math and science in a productive capacity in society.

In 1997, I retired from the Army, went to work for United Airlines, and spent the next year as a flight engineer on the B-727, and then upgraded to first officer on the B-757/767. I wanted to fly internationally, so I bid for the B-777 and enjoyed piloting that immensely. After the events of September 11, 2001, I was bumped to the Airbus 320, but, in 2007, happily returned to the B-777. My favorite trips are the military charters, where we transport soldiers to destinations in Europe and the Middle East. Recently, the economic tides have turned again, and I've moved back to the B-757/767. I hope to eventually gain enough seniority to upgrade to captain before I retire.

Our older sons—our twins—are busily embarking on the rest of their lives. David graduated in 2010 from Illinois State University with a degree in accounting. Trevor graduated in May 2009 from the Air Force Academy and, in an unusual twist, cross-commissioned with the Army. He is now an Army second lieutenant in the Armor Branch, assigned to Fort Bragg, North Carolina, and preparing to deploy to Afghanistan.

Frank and I have always worked in jobs that had uncertain hours and irregular absences from home. When the twins were born, we decided to hire a nanny to live with us, to provide some stability to the home in case we were both working extended hours. Our first nanny lived with us until Trevor and David were six. Our current nanny, Vilma, has been with us since before Mike was born. She is now an integral member of the family and will have a home with us for as long as she desires.

As I think about the legacy I want to pass down to my sons, I remember a letter I wrote to my twins for a high school English assignment entitled "What I Wish Someone Had Told Me About." In it, I encouraged my sons to be tenacious and to never let a person or thing stand in the way of their goals; to have fun and enjoy life; to find a career that would make them happy to go to work; and to be decent human beings and know that credentials on the wall do not make one a decent human being. Morality and integrity are not measured in awards and achievements, but in the depth of one's conscience and soul.

Mom to Mom:

The thing that surprised me the most about being a mom is how my priorities have changed as my children have grown. When they were babies, I was primarily concerned with their safety (choking, falling, etc.); then throughout their childhood until they were teenagers, I paid particular attention to their development and growth; finally, as teenagers and now, young adults, I am again primarily concerned with their safety.

"Motherhood is like Albania—you can't trust the descriptions in the books; you have to go there."

—Marni Jackson

Rank:	Army Major
Years Served:	21
Current Military Status:	Retired
Number of Children:	3

Susan (Decker) Allen

C-130 *Hercules*, P-3 *Orion*, C-9 *Skytrain*

AFTER GRADUATING FROM BUCKNELL UNIVERSITY, PENNSYLVANIA, IN 1986, I TAUGHT MATH AT A LOCAL HIGH SCHOOL FOR a short time, but the itch to experience new places and things became more intriguing than the experiences offered by teaching.

I decided to follow in my dad's footsteps and join the Navy. I figured I would enjoy a brief career in the service, travel the world, and then come back home a few years later to settle down and go back to teaching. In February 1988, I packed my bags and headed to the Navy's officer candidate school, then Navy Supply Corps School, and finally reported to my first duty station, the USS *Yellowstone*, as a supply officer.

A fellow female supply officer had always wanted to be a pilot, and had applied to flight school. This gave me the idea and the confidence to apply as well, although, to be honest, it was probably more for the adventure than really wanting to be a pilot. Little did I know that just seventeen months after joining the crew of the *Yellowstone*, I'd be packing my bags again and heading to flight school.

Learning to fly wasn't the easiest thing for me—I can't even drive a stick shift, and I was never really interested in the mechanics of a car, let alone an airplane! My first flight instructor was a Marine Corps officer named Captain O'Rourke, who used to get so excited each time I mastered a new skill in the airplane. I always thought he deserved hazardous duty pay for flying with young and very inexperienced student pilots.

Captain O'Rourke would always say that flying among the clouds was "flying in God's country." I have thought of that many times over the years.

Another memory of flight school is significant because of an aircraft mishap. My training flight had been delayed because the squadron commanding officer took our aircraft to use for his own flight. Consequently, my instructor pilot and I were assigned another airplane. As we waited for this plane, my instructor and I discussed a recent helicopter crash. The event had affected me personally, because I knew people involved in the crash. My flight instructor told me, "You cannot have a career as a Navy pilot and not know someone who was in a crash or be in a crash yourself." That afternoon, while we were flying, one of our squadron's planes went down (crashed). Unbelievably, it was the plane that the commanding officer was flying. It could have been me on that plane. The danger of flying took me aback, and I was forced to face the reality of the dangerous career I had chosen.

In June 1992, I received my wings of gold and then learned to fly the C-130 *Hercules*. I reported to a squadron in Point Mugu, California, flying in support of the Navy's Antarctic mission. At this time, most women military aviators were flying in support squadrons because the combat exclusion law prohibited women from flying combat missions. All that changed in April 1993 when the ban was lifted. I was among the first women selected to fly the P-3 *Orion*, and I soon transferred to Jacksonville, Florida, for training.

Afterwards, I joined a P-3 squadron, which proved to be a very challenging and stressful tour. I was one of the first two women ever assigned to the squadron, and the idea of women flying in combat was not universally accepted. My commanding officer was not very supportive of having women in his squadron, but, within two years, a

Susan, her father, and her daughter at Susan's change-of-command ceremony at Navy Reserve Center Avoca, Pennsylvania, May 2005.

new commander took over and attitudes changed for the better. Overall, I really enjoyed my time. I decided at the end of my tour in 1997 to switch to working full-time in the Navy Reserve. There were a couple of great benefits with the new change. I learned to fly a new aircraft—the C-9—and I transferred to Naval Air Station Willow Grove outside of Philadelphia, Pennsylvania. As a C-9 pilot, I flew logistics flights, transporting people and cargo all over the world. It was like being a commercial airline pilot, yet still in the Navy. Perhaps the best part of this tour was that I was stationed near my family.

I also reconnected with friends, including a former friend named Dan, whom I knew from my teenage life-guarding days. I had just joined the local U.S. Masters swim team; Dan, also a Masters swimmer, and I encountered each other at a swim meet. We talked for a little while at the meet before I realized he had absolutely

no idea who I was. Before long, we exchanged phone numbers with promises to keep in touch—but he never called. Almost exactly a year later, I ran into him again at the annual swim meet. This time, I took matters into my own hands and invited him to a dinner party at my house. One week later we had our second date, and four months later we became engaged.

We married in April 2001. Six months later, I received orders to fly the C-12 aircraft at Naval Air Station Atlanta, Georgia. As before, I flew mostly logistics missions, transporting passengers and cargo.

Shortly after arriving in Atlanta, Dan and I learned we were expecting our first child. I flew up until twenty-seven weeks pregnant. Being pregnant while flying was quite the experience! I had to keep getting bigger flight suits as my belly expanded. Eventually, my belly got so big that I was unable to bend over to reach the emergency gear extension handle. Our son, Kevin, was born and, shortly before my tour in Atlanta was over, we had our second child, daughter Jessica.

I was selected to become the commanding officer of the Navy Reserve Center in Avoca, Pennsylvania. The move marked the end of my flying career, but it's a decision I'll never regret. I've had the chance to travel to places most people never even dream about and experience life in a way that no nine-to-five job could ever replicate.

Dan and I also decided that I would retire from the Navy after this tour. He has been so supportive of my career and encouraged me to stay in the Navy for twenty years. He has also been very supportive of my next step—becoming a teacher.

On January 5, 2008, my family escorted me across the quarterdeck as I retired from the Navy. My daughter fell asleep during the ceremony, and my son was more thrilled with his Webkinz toy. The ceremony was fun—no tears and a lot of smiles.

My kids are still getting used to the fact that I don't work in the Navy anymore. They still sometimes ask when they can go back to where "Mommy works." It was quite an adjustment at first—for all of us. Shortly after retiring

Mom to Mom:
Being a mom is the most challenging and most rewarding job I have ever had; I wouldn't trade the experience for anything.

from the Navy, I started teaching at a local high school and plan to continue in the years to come. For me, it was the first time in twenty years that I had to think about what I was going to wear every day.

For women considering joining the military—it is tough but challenging. The military provides a great experience, pays for education, offers amazing opportunities, and offers wonderful travel adventures. I have gained so much, and my life experiences are broader than if I had not joined the military. I want my children to know they can do anything they have their hearts set on, which is the very same thing my parents told me. Of course, I also want my kids to think their mommy was cool flying airplanes.

I've had the honor and privilege of serving in the U.S. Navy and also the absolute thrill of being someone's mommy.

Rank:	Navy Lieutenant Commander
Years Served:	20
Current Military Status:	Retired
Number of Children:	2

Karen (Stottlemyer) Baetzel

H-46 *Sea Knight*, C-9 *Skytrain*, C-12 *Huron*

WHAT MAKES A BLUE-COLLAR GIRL FROM THE MIDDLE OF NOWHERE THINK SHE CAN FLY FOR A LIVING, LIVE IN EXOTIC COUNTRIES, AND see the world pretty much on her own terms? I honestly do not know. My options after local college in 1978 seemed pretty predictable. I was nearly six grand in debt, and the military recruiting center seemed like the perfect escape hatch. The Air Force wasn't interested, and the Marines were at lunch—that left the Army and the Navy, and the sailor made the first eye contact.

Three days after graduation, I was on my way to officer candidate school in Newport, Rhode Island, with all my worldly possessions packed in my 1972 Pinto. The recruiter had asked in passing if I thought I wanted to test for flight school. Way beyond my reach, I thought. I felt lucky to get out of small-town USA. After a few weeks at officer candidate school, I reconsidered, but I headed off to see a little of the world first. It took more than two years to finally get to Pensacola for flight school, during which I took a wonderful detour through Japan. Looking back, flight school turned out to be a bit surreal. My complete naiveté worked to my advantage. I didn't know enough to be terrified, never worried about getting the NAMI whammy (occurs when you are found to be physically disqualified to become an aviator), didn't experience motion sickness, and never had checkride-itis. I just blissfully showed up each day for the earliest flight I could schedule and kept at it.

In those days, with very few women in naval aviation, keeping a low profile proved difficult, and we experienced a marginally hospitable environment. Instructors occasionally refused to fly with women, and one Marine Corps instructor threw a small fit when I showed up to a briefing because he "had not been properly informed." This stuff is hilarious now, a mild pain in the neck then, but I never thought or felt that I would fail. It also never dawned on me to make an issue of that sort of silliness, but, by today's standards, I think it fair to say that every early female aviator must have had a catalogue of "actionable offenses" in the harassment arena— simply part of the culture then and part of our stories now.

In 1981, women aviators were still very carefully managed. Halfway through my initial phase of flight training, I was called to the commodore's office—not a place most flight students wanted to visit. He more or less told me I would be flying H-46 helicopters, and gave me the choice of the West Coast or East Coast. Ever the pragmatist, I was leaning toward H-46s anyway, as I figured the helicopter's logistics and replenishment missions would be the least restrictive community for women aviators. In the end, I was proved correct.

I had a fabulous tour in Norfolk, Virginia, flying H-46s. I really loved going to sea and cruising on several ships. I felt privileged to cruise with some amazing women, including Kathy O'Keefe and Wendy Lawrence (Wendy later went on to the space shuttle program). My time at sea has provided some of the best memories of my life. My greatest military moment was the serendipitous rescue of two fellow naval aviators who ejected from a crippled A-4 into the frigid Chesapeake Bay one cold February day. Their life expectancy in those waters was measured in minutes, and no other rescue platforms (aircraft or ships) were anywhere close. We picked them up seconds after they hit the water, and had them on the ground and in an ambulance within minutes. Of all my thirty years of military service, I mark that day as the most significant. While it was entirely engineered by fate, my being in the right place at the right time with the right training and skill set unquestionably saved those lives. I sure felt good that night about being a Navy pilot, and I still do.

Baetzel Family, October 2001.

Between detachments in mid-tour, I met a squadron mate, Bernie Baetzel, who had been on opposite cruise cycles. We managed to weather the frequent separations and build a relationship over the next year and a half and sought compatible shore duties. We married in May 1985. We welcomed our son, Chapman, in April 1986 and, less than two years later, our daughter, Victoria.

Bernie decided to pursue an airline career, and it was time for me to go back to sea. Since it seemed incomprehensible to me to be away from an infant and a toddler, I reluctantly transferred to the Navy Reserve, which turned out to be yet another remarkable door that the Navy threw open.

The years passed, and the Navy Reserve was extremely good to me. The Navy recalled me to active duty for three years, and I completed a fixed-wing transition to fly C-12s and, later, C-9s in Memphis, Tennessee. I enjoyed the flying but the pace of my job required that Bernie and I import my sister, Kay, to live with us for a year during *Desert Storm*. We could not easily find the kind of childcare we needed, short

of an au pair, so we were fortunate Kay was willing to disrupt her life and help us.

When the squadron in Memphis was decommissioned, I returned to reserve status. However, not long afterward, I was selected for a year of graduate study at the Naval War College, and moved to New England. Next, I served in the emergency preparedness field, which found me at the Disaster Field Office in New York City after the September 11, 2001, attacks and assisting the Federal Emergency Management Agency (FEMA) during Hurricane Katrina.

I have truly lived the American dream, courtesy of the Navy. It has given me tenfold for the service I have rendered and has been the golden thread intertwined in every good path I have walked. When I speak to young women who are considering military service, which I am frequently asked to do, my thoughts are often hopelessly idealistic. I believe the military is a true meritocracy, but, like all things of value, makes extraordinary demands on time, dedication, and character. Because the rewards extend beyond money, career training, or travel, a military career is not meant for those who care primarily for themselves, for wealth, or advantage.

As to combining the military and motherhood, I believe it can be successfully done, but it is an exceptional challenge. Many times I felt I was compromised in every role in my life—I wasn't the officer, mother, or wife I wanted to be. I have come to believe that is a price women pay when they choose to combine a demanding career, a marriage, and children. I believe the women who do it well have extraordinarily supportive husbands and extended families, are women of faith with extremely well-grounded personalities, and draw on a real measure of providential luck in terms of healthy kids.

I also like to say that you can have it all, but never all at the same time. My service in the Navy Reserve allowed a measure of flexibility that I don't believe would have been available in a thirty-year active-duty career. The continued integration of active and reserve components in the Navy may make this sort of career more common in the future.

I can serve the rest of my life and never repay this country for the opportunities that it has offered me, both as a citizen and a woman. The visionary geniuses who championed our form of government more than two hundred years ago could never have understood in what an extraordinary way it changed the course of human history. At a personal level, it has never been a better time to be a woman, and never a better time to be an American woman.

I sent my kids off to school every day of their lives with the following mom-ism: "Work hard and keep your promises," and their dad and I raised them using leadership principles we learned in the Navy. The most profound leadership principle that I used for childrearing I had learned as a division officer (manager in a Navy squadron responsible for ten to fifty personnel): "If they don't hate you once in a while, you aren't doing your job." The significance of this as a parent

Mom to Mom:

The thing that continues to surprise me the most about being a mom is what compelling teachers my children are. Each day that I walk this planet as a mother, they offer me a subtle but powerful lesson and invitation to live in integrity, to set an example of perseverance, and what it really means to be a decent human being. I have never had any teacher or leader who came remotely close to inspiring me to excellence as my own son and daughter have.

cannot be overstated. The easy way is to soak up all the love, to pamper and indulge. It's hard to be "the heavy," to say no and then stick by it.

Parenting is excruciatingly hard—occasionally heart-breaking—work for all mothers when done well. It is difficult to remember that our job is to make ourselves obsolete, and to prepare our children to grow up whole and healthy as independent people in a world that will not see them as we do.

The Navy taught me not to indulge my sailors or attempt to win the squadron popularity contest. That was the cheapest sort of leadership and failed the mission. Likewise, I do not believe we are put on this planet to be our children's friends. We need to ready them for the "missions" of life the same way.

Looking at my accumulated accoutrements of a military career, I would like to pass on my officer's sword to my son, Chapman, to symbolize my dreams for him to be an honest and righteous man, to believe in the power of integrity, and to never be afraid to do the right thing. To my daughter, Victoria, I would like to give my gold wings to symbolize her soaring potential, her future growth into amazing womanhood with strength and courage, and her freedom to explore the galaxy as she finds it. What's left after that is simply me—not an officer or a pilot. How extraordinarily lucky I am, as that's all my beloved husband ever wanted in the first place.

The core values I learned in military service are those gifts I want to pass down to my children—honor, courage, and commitment.

Rank:	Navy Captain
Years Served:	30
Current Military Status:	Retired
Number of Children:	2

Barbara Bell

A-3 *Skywarrior,* F/A-18 *Hornet,* F-14 *Tomcat,* EA-6B *Prowler*

ROWING UP IN THE SMALL TOWN OF TRAVERSE CITY, MICHIGAN, I WAS NOT EXPOSED TO MANY WOMEN WHO CHOSE PATHS OUT OF THE ordinary...except for my mom, a World War II cadet nurse who has been a strong influence in my life. She did not have the opportunities I have had, but she always wished them for me. I remember being frustrated in high school because I always felt different from most of the girls. I *needed*—not just wanted—so much more out of life. I have become the strong woman I am today because of the unusual path I chose while in high school.

When I watched my brother, Dan, go off to the Air Force Academy and saw the immediate effect upon his future, I wanted the same for myself. Women had just been accepted to service academies in 1976, so the integration of women was still in its infancy when I arrived in 1979 as a member of the fourth class of Naval Academy women. Clearly, the road would be rough, but I learned to survive, and later excel, in my Navy career because of my academy experience. I learned to pick my battles selectively, how to fight them well, and how to enjoy the ride (or flight) along the way.

While at the academy, I started taking lessons with the local flying club and flew the Cessna 150 and 152. I was hooked! During my senior year, I met Lieutenant Colleen Nevius, the first Navy woman to graduate from the Navy's test pilot school. Completely enthralled with her, I asked her a million questions about how she was selected for test pilot school. Her advice was to graduate at the top of my flight school class, get as many qualifications as soon as possible, rack up one thousand hours of flight time, and tell all commanding officers along the way about wanting to go to test pilot school. I decided that very night to follow in her footsteps. I graduated from the academy in 1983 and reported to flight school in Pensacola, Florida. Following Colleen's advice, I spent extra hours studying and flying in the simulators, and graduated at the top of my flight school class. When I received my wings of gold as a naval flight officer in 1984, I was well on my way.

In my first squadron at Naval Air Station Point Mugu, California, flying the A-3 *Skywarrior,* I acquired the hours, experience, and the commanding officer's endorsement needed to apply to the Navy's test pilot school. I was accepted in 1988—the turning point of my career. With the opportunity to use my undergraduate engineering degree, combine it with flying, and compete with the best aviators the military had to offer, I thrived.

After graduating from test pilot school, I went on to fly several different aircraft including the F-14 *Tomcat,* EA-6B *Prowler,* and F/A-18 *Hornet,* and began a career in the testing and acquisition of Navy aircraft.

I recently retired as a Navy captain after twenty-eight years in uniform, having flown thirty-five different types of aircraft and having lived all over the United States and in Australia. I cannot think of a grander adventure.

I could list my accomplishments and firsts in the Navy, but that no longer defines who I am today. Did I mention always wanting more out of life? I met my husband, Lieutenant Andy Kirschbaum, at graduate school in Monterey, California, and we married in 1994. He was a helicopter pilot, an athlete, a kind and gentle man not threatened by my many successes. (My first husband, a Navy fighter pilot, could not say the same, and we divorced after a short marriage.) I remember Andy's dad asking him if he could handle marrying someone so accomplished, and Andy simply replied, "Well, someone has to love her, and I do."

Barb with her family, 2010, Hood River, Oregon.

Andy has truly been the wind beneath my wings. He has traveled the world with me as my best friend, copilot, and husband. After graduate school, he left the Navy and agreed to follow me around for the remainder of my Navy career. I know he is one in a million, because not many men would agree to step aside to follow a woman. Andy has done just that for the past fifteen years. I am forever indebted to him.

Six years ago, Andy and I began a new adventure, into parenthood, with the adoption of our son. After mountains of paperwork and a year-and-a-half wait, we traveled to Romania in February 2004 to pick up four-year-old David. He gets us up in the morning with a thousand-watt smile and the energy to match. He delights in every moment of the day (except when sent to his bedroom) and keeps us flying at high speed. We adopted our second child, Kim Anh, from Vietnam in March of 2009, when she was five and she is also a ball of energy. We traveled to Hanoi and were amazed at how welcoming

the Vietnamese were to us. We stayed at a hotel adjacent to the infamous "Hanoi Hilton" prison where American POWs were kept during the war. How life has changed for all of us.

For women interested in pursuing military aviation, the adventures of flying are indescribable and the people are fantastic. Flying teaches independence, competence, and the ability to make quick, solid decisions. There is an unrivaled power in the sisterhood of women aviators. I am tremendously proud to be one of them. I am proud to be part of a long legacy of women flyers, from the World War II Women Airforce Service Pilots (WASP) to the women who fly today in combat operations in Iraq and Afghanistan.

For my next career, I'm still a bit undecided, though I am seeking more balance between family and work life. Enjoying the break after all these years, I'm re-exploring my creativity, and who knows what will result? I do know that my next job will have two requirements—it will be important and it will be fun.

I am many things today, all of which define me—a mom who flies, a wife, a (now retired) naval officer, a test pilot school graduate, an artist, and a woman who chose the path less traveled.

My hopes and dreams for our children are many. I want them to know God, be good citizens, value honesty and hard work, and find their own path to their own dreams. I want them to experience different cultures, different friends, stay close with their family, and know themselves. I want them to revel in their native heritage and appreciate the freedoms and independence valued in their adopted country.

I can't change the world, but I can change my little piece of it and hold my ground.

Rank:	Navy Captain
Years Served:	24
Current Military Status:	Retired
Number of Children:	2

Pamela (Lyons) Carel

A-7E *Corsair II*, F/A-18 *Hornet*

AS THE OLDEST OF THREE CHILDREN, I WAS THE BOSSY ONE. MY DAD ALWAYS SAID I WAS BORN WITH THREE STRIPES ON MY SHOULDER! I wanted to be an engineer and an astronaut, so I majored in aerospace engineering at the University of Texas at Austin. I got to know several ROTC students, mostly guys, in my engineering classes, and they would often talk about the aircraft they might fly once they were in the military. I thought to myself, "If they could fly, why couldn't I?" It sure sounded like a lot more fun than sitting in a cubicle designing a rocket engine.

I rushed to see the Navy and Air Force recruiters on campus. The Air Force informed me there weren't many Air Force aircraft for women to fly. The Navy said, "Sure! We'll let you fly."

After college graduation in 1986, I attended the Navy's aviation officer candidate school in Pensacola, Florida. The first day of class started out with more than sixty wannabe aviator officers. Of these, five of us were women. One had four older brothers, all in the Marine Corps. Her name was Marine. She knew all about marching, military life, and what would take place over the next few months. She scared me to death! My only hope was to make it through the first night in the barracks.

She, along with almost half the class, was NAMI-whammied, meaning they were physically disqualified from becoming aviators. Only twenty-three of the original members graduated from that class, and I was the only woman.

I knew I wanted to fly jets and, after I received my wings of gold in 1988, I got my wish. Though I'd hoped to be assigned to a squadron in Hawaii, I was assigned to one of the Navy's trainer squadrons as a T-2 instructor pilot for a few years in Texas, and then got orders to fly the A-7E *Corsair II* in California. As the only woman in my A-7 training class, I was not well received. I was issued training manuals and told to study on my own. My mail was tossed on the hangar floor as a method of delivery. I was handed a plain manila folder with my military awards and citations from my previous squadron, instead of being presented with them at an official ceremony, as was the norm. Glad to be done with training, I was on my way to my fleet squadron—the Flashbacks of VAQ-34 at Naval Air Station Point Mugu, California.

Although the A-7 was a combat aircraft, women were unable to fly in combat squadrons due to the combat exclusion law. This presented me with limited choices in the types of aircraft and squadrons from which I could choose. VAQ-34 was an electronic warfare support squadron—we used our A-7s to mimic enemy aircraft and missiles in training Navy ships. I would have much preferred to be in a combat squadron, but I loved my time at VAQ-34—it had more female aviators than I had ever before seen in one room.

Although our squadron was not involved in combat operations, we flew all over the country, training combat squadrons and Navy ships. We flew to Roosevelt Roads, Puerto Rico, often. During one detachment to Roosevelt Roads, a flight of two A-7 *Corsairs* from my squadron took off for the start of training exercises—both pilots were women. On a fuel stop at Kelly Air Force Base, Texas, one of the A-7s blew a tire on landing—not an uncommon occurrence in the *Corsair*. I was scheduled to take off a few hours later for Puerto Rico and since my A-7 was outfitted with a "buddy store"—an extra tire and a

VFA-22 Squadron photo of Pam, 1994.

torque wrench—I was sent out as the rescue. Apparently, the men at Kelly Air Force Base were not accustomed to Navy female jet pilots, let alone those who conduct maintenance! You can imagine the surprise after the first two female pilots landed, I show up with the rescue equipment. They were convinced the squadron was all female! The Kelly transient maintenance crew tried to be helpful, but after they broke their torque wrench, we ended up changing the tire ourselves. It was a success, and we all arrived safely at our final destination with a good laugh!

We did not fly the A-7 for very long, because it was soon decommissioned. The squadron moved to Naval Air Station Lemoore, California, and transitioned to the F/A-18 *Hornet*. Once again, although the *Hornet* was a combat aircraft, VAQ-34 still flew in a support role.

Finally, in 1993, the combat exclusion law was repealed. I transitioned to a combat F/A-18 squadron

(VFA-22) at NAS Lemoore soon after and became the first female Navy fighter pilot. Several women who had been in the support squadrons were now stationed onboard the aircraft carrier USS *Abraham Lincoln* flying combat aircraft. What was more, we were the first group of women aviators ever to deploy on a West Coast aircraft carrier. We had formed a tight bond amidst the controversy of being the "first."

During this tour, I lost several good friends to aircraft accidents. One of those very good friends was the Navy's first F-14 pilot, Kara Hultgreen, who died in October 1994 while attempting to land her F-14 on the *Lincoln*. Not only was Kara's death a very sad time for all of us, but the entire tour was also fraught with change, turmoil, and frustration because of issues surrounding the integration of women into combat squadrons. Most of the men were supportive, but the few who weren't made life difficult. The situation did improve, but slowly.

While on a work trip to San Diego during my VAQ-34 tour, I met fellow aviator, Ken Carel. He was a radar intercept officer in the F-14 *Tomcat* and flew in a combat squadron stationed in San Diego. What was not to love? We married in 1995, but I was still stationed at NAS Lemoore and Ken was still in San Diego.

Ken decided to leave the military to focus on his career in the aerospace industry and so that we could live in the same location. Even so, I spent nineteen months of our first two years of marriage on an aircraft carrier at sea. After this tour, I asked for orders to return to Texas and once again instruct student pilots at one of the Navy's training squadrons. Since this was shore duty, it was the perfect time to start a family.

At this point, I still planned to make the Navy a career, but I was unsure how we would make it work after having children. If I stayed in, I knew that I would be on sea duty numerous times throughout the rest of my career.

Near the end of my instructor tour, I became pregnant with our first son, Kenny, and although it was a difficult decision, I chose to leave active duty in 2001. I transitioned immediately to the Navy Reserve, which provided a wonderful opportunity—I could be a full-time mom and work part-time for the Navy. This led to a new discovery—being a stay-at-home mom is not for the weak, and taking care of a newborn 24/7 is extremely challenging! As soon as I started getting used to baby number one, baby number two was on the way. Our son, Jackson, was born the following year, and I learned a new skill—the art of juggling two children under the age of three.

I have really enjoyed my varied tours in both the active-duty Navy and the Navy Reserve. The best part

Mom to Mom:

The most rewarding thing about being a mom is watching two little babies grow and learn and become wonderful, curious, and fun human beings. They never cease to amaze me with their uncanny insights and their independent spirits.

about the Navy Reserve has been that I can be a stay-at-home mom as much as I want and work only a few days each month, or I can request extended-duty assignments. Since Ken also works for the Navy Reserve in addition to his full-time job, we are constantly juggling schedules and assignments to make it all work for our family.

So far, our young sons, Kenny and Jackson, are unfazed by our comings and goings and are totally unimpressed with our flying careers. As a naval officer, I would be very proud if either of them wanted to join the military. On the other hand, as a mom, I would be just as apprehensive as my mother was!

Being a mom has definitely been the hardest, albeit the best, job I have had. I've been thrilled to share my children's every milestone with them. I have experienced the elation of being their sole source of comfort and chief problem-solver, as well as the humbling realization that, to them, I am just a mom and had no other life before they came into existence!

I'm sure that after Little League, Cub Scouts, and science fair projects are over, I will once again have my own time. For now, I enjoy all the time that is theirs.

. . . .

"Don't look back. Something might be gaining on you."

. . . .

—Satchel Paige

Rank:	Navy Captain
Years Served:	23
Current Military Status:	Reserve
Number of Children:	2

Sally deGozzaldi

H-2F *Seasprite*, H-46D *Sea Knight*, TH-57 *Sea Ranger*

MY MOM IMPRESSED UPON MY THREE SISTERS AND ME THAT A WOMAN COULD DO WHATEVER SHE WANTED. FOR AS LONG AS I CAN REMEMBER, I have wanted to fly. I attended Amherst College in Massachusetts, figuring that, once I graduated, I would find a good job and make enough money to take flying lessons. Although I didn't know much about the military, when a member of my college hockey team went into the Navy flight program, I wrote her about my interest in flying. She replied with an encouraging and motivational letter, and from that point on, I was determined to become a Navy flier.

In 1985, I received my commission as an ensign through the Navy's aviation officer candidate school—a challenging program both physically and mentally. Flight school was a blur and took a year to complete. When I first joined the Navy, most ships and many aircraft were not open to women. Women could fly helicopters, which provided the only opportunity to compete on an equal playing field. In addition, flying helos gave the best opportunity to deploy on naval ships, so it made sense to fly them!

After earning my wings of gold in 1986, I learned to fly the H-2F helicopter and I deployed to the Indian Ocean on the USNS *Chauvenet*, where our mission was to create coastal maps for Somalia and Kenya. The H-2F transported mapping equipment to and from coastal sites so that ships could determine their positions from sonar readings.

I loved flying, I loved deploying on ships, and I loved the opportunities the Navy provided. I moved every few years, and my tours included flying as an instructor pilot at a couple of the Navy's training squadrons and a couple of non-flying positions. My first non-flying job was as an admiral's aide in Florida, a very busy and dynamic job,

and then as a student receiving my master of science in aeronautical engineering at the Navy's postgraduate school in Monterey, California.

After graduation I returned to flying and to sea duty, this time flying the H-46 helicopter onboard the USS *Savannah*, transporting supplies, and then on the USS *Wasp*, flying search and rescue. It was back to school again, after sea duty, to the Air Force's Air Command and Staff College in Montgomery, Alabama, where career military officers learn about military history, operations, and tactics.

I had begun to make plans for being single for the rest of my life when I met a man who seemed to be the perfect fit. During my tour at Command and Staff College, we married and, soon after, had a beautiful son, Douglas. After this tour, I was transferred to Guam to fly helos for helicopter squadron HC-5, primarily transporting supplies and providing search-and-rescue support.

I became the squadron's aviation safety officer during this tour and assisted the National Transportation and Safety Board after the Korean Air Lines crash in 1997. I walked the wreckage with the base safety officer to locate and identify the different aircraft parts.

My husband and son also moved to Guam with me but, unfortunately, my husband and I divorced. I obtained full custody of my son and was extremely fortunate to have very supportive parents. My mother traveled from Maine to Guam a few times to help watch Douglas when I deployed. I finished up my assignment on Guam as a single parent.

That was probably the toughest time in my life, reeling from a failed marriage, holding down positions as

Sally with her three boys, Douglas, James, and Philip, 2005, when she was the commanding officer of a helicopter training squadron at NAS Whiting Field, Florida.

officer in charge and maintenance officer, and trying to be the sole parent. My close friends and family were instrumental in helping me balance all of my priorities. Moreover, becoming a single parent helped me decide what was important in my daily activities and guided me in the choices I made for the future.

At the end of this tour, I left Guam, with my son, for a job at the Pentagon. I was working there on September 11, 2001, during the terrorist attack, but, thankfully, I wasn't injured.

When I had returned to the States in 1999, I re-kindled a friendship with one of my best friends from college, Christopher Knowlton, after our school's fifteen-year reunion. Having just survived a divorce, I wasn't ready to even think about another relationship, but eventually we started dating. We had some considerable

geographic obstacles to overcome—Chris owned a business in Connecticut and I was in Washington, D.C. My son always asked when we were going to get married, as he was a big supporter of Chris even before I knew my own mind. Chris proposed, and we married in February 2001.

A short time later, I received orders to be the commanding officer of Helicopter Training Squadron Eight (HT-8) at one of the Navy training bases in Florida. Since I had already turned forty years old and would be on shore duty, Chris and I immediately tried to add to our family. By the next year, our son, James, was born. Chris still had his business in Connecticut but traveled to Florida one week each month. We decided we needed help, so we splurged for a full-time, live-in nanny.

I first served as the executive officer for HT-8 and, right before I took over as the squadron commander, I became pregnant with my third son. Since I was on shore duty, no rules prevented me from taking command of the squadron, but I was required to stop flying when five months pregnant. I set a precedent as the first Navy female to have a child while serving as commanding officer. My immediate chain of command was very supportive, but farther up the chain there was some concern; in the end, the Navy supported me in my position.

In 2005, at the end of my command tour, I retired from the Navy. I had spent twenty wonderful, challenging years in the military and, although it was stressful at times, it was definitely worth it. Serving as a squadron commanding officer was the highlight of my career. Being happily married was the major factor that helped to balance work and family. I found that a positive attitude, contributing to the team, and working hard were keys to a successful career.

After I retired from the Navy, we moved back to Connecticut, and I was a stay-at-home mom for a few years while earning my teaching degree. I am now a high school math teacher teaching algebra and geometry.

If any of my sons are interested in the military, I will encourage them to go into aviation. Both Chris and I stress the importance of education to our boys. We also stress the importance of being a strong, capable person who can make decisions on his or her own.

Mom to Mom:

The best thing about being a mom is the wonderful feeling I get when I watch my sons express themselves in thoughtful and caring ways.

**Never let it rest
Until the good is better
And the better is best.**

—James Casey

Rank:	Navy Commander
Years Served:	20
Current Military Status:	Retired
Number of Children:	3

Catherine (McCann) Gillies

H-3 *Sea King,* H-1 *Huey*

I GREW UP IN A SMALL COMMUNITY JUST OUTSIDE OF ANNAPOLIS, MARYLAND, NOT FAR FROM THE NAVAL ACADEMY. HAVING SPENT MY SUMMERS near the Chesapeake Bay, I developed a deep love for the water. The sharp uniforms of the Naval Academy impressed me greatly, so I was delighted to discover that women were now part of the midshipmen brigade. When I later learned that the academy had a good reputation for a rigorous academic program and that graduates often had opportunities for careers at sea, I became convinced that should be my future.

I started the academy in the summer of 1985 and dreamed of life onboard a ship as a naval surface warfare officer. Although two of my academy roommates encouraged me to consider a Navy career as a helicopter pilot, I initially shunned the idea, preferring to follow my romantic ideas of life at sea. They reminded me, however, that helicopter pilots could often go to sea onboard ships, but also had the freedom to fly off the ship from time to time. I liked that logic and thought perhaps they were correct, that helicopter pilots had the best of both worlds in the Navy—flying and sea time.

After graduating in 1989, I started flight school at Pensacola, Florida. I especially enjoyed the night cross-country navigation flights flying the T-34 trainer, but the aerobatics flights were challenging; I got sick on every acrobatic flight. I was definitely much more suited to helicopters than jets.

After flight school, I trained in the H-3 *Sea King* helicopter and got my first fleet assignment to the HC-16 squadron in Pensacola flying search and rescue. While there, I flew off of five different aircraft carriers. Navy policy had not yet changed to allow women to be permanently assigned onboard combat ships, including aircraft carriers, but we conducted missions with the carriers and regularly flew on and off.

I have many amusing memories from these early days when there were very few women in aviation. When a fellow woman aviator and I once drove from Baltimore to Philadelphia in a blinding snowstorm to report to the USS *Kitty Hawk* for our first carrier-at-sea deployment, the Marine Corps guards posted at the entrance to the ship's pier wouldn't let us through the gate. They announced, "There aren't any women aboard this ship!" After showing them our military identification cards and orders, a rash of apologies and flurry of saluting followed, and we were let onboard.

Most of our early days onboard carriers meant Marine Corps guards posted outside our (locking) stateroom doors. My fellow female pilot and I couldn't stand the thought of them being there 24/7 listening to everything we said and every noise we made. That got old pretty fast, so I ordered them away from my door. They'd stay away for a while until they got caught by their supervisors and were ordered back. Several days of this on each ship—with a few, "I outrank your boss, now scram!" remarks from me—finally wore them down, and they stopped coming back.

On another at-sea period on a different carrier, I called the ship's weather forecasters to ask for a weather briefing for my flight. When the sailor suppressed his laughter at my request, he asked me how I made the call to him and who put me up to it because "there aren't women on this ship." He then hung up on me, still laughing. The other female pilot in our squadron and I were definitely novelties.

Catherine and a flight training instructor pose after the training squadron
VT-2 "tie-cutting" ceremony, 1989, NAS Whiting Field, Florida.

I like to sew and had taken a quilting class, and I would take small quilting projects onboard my carrier detachments. The guys would take their same old movies (and be bored to death in three days) while I had tons to do and was even able to make a few nice gifts and holiday decorations along the way. I'd quilt at night or whenever I had the ready-room phone watch for hours on end. At the end of one very long phone watch, a fellow pilot came into the ready room and saw what I was doing. To this day I can't remember who it was, but he muttered, "$%&%$, there are dead aviators the world over turning in their graves tonight because some chick is knitting in their ready room!"

Flying the search-and-rescue mission off the aircraft carriers was absolutely thrilling! I loved listening to the other carrier aircraft conduct flight operations, while we circled alongside in case an accident occurred. In addition, I flew on several medical-evacuation missions, including

transporting a diver with the bends to a decompression chamber. During one rescue mission at sea, I was the copilot during a rescue of a ship crewmember who had jumped overboard. I also enjoyed flying at night and loved the excitement of working up on the flight deck.

Near the end of that tour, the combat exclusion law was lifted, creating many more exciting and career-enhancing opportunities for women in the military. Women could now fly in combat squadrons and participate in several combat occupations in the military.

My current squadron decommissioned, and several of our squadron pilots transferred to HMT-303, the UH-1N *Huey* helicopter training squadron, which relocated around the same time to Camp Pendleton, a Marine Corps base in California. Although HMT-303 was a Marine Corps squadron, they would train both Navy and Marine Corps student helicopter pilots. I asked to transfer to the new squadron also. Women weren't yet allowed to fly in the Marine Corps, but my commanding officer found a way for me to join HMT-303, and I became the first and only female pilot at that time flying in any Marine Corps squadron.

I was thrilled to see the first female Marine Corps aviator—Sarah Deal—complete flight training about the same time my tour at Camp Pendleton ended. Flying with HMT-303 was like a dream, and I really enjoyed flying the *Huey* and teaching students how to fly.

Several months after I left Camp Pendleton, I found myself volunteering at the Miramar air show and swapping flying stories with some H-3 pilots, who were reservists attached to a local reserve squadron. I didn't give the conversation too much thought until my boss asked me if I had ever considered supporting the Navy Reserve full-time. I decided I would, and, with his very strong endorsement letter, I was accepted to fly the H-3 in the reserve community, which allowed me to stay in San Diego. Professionally, I really enjoyed this tour because I flew a lot of utility flights in which I carried external loads suspended below my helicopter. I had a passion for flying external loads and enjoyed nearly every minute flying around with things hanging below my helicopter. It also turned out to be a good personal decision to stay in San Diego because it allowed me to finish up my master's degree, earn a second, and, finally, earn a doctorate. I didn't realize it at the time, but this turned out to be my last flying job.

I continued working in the Navy, supporting the Navy Reserve in a non-flying support role. Before retiring from the Navy in 2009, I had gotten married and started my family—two daughters and a son. However, I spent the last few years in the Navy as a single mom—it was hard juggling my Navy career with a family. I wanted to be the best at both, and I hated it when I had to make either take a back seat to the other for a while. I survived because I had good support. I moved back home to be near my mom for my final active-duty tour, and her support was invaluable.

I loved my Navy career and all its adventures and educational opportunities. My motto has always been "Never give up!" Sometimes it's life's little challenges that make things so interesting! I learned long ago that we are more likely to succeed in reaching our goals if we have a mentor to guide us. I've taken that philosophy another step and I make myself available to mentor Navy junior officers and enlisted members to help them follow their dreams. My advice to other working moms is that support is absolutely key, especially juggling parenting and career responsibilities.

Now that I'm retired from the Navy, I'm thrilled to be home and to be there for and with the kids. I love being a mom! I teach part-time for a couple of colleges and both jobs fit nicely with my other adventures. Last year we started homeschooling, which I really enjoy—we've grown so close together as a result, and we've done a lot of cool things as a family. The kids and I are very active with school field trips, sports, and Girl Scouts, and I also sponsor and coach a kid's Lego League.

I hope to pass to my children that they can do whatever they want and be whatever they want. Life is full of choices and fantastic opportunities. I hope they find life to be as much of an adventure as I have, and that they will be well-rounded and happy.

> **Mom to Mom:**
> The most rewarding thing about being a mom is seeing my kids try out new things and succeed. I'm really amazed at how strong and resilient they are.

Roadblocks along the way to success are only speed bumps if you look at them from the right perspective.

Rank:	Navy Lieutenant Commander
Years Served:	20
Current Military Status:	Retired
Number of Children:	3

Kristin (Burke) Greentree

F/A-18 *Hornet*, F-16 *Fighting Falcon*

I'LL NEVER FORGET MY FIRST AIRLINE FLIGHT—I WAS TWELVE AND FLEW ALONE. WHEN I RETURNED HOME AND SAW MY MOM, THE FIRST WORDS OUT of my mouth were, "I want to be a pilot!"

Although I contemplated going to college to study how to become a pilot, my dad wisely encouraged me to get a degree in engineering first, so I attended Virginia Tech and studied aerospace engineering. Having great support from my mom and dad has been priceless, and I attribute my learned ability to set and achieve goals to their constant encouragement and confidence in me.

Approaching college graduation in 1999, I began to feel the pull of flying once again, so I started the process of applying to the U.S. Air Force for officer training school and eventually pilot training. During that process, I was offered an excellent job as a civilian working for the Navy as an engineer. I decided to take the job and learn what the Navy was all about. Wow, am I glad that I did! It didn't take me long, working around F/A-18 test pilots who landed their aircraft on moving ships, to realize that flying Navy aircraft was what I wanted to do!

A few months later, I entered the Navy's officer candidate school—an amazing experience—which reinforced my belief that the military and naval aviation were for me! Soon after, I started flight training in Corpus Christi, Texas, elated to be there. I worked to keep my grades high so that I would get to fly what I wanted after graduation—jets! Thankfully, my hard work paid off, and I received my first choice.

During the early stages of jet training, I discovered I was pregnant and had to stop flying immediately. I wasn't sure what to do about my career in the Navy. Fortunately, one of the flight instructors in my command was a new

mom and a Navy F/A-18 pilot. She stressed to me that it would be extremely difficult, but that I could make both parenting and my aviation career work, as long as I had a lot of support.

I prayed, and I struggled with the choice of whether or not to stay in the Navy. In the end, I chose to continue my path of becoming a Navy pilot. I knew that if I backed out of my lifelong dream, I would regret it. I also knew that if things got too tough along the way, I could leave the military at my end-of-service commitment. Finding out I was pregnant and putting off flight training was initially very difficult, but having my son, Austin, turned out to be the best thing that has ever happened. I was scared about being a mom, a role I did not believe I was ready for, and I was selfishly afraid that I might never fly again. However, Austin's first year of life was one of my most memorable years, and I experienced more joy than I had ever known. I felt like I had it all—the absolute joy of flying, and the amazement of being a mom to this little boy. He was and continues to be my most cherished blessing in life.

After Austin was born, I continued jet training in Texas, while his dad, also a Navy pilot, transferred to Virginia. Eventually, we all ended up in Virginia together, where I trained to fly the F/A-18C *Hornet* and joined VFA-37. After joining the squadron, it quickly became apparent that I would soon deploy on an aircraft carrier and fly missions in a combat zone.

For my first combat experience in the F/A-18, I flew on the wing of my squadron commander into Iraq—extremely nervous and a little scared, as we searched the ground for surface fire, which, thankfully, was not as imminent a threat as I had thought—in our role of supporting the troops on the ground.

Kristin and son, Austin (5 years old), 2008, Fallon, Nevada.

Of course, I would be remiss as a naval aviator if I didn't mention the amazing experience of flying from a Navy aircraft carrier. I honestly love it and it is the most exciting part of my job! There is nothing like attempting to land on the flight deck of a moving ship.

Flying around the carrier was amazing but I also loved participating in air shows and talking with people about aviation and the military. I still laugh about an encounter I had with a man at the Pittsburgh air show. I was very lucky to get to take an F/A-18C to the air show as a static display. I stood by the aircraft for both days of the air show and remember a man in his fifties looking at the airplane. I approached him and asked, "Can I answer any questions for you, sir?" He stared at me with a puzzled look on his face, and then asked, "They let you fly this thing?!" I answered, "Yes, sir." In perfect Pittsburghese, he exclaimed "Naahhh!" (Translation: No!). I still laugh at and

imitate the exchange I had with this man on many occasions. It is amazing that there are still so many people in this country who don't realize that women are permitted to fly in combat.

After my F/A-18 tour, I was given the incredible opportunity to become a Strike Fighter instructor at the Naval Strike and Air Warfare Center in Fallon, Nevada, flying both the F/A-18 and the F-16. I trained other naval aviators in advanced aviation combat tactics, techniques, and procedures. Flying the F-16 has been a highlight of my career—it's comparable to strapping on a sleek sports car with nothing ahead but open road.

Austin is a trooper regarding the crazy military schedules! Some days I take him to daycare at 5 a.m., while other days I can't pick him up until well after dark. I am so thankful for the very flexible caregivers, most of whom are military wives. They have sacrificed so much of their own time to help care for my son while I work, and I hope they know how grateful I am.

Although the experiences of a military mom are somewhat different from those of other working moms, I suspect the emotions we experience are very similar—guilt, worry, and fear, especially for moms who work outside of the home. Will Austin be angry with me for being in the military or for being away so much? Will he be negatively affected by my sometimes ridiculous work schedule? And my biggest fear: will he grow up feeling as if I didn't love him because I was taken away from him so much during my service in the military?

Making sure my son knows that I love him is my priority in life. Balancing that with trying to raise a respectful and considerate young man is the greatest challenge a military parent faces. I pray a lot and trust God to help us through it.

When young women ask me about being a naval aviator and a mom, I tell them I do not recommend doing both. Although some women feel that they can "have it all," I do not believe I can give my child my best if I am trying to do it all. Each woman has to make her own decision for herself and her family. That being said, I am not certain what the future holds for me, but I have decided this—I do not want to miss any more of my son's life. I

Mom to Mom:

The thing that surprised me most about being a mom is the reality of how important it is! Even flying a multi-million-dollar aircraft pales in comparison to the awesome responsibility of raising my child to be a kind, loving, caring, responsible, and wise young adult; all the while he is watching to see if I am doing the same!

love what I do and I love serving in the military, but I love Austin so much more and want to be there for him and to watch him grow up.

During my first deployment, in the skies over Iraq, supporting our troops on the ground, I realized that what I was doing was important and a worthy service. I pray that my son grows up to learn that serving in the military is a noble choice of duty. Some are called to do it, others are not. For now, I feel blessed every time that I climb into a fighter jet and go flying. It is an amazing feeling and a freedom that I will always cherish.

I am grateful to God for blessing me with my son, the greatest gift I could have ever imagined. He is and will always be my greatest accomplishment in life!

Rank:	Navy Lieutenant
Years Served:	9
Current Military Status:	Active Duty
Number of Children:	1

Michelle (Guidry) Hickie

S-3 *Viking*

SINCE MY DAD WAS AN ARMY HELICOPTER PILOT, I GREW UP AROUND THE MILITARY AND AVIATION. MY MOTHER WAS DETERMINED I WOULD go to college! Her strong work ethic and loving persuasiveness kept me focused on long-term goals when I was ready to give up and take the easy road.

In 1988, I graduated from Auburn University with a degree in aerospace engineering and received my commission in the Navy. Initially, I could not apply to flight school because of a medical issue that disqualified me—a childhood allergy to bee stings. I took a job at the Space and Naval Warfare Systems Command in Washington, D.C., where I worked as a test engineer on a communications satellite program. During that tour, I received a medical waiver for my allergy issue and finally was on my way to flight school.

I started flight training in February 1991 and initially hoped to fly helicopters, but ended up selecting jets. Because the combat exclusion law prohibited women from flying in combat squadrons, I would be limited to a support squadron once I got to the fleet. Before graduating from flight school, I learned those support squadrons were to be decommissioned soon. Instead of getting flying orders, I went to the aircraft carrier USS *Forrestal* to be a fuels officer, a non-flying job.

Finally, in April 1993, the combat exclusion law was repealed. That meant I could now fly in a combat squadron, and the Navy told me I would fly the S-3 *Viking*, a carrier-based antisubmarine-warfare jet.

After training to fly the S-3, I joined an S-3 squadron in San Diego, California, and deployed aboard the USS *Carl Vinson* in support of Operation *Enduring Freedom*. The flying was some of the best of my life. Sunset and sunrise were my favorite times to fly—always so quiet and tranquil.

In addition to the antisubmarine-warfare mission, the S-3 also performed tanking missions for different carrier aircraft. The "night hawker" tanking mission was my favorite—we followed a jet around the aircraft carrier landing pattern in a position for them to refuel immediately if they couldn't land on the carrier.

Life on the boat (what naval aviators call an aircraft carrier) was difficult at times because you could never escape work since you were there 24/7. Being one of two women aviators in the squadron—and one of only a handful of women on the entire aircraft carrier with more than 6,000 men—made life interesting.

After my squadron tour, I had the incredible opportunity to attend the Navy's Postgraduate and Test Pilot School (TPS) Cooperative Program. First stop in 1997 was to Naval Postgraduate School in Monterey, California, and then on to the Navy's test pilot school at NAS Patuxent (Pax) River, Maryland, a challenging program that included both academics and flying. I flew twenty-five different aircraft during test pilot school, including jets, helicopters, sailplanes, and floatplanes. Once I finished this phase, I received my master's degree in aeronautical engineering.

I met my husband, Ty Hickie, while attending school in Monterey, and we married after I moved to Pax. After TPS, I transferred to one of the test squadrons at Pax and thoroughly enjoyed flying several different aircraft. I even received the test pilot of the year award! My favorite flight was flying the PBY-6A *Catalina* patrol bomber that could land on a runway or on water.

Soon after joining the test squadron, I became pregnant with my son, Garrett. Military rules restricted me from

Michelle and husband, Ty, dressed up for a Navy "Dining Out" function, October 2006, NAS Patuxent River, Maryland.

flying ejection-seat aircraft while pregnant, but I was able to fly the C-130 *Hercules*, a non-ejection-seat aircraft. My last flight while pregnant occurred on September 11, 2001. We were conducting a tanking mission for some F/A-18 *Hornets* off the East Coast when the terrorists attacked. I remember wondering what was going on and how this could be happening! It was even more terrifying watching the news coverage once I landed.

In addition to Garrett, we also have three other children—my stepdaughter, Jennifer, and my stepsons, Timothy and Justin. Jennifer lives in Iowa with our grandsons, and, recently, our son, Justin, also had a son.

After leaving the squadron, I transferred to a desk job at Pax, employing my aviation, engineering, and test pilot skills. In 2007, I deployed to Iraq for a year and worked with the Army, serving as the director of engineering for the equipment used to keep improvised explosive devices from killing our troops. This was the longest I have ever been away from my family. While it was a rewarding

experience, it was difficult to be separated from my husband and kids. I sent daily emails to Ty and text messages to my teenage sons' cell phones. I also put together monthly presentations that included photos and updates on my daily life in Iraq and sent it to family and friends back home. Ty and I never tried to shield our kids from the knowledge of the dangerous work I was involved in during my deployment, but we also didn't provide a lot of details, especially to Garrett. During the deployment, support from friends and family was essential for Ty and the boys. We were thankful that several family members came to help for a few months at a time.

I have not flown a military aircraft in more than nine years, and I don't know if I will ever fly for the military again. I would love to, but it all depends on the needs of the Navy. Flying—hands down—has been the highlight of my career, and I miss it every day. The Navy recently promoted me to captain. I feel honored, never thinking I would go this far. I still enjoy my career and plan to stay in for several more years. The Navy has taught me so much over the years—discipline, organization, respect, confidence, compartmentalization, commitment, teamwork, and integrity.

Raising a family with both parents working takes dedication and communication to coordinate all the comings and goings of school events, sports, and family fun time. It is a team effort! Our family plans the daily and weekly activities when we gather for meals. We make it a point to dedicate dinnertime to communication, meaning no television, no telephone, and no outside distractions. Everyone pitches in and does their share of the work to keep the household running smoothly; otherwise, it would be chaos. As a career-oriented woman, I was not sure how a family would fit into my life. I find it amazing that I met a wonderful man who was a great father already and understood my goals to continue in my career. I had never thought I would meet someone who would be so giving and willing to support me in my endeavors.

Mom to Mom:

The thing that surprised me the most about being a mom is how much love I have to give. I have even more love for everyone else because of the love I receive from my children.

I'm trying to instill in my children the old Army slogan, "Be all you can be." I think it is important to set high goals and then strive to reach them. I tell my kids that they will never know what they can do until they try. Succeed or fail, they must at least try! Our two older boys have recently graduated from high school, and I keep telling them how important it is for their future that they excel now. Excelling now may or may not be cool or fun, but the rest of their lives depends on it. Right now, my youngest son only cares about who he is going to be for Halloween.

Reach for the stars. If you don't try to reach as high as you can, you will never know how far you can go.

Rank:	Navy Captain
Years Served:	21
Current Military Status:	Active Duty
Number of Children:	4

Jamie (Edwards) Johnson

F/A-18 *Hornet*

I WAS BORN AND RAISED IN HAWAII AND NEVER DREAMED OF FLYING AIRPLANES FOR A CAREER. MY DREAM WAS TO BECOME A FOREIGN DIPLOMAT and ambassador. So my flying career happened by chance.

With only enough money to make it through one year at Boston University studying international relations, I decided a military scholarship was the only way I could stay in college. Thankfully, the Navy saw it my way, and I was picked up for Navy ROTC.

During the summer following my sophomore year, I toured a Navy helicopter squadron and rode in an H-2 *Sea Sprite*. It was love at first flight! To fly through the air, stop, hover, and skim over the trees was amazing. I knew I wanted to be a helicopter pilot...until I saw two F/A-18 *Hornets* race like lightning into a nearby fighter base. Watching pure beauty and power in harmonious motion was mesmerizing. So I changed my mind and decided to shoot for the top—jets!

I headed to flight training in the early 1990s. With hard work and diligent study, I graduated high enough to get a coveted jet slot. After training in the T-2C *Buckeye* and the TA-4J *Sky Hawk*, I fell in love with fast movers and high-speed flying. INCREDIBLE is the only word that describes the first time I landed on an aircraft carrier for carrier qualifications, followed by getting a kick-in-the-pants catapult shot takeoff. I adored the A-4 and, to this day, still remember the first time I sat in the cockpit of the *Sky Hawk*, marveling at the thrill of being in that powerful jet—I felt like rocket woman!

When I graduated from flight school in June 1994, Congress had just changed the law, now allowing women to fly in combat squadrons. I was assigned to a combat F/A-18 *Hornet* squadron in Lemoore, California. The *Hornet*, my first choice of a fighter, is an absolute beauty. In December 1995, I joined the squadron, and a year later deployed to the Arabian Gulf aboard the aircraft carrier USS *Kitty Hawk*.

One night, while flying over the Indian Ocean en route to the Gulf, I wondered what combat would be like. Would it be easy to face after all of my training, or would it be devastating? Would I be able to handle it and do my duty? A friend recommended reading *The Heart of a Man: A Naval Pilot's Vietnam Diary* by Frank Callihan Elkins. It is the personal diary of a young A-4 naval aviator who was shot down in October 1966. His thoughts and conclusions about flying combat missions helped me to calmly face my own thoughts and make solid decisions about the reality of flying a powerful, lethal warfighting jet in a time of combat. In the end, I flew twenty-three combat missions over Iraq. After completing my squadron tour in 1998, I joined the F/A-18 training squadron as an instructor pilot.

I met my future husband, Stevin Johnson, while we both were going through the *Hornet* training squadron as students. He likes to say that he fell in love with me at SERE school (Survival, Evasion, Resistance, and Escape), training that prepared aviators how to respond if taken as a prisoner of war by a hostile country. For a few days during SERE school, I was the senior-ranking officer for our class, and Stevin says he was impressed by my calm demeanor and good decisions.

Stevin, on the other hand, was the most humble, calm, and loyal man I had ever met. Calm and humble

Jamie and husband, Stevin, with their first child, son Sean, in 2002, NAS Lemoore, California.

are not adjectives generally used to describe fighter pilots, so to find one in that crowd was truly a treasure. Plus, he has the tenacity of a bulldog and brushed off the criticism he received for dating and then marrying a "chick" fighter pilot. I had to love that about him, a real knight in shining armor! Only, his white horse was just like mine, an F/A-18!

Before we married, we were mostly concerned about being stationed apart. We feared one of us would be sent to the opposite coast, or that he would be sent to a Japan-based squadron that was not available to female pilots at the time. Looking back, if I had known how hard squadron life would be—long hours, studying, pressure of performance, deployments—I might have waited a lot longer to marry.

My plan was to not have children while I flew ejection-seat fighter aircraft. Women are not allowed to fly while pregnant in ejection-seat aircraft, so that would have meant ten months of no flying during any pregnancy and postpartum recovery. Not an option in such a competitive field, especially as I was the only female pilot in my combat squadron.

Honestly, I was not sure I wanted kids. I was the youngest of six children and never had to take care of another soul in my life—I never even babysat! But my husband wanted kids, so after seven years of flying fighters and debating this important subject countless times, we decided to start a family. However, as fun as flying was, the toll of being married to another fighter pilot and spending months apart for years to come began to weigh on my mind. I didn't think I could continue both my intense military flying career and step into the mysterious world of motherhood, while giving either job the full attention they both deserved. Therefore, I left active duty.

Leaving a fast-paced, exhilarating flying job and being suddenly unemployed, I was now *just* a Navy wife. It was one of the most depressing times of my life. I struggled to identify myself as something other than a fighter pilot. Fortunately, I had joined the Navy Reserve and continued flying with the F/A-18 training squadron as an instructor pilot.

A few years later, in the summer of 2001, I decided to pursue a career with American Airlines as a commercial pilot. Then the September 11, 2001, attacks on the World Trade Center changed my plans. The airlines stopped new-hire trainees three days later, so I began working for Boeing Aerospace Operations as a simulator instructor and started pursuing a second college degree, in addition to continuing to serve in the Navy Reserve.

We started our family in 2002 with the birth of my son, Sean, and then a few years later, in 2005, we had our daughter, Sydney, and then our third child, Sofia, in 2007.

Looking back, I think that raising children is a much tougher assignment than flying 500 knots at 200 feet or yanking and banking in a challenging dogfight. My kids have made me appreciate the true meaning of sacrifice and duty. Being a mom also makes me appreciate the love, support, and encouragement my mother gave me. I hope to give my children the same. I also hope to inspire them to reach for the stars and to dream big.

Mom to Mom:

Being a mom is the closest thing there is to understanding how God feels about us, His children.

As I look back at my flying days, I gloss over the hard times and remember the wonderful experiences and the incredible opportunities. I remain amazed and grateful to this country, my America, which has allowed me to fly such a great aircraft, trusted me to conduct combat missions, and helped me prove that both men and women can fly these electrifying jets and withstand the rigors of carrier aviation.

Would I recommend naval aviation to the next generation of women? Absolutely! It is the opportunity of a lifetime, a challenging, consuming, and fulfilling place to be. Yes, it is hard and there is a lot of blood, sweat, and tears behind building the skills to fly so effortlessly. It demands the very best, but the satisfaction is worth the price.

I had no idea how much having kids would change my life, my perspective, my self-worth. Three kids later, I can say that I loved flying in the Navy, flying fighters, and would still be doing it today if I were single or didn't have kids. But, now, I consider being a mom my greatest duty and my greatest honor of all.

"You become successful the moment you start moving toward a worthwhile goal."

—Samuel Johnson

Rank:	Navy Commander
Years Served:	19
Current Military Status:	Navy Reserve
Number of Children:	3

Margaret (DeLuca) Klein

EC-130 *Hercules*, E-6B *Mercury*

I WAS BORN IN BOSTON, MASSACHUSETTS, IN 1957, THE OLDEST OF FOUR DAUGHTERS. MY DAD SERVED IN THE NAVY RESERVE AND BELONGED to the Navy flying club when I was growing up. I remember being ten years old, sitting in the flying club office on Saturday mornings while my dad was flying or in a class. I couldn't wait until he earned his license so I could fly with him!

My parents always encouraged me to excel in school, and my high school experience reinforced the notion that there was no limit to my choice of career fields. As I finished high school, I applied for college ROTC scholarships. I knew I wanted to join the military, but wasn't sure exactly what I wanted to do. All I knew was I wanted to major in oceanography.

I attended civilian colleges until the spring of 1977 when I was accepted at both West Point and the Naval Academy. After much deliberation, I decided on the Naval Academy. I saw how much my dad loved his time in the Navy Reserve, so I decided to pursue a Navy career.

Only one year earlier, in 1976, the Naval Academy had started accepting women. In 1977, women comprised less than 10 percent of entering freshmen. During my four years there, I made friends I treasure to this day. Not a week goes by that I don't hear from or read about a classmate.

Two important things shaped my life during my four years at the academy—I met my future husband, Frank, and the Navy opened up the naval flight officer program to women. Just before I graduated from the Naval Academy, Frank and I became engaged. Frank had graduated from the academy two years earlier and was a naval flight officer flying the P-3 *Orion*.

Aviators in the Navy are either pilots or naval flight officers. Pilots fly the airplanes, and naval flight officers handle the radios, navigation equipment, and associated aircraft systems. My eyesight prevented me from being a pilot, so when it came time for me to choose what I wanted to do, and there was only one naval flight officer slot left, I took it.

I graduated in 1981, attended flight training, and then received orders to fly the C-130 at a squadron in Hawaii. Frank and I were now married, and we transferred to Hawaii together. We had an additional passenger with us—we discovered I was pregnant. I showed up at the squadron six months pregnant, and, although our timing could have been better, I was overjoyed to be having our first child. Since I was so far along in my pregnancy, I couldn't fly due to Navy regulations, so I made a point of working twelve-hour days to compensate.

Our son, Brendan, was born in January 1984, and what a blessing he was! After Brendan's birth, I was again able to pull my weight when it came to flying, and my career took off from there. Finding good daycare for Brendan was difficult and, since we lived so far from home, no family was available nearby to help. Fortunately, I found a wonderful woman who treated my son like one of her own, and thus I survived my first assignment as an aviator mom.

After our tours in Hawaii, we moved to Norfolk, Virginia, where I worked at a non-flying staff job. My daughter was born during this tour. I was very concerned about who would take care of my job while I stayed home for six weeks of maternity leave. As it turned out, a dear friend covered my job while doing his. It was really hard asking for help. No one ever turned me down when I asked, so my advice is to ask sooner rather than later.

Peg and family at Peg's change-of-command ceremony, 2004, when she took over command of the Navy's TACAMO Air Wing at Tinker Air Force Base in Oklahoma City, Oklahoma.

Since this tour was Frank's turn for sea duty, he had two deployments onboard aircraft carriers, the USS *Saratoga* and the USS *Theodore Roosevelt*. That was when I found out that we who deploy have it much easier than the loved ones we leave behind. The Army used to have an ad campaign that talked about soldiers doing more by 9 a.m. than most people do in a day. That's how I felt getting kids out the door to daycare. Once I made it to work, my day was easy. Shore duty was great, and I spent lots of weekends visiting family, which made my husband's deployments go by quickly.

Frank and I both enjoyed great careers, which included each of us commanding operational flying squadrons. I don't know if that's been done by many other couples in the Navy. Frank served as the commanding officer of a P-3 squadron out of Brunswick, Maine, and then retired a year after his squadron command. I became the commanding officer of the Navy's E-6 aircraft wing at Tinker AFB in Oklahoma.

I turned over command in December 2005 and headed to sea onboard the aircraft carrier USS *Dwight D. Eisenhower*, serving as the chief of staff for the *Eisenhower* strike group that had more than 6,000 sailors and officers. Just a few weeks into the ship's deployment, I found out I had been selected to be the commandant of midshipmen at the Naval Academy. Prior to leaving the *Eisenhower* for the academy job, I finally realized my lifelong dream of flying in the backseat of an F/A-18 *Hornet*, and got catapulted off the carrier and then made an arrested landing.

As the Naval Academy commandant, I was the dean of students, responsible for the professional development of 4,300 midshipmen. I also led a staff of more than 600 military and civilian professionals. I very much enjoyed this tour leading and mentoring future naval officers. Midshipmen are an amazing group of young men and women—smart and dedicated to serving this country. Shortly before leaving the academy for my next job in Norfolk, Virginia, I was selected to the rank of rear admiral!

My advice to young men and women—find something you can be passionate about, then stay in dogged pursuit of it. If you run into roadblocks, craft a way around the obstacles. If they are insurmountable, come up with plan B, but keep your plan A options open.

Frank and our children have been my biggest source of inspiration. They encouraged me to take on every challenging assignment that came my way. There has always been give and take—my son and daughter were in three high schools because of my career. Though there were bumps and bruises along the way, they have gained some great experiences from moving around the world. Both are interested in service to their country, are extremely patriotic, and have a profound appreciation for life in the greatest country in the world.

Mom to Mom:

I love being a mom because bringing two children into the world was probably the closest thing to a miracle that I will ever be blessed to see. The responsibility of being a mom was daunting because the "mom" training track is non-existent. But, when my children were born, they were such a blessing from God and the most inspirational events in my life.

My hopes and dreams for my children are that they find a career where they can be successful and productive. I hope they use the gifts God has given them, and I hope they each find a life partner who will be as supportive and loving as my husband has been to me. It has made my life incredibly fun and exciting. I wouldn't have traded any of it.

. . . .

Work hard, enjoy your work, and infect others with your positive attitude!

. . . .

Rank:	Navy Rear Admiral
Years Served:	28
Current Military Status:	Active Duty
Number of Children:	2

Karin (Klose) Kulinski

EP-3E & RP-3 *Orion*, C-130 *Hercules*

WHEN I JOINED THE NAVY IN THE SUMMER OF 1985, I WANTED TO ATTEND THE UNITED STATES NAVAL ACADEMY MORE THAN anything else in life. I didn't even really know what women could do in the Navy, but I wanted a different and challenging college experience. The academy seemed to be the top academic, athletic, honorable, travel-intensive, patriotic, and prestigious experience. My parents were surprised with my career choice because no one in our family had any connections with the military.

Immediately after high school graduation, I participated in the Naval Academy's plebe summer, their transition course for all incoming freshmen. However, plebe summer is no gentle easing into the military routine and proved to be the hardest summer of my life. Soon after entering the academy gate on induction day, I put on my first military uniform, learned how to salute, and then was yelled at every day for the next six weeks. The challenges and stress of that summer built not only the foundation of my naval career but also the start of lifelong friendships.

During the summer before my senior year, I worked at the Pentagon, experienced life with a P-3 *Orion* squadron in Iceland, and then spent a month as part of the crew on a Navy destroyer tender. The stark comparison between ship life and aviation life quickly convinced me that aviation was the way to go.

Flight school, simply put, was tough. I strove to get the best possible academic and flight grades. Upon receiving my Navy wings of gold in December 1990, I had limited choices for the type of aircraft I could fly. The combat exclusion law prohibited women from flying combat aircraft or flying in a combat squadron. Therefore, I based my flight selection on location—I chose Rota, Spain, to

fly the EP-3E *Aries-II*, a reconnaissance version of the Navy's P-3 *Orion*.

In 1991, I arrived in Rota and spent the next three years flying for VQ-2 (Fleet Air Reconnaissance Squadron Two). The squadron's mission was to conduct airborne electronic reconnaissance to obtain information on areas and targets of naval and national interest.

We worked sixteen-hour days, deploying for three weeks at a time to Souda Bay on Crete. At age twenty-six, I was in charge of a $60 million aircraft with a twenty-six person crew. The Navy gives its young officers tremendous responsibility, which in turn teaches confidence and the basic tenets of leadership.

Although my squadron duties kept me extremely busy, I lived on the beach with a couple of roommates and enjoyed the incredible hospitality and liveliness of Spain, which I sorely miss to this day. The work-hard/play-hard lifestyle the Navy offers continued into my next tour.

In 1994, I moved to Alexandria, Virginia, to fly the RP-3 for the Naval Research Laboratory. We measured the ocean temperature, tested new radar systems, and completed other airborne naval research throughout the world, including Thailand, England, United Arab Emirates, Japan, the Maldives, Italy, Australia, Djibouti, Singapore, and Kazakhstan.

The mission to Kazakhstan was my most challenging in the Navy. Told only that the Department of Energy would like to take a P-3 to Kazakhstan, I had to arrange payment of $138,000 in cash for fees, billeting, in-flight air-traffic-control translation, and training on Soviet flight procedures. In between my travels with the Naval Research Lab, I worked as a White House social aide,

Karen with two of her daughters, Katrina and Stephanie, on VR-53 flight line, 2007.

assisting presidential guests during state dinners, receptions, and parties.

I loved the Navy life and enjoyed moving every few years. However, as I entered into my thirties, I wanted to settle down a little more. I decided to leave the active-duty Navy and, in 1997, joined the Navy Reserve to fly the C-130 *Hercules* aircraft at VR-53, based at Andrews AFB. I typically worked a few days each month.

Flying the C-130 has been even more rewarding than my previous P-3 tours. As a pilot of the Navy's largest cargo aircraft, I have flown troops and cargo to every corner of the world, deploying to such places as Sicily, Japan, Iwo Jima, Bahrain, and Qatar, and often to runways so short that *only* a C-130 could land. I've brought fifteen tons of ammunition into the Balkans, tsunami-relief supplies to Indonesia, and Christmas presents to sailors in the Persian Gulf.

In addition to flying for VR-53, I also joined United Airlines in 1998 and spent five enjoyable years flying the 737 throughout the United States and Canada, but was furloughed at the end of 2003.

During my first tour in Washington, D.C., one of my running buddies insisted upon introducing me to his college friend, Stephen Kulinski, an architect who spent more than twenty years in Old Town Alexandria, designing and rebuilding various parts of Northern Virginia. Our three years of dates included a camping trip to Yellowstone National Park, a Cessna flight across the Chesapeake Bay, and my squadron copilot's wedding in Spain.

After answering several hundred questions from my friends and family on how I could possibly have met a civilian (someone not in the military), I married Steve in 2000. Steve agreed to love, honor, and take at least one international vacation per year. He has been incredibly understanding of the Navy, and has made both of my careers possible.

Steve and I greeted our first daughter, Katrina, in 2003, then Stephanie in 2006, and Natalie in 2010. The irregular work hours have often allowed me extra time at home with my daughters. The drastic differences between the two halves of my life make me appreciate and look forward to each half even more. By the time my first daughter, Katrina, turned one, she proudly pointed at every airplane, exclaiming "Mommy!" The best memory has been the look of awe the first time Katrina saw the C-130 I am now flying and declared, "It's so big!"

Although United offered me the opportunity to return to work in 2005, I chose to remain voluntarily furloughed for two more years to pursue my Navy career and family life instead. In the meantime, I enjoyed my time home with my daughters and also continued to fly for VR-53 on a part-time basis.

In 2007, I was selected as the executive officer of VR-53, the second in command of the squadron, and I also returned to fly the 767 with United. I took command of VR-53 in March 2008. My command tour was exceptionally rewarding, not just because I was in command, but because I was commanding my favorite unit in the Navy. I had already spent ten years in VR-53. I loved the mission of the squadron—airlifting supplies to people who really needed them or flying people to places they needed to go. Flying a sturdy old plane like the C-130 with a very experienced and motivated crew makes it even better. Add some great international travel and camaraderie to this patriotic mission, and it's just downright fun.

I hope to pass down to my daughters the drive necessary to succeed in life and the understanding of long-term discipline. While I don't specifically want to motivate them to become pilots themselves, I do want to instill in them certain aspects of aviation. I hope to encourage them to be confident in taking risks and to have the wisdom to know which risks are worthwhile.

I also hope I can dissuade any gender-related apprehension about physical and mechanical challenges, and I hope to inspire them to tackle any career they truly desire, no matter how daunting or out of the ordinary it may at first seem.

Mom to Mom:

Being a mom makes my life more complete. It's wonderful to see another small part of you take part in the world and enjoy life, and to know that they will continue to do so long after you're gone.

. . . .

If you can learn how to fly a C-130, you can certainly figure out how to handle a newborn.

. . . .

Rank:	Navy Captain
Years Served:	20
Current Military Status:	Navy Reserve
Number of Children:	3

Lori (Bolebruch) Lindholm

SH-3 *Sea King*

IF ANYONE HAD TOLD ME WHEN I WAS A LITTLE GIRL THAT I WOULD BECOME A CAPTAIN IN THE UNITED STATES NAVY, FLY HELICOPTERS, AND LIVE in the Philippines, I wouldn't have believed them. But I experienced and accomplished those things because no one ever told me I couldn't.

I grew up in a small town in upstate New York that left little opportunity for its college-bound youth. I fancied myself an actress and headed off to a New York state college to study theatre, earning a bachelor of arts and wondering what I should do with that degree. In my course of study, I realized acting was not my deepest desire and thought a career in arts management might be something to try.

I enrolled in a master's program at American University in Washington, D.C. My first taste of the nation's capital was overwhelming for this small-town girl, so I headed home after about a month. I found a job bartending at my hometown's American Legion. The town's recruiters—Army, Navy, Marine Corps, and Air Force—frequented the American Legion for lunch. Convinced by the Navy recruiter that I should join the Navy as a public affairs officer due to my interest in theatre, I decided to give the Navy a try. Four months later, I left upstate New York for officer candidate school and began a journey that had a few more surprises in store than I expected.

I started out my Navy career as a public affairs officer at Fleet Logistics Support Squadron Thirty (VRC-30) in San Diego, one of the first Navy squadrons with women aviators. I met some incredible pioneers, both men and women, including my squadron commanding officer, a man who thought it was just fine for women to fly—an idea I would discover over the course of my career was not a mainstream idea. After a year in the squadron, I

applied to flight school and, in March 1982, I headed eastbound to Pensacola, Florida, to start my flying career.

While in flight school, I trained with women and men who had dreamed of flying their entire lives, others who were following family tradition, and a few like me, who happened to get there because it seemed like the thing to do at the time and someone had confidence in us that we could do it.

Flight school taught me some incredible lessons I have carried forward in all facets of my life, including "power plus attitude equals performance," a nugget from one of my squadron mates that I've never forgotten. I earned my wings of gold in August 1983 and headed back to San Diego, to fly the SH-3 *Sea King* helicopter.

After a year in the squadron, I received orders to Fleet Composite Squadron Five (VC-5) in the Republic of the Philippines, again to fly the SH-3. I was not initially enamored and thought to myself, "Leave San Diego for *where*?" My tour in VC-5, however, was nothing short of fantastic—hard work, incredible experiences, a bonding with folks who have remained steadfast friends for the past twenty years, sadness in the loss of fellow aviators, and a realization that a life of freedom is so very precious.

In the spring of 1986, I returned to San Diego and HC-1. This time, the squadron had a handful of women pilots. Anytime more than three of us gathered, our male squadron mates remarked that we were up to something. But I do believe the squadron as a whole was better with a more diverse group of officers and sailors.

After this tour, I received orders to the aircraft carrier USS *Lexington* as ship's company, which meant I wasn't flying but was part of the carrier crew. Assignment as part of the ship's company was fascinating, and getting

Lori, husband Ross, and son Adam, September 2005.

a World War II–vintage carrier out to sea was sometimes miraculous.

During this assignment, I was again reminded how fleeting life is. One Sunday afternoon, flight operations were in full swing with student naval aviators practicing landing on and taking off from the carrier. One of the student pilots started his first pass at the boat, attempting to land. He stalled his aircraft just before landing on the carrier deck and cartwheeled down the flight deck, landing on the starboard jet blast deflector. Five people were killed that day, including three in my division. I carry their faces with me still, and always will.

My life would take another significant turn during this tour—I met my future husband, Ross, in the middle of the Gulf of Mexico when he was onboard to see flight operations as a Navy cruise guest. When my tour on the *Lexington* ended, I moved to Washington, D.C., for my last active-duty tour. Ross, who'd been working for Senator Connie Mack in Pensacola, was also reassigned to the senator's staff in Washington—guess that's when we knew God must have a plan for us.

During this tour, during one week in 1991, I worked with a group of active-duty and reserve military women, several members from the DACOWITS (Defense Advisory Committee on Women in the Services) organization, and also the National Organization for Women to help bring about the repeal of the combat exclusion law. I was particularly interested in helping to change this law to allow women to fly in combat. During the week, we met with numerous members and staff to brief them on how important and necessary women were to the military and why this law should be repealed. I am proud to say that we changed a number of conservative lawmakers' minds about this law, and by the end of the week, they too became supporters of repealing the combat exclusion law. The combat exclusion law was repealed in 1993, and I am proud that I was part of that significant change in our military history.

In 1993, I left active duty, got married, and found my first civilian job as a government contractor. I joined the Navy Reserve and began supporting the Navy with a series of Pentagon assignments, mostly on weekends.

Mom to Mom:

I love being a mom and hearing my son laugh over the silliest thing and sing with full voice in the shower—there is no greater joy than that.

Ross and I had spent several years trying to start our family, including two years working with fertility doctors, when the true miracle of our lives happened. In September 2000, we were blessed with our wonderful son, Adam. He knows his mommy is a helicopter pilot, as I share my stories with him. He is fascinated with science and math and loves to figure out how things work. We often discuss the physics of flying, which he couples with the magic of Harry Potter and the imaginary world of *Star Wars* to design light-speed, magically disappearing aircraft. And he's trying to figure out how to have a pool in an airplane so he can bring a pet dolphin along on his adventures.

My fondest Navy flying memory was preflighting the aircraft at dawn and flying into the sunrise for operations in the Philippine Sea. Today, I fly a desk for Lockheed Martin, but I work with very bright, engaging people who build equipment to keep our military the best in the world. So, while it's been a few years since I have piloted an aircraft, I know what I do contributes to those who are flying.

My life is so much richer for saying, "Why not join the Navy?" in January 1980, and all the "Why nots?" that continued to present themselves. I have had the opportunity to follow some fantastic leaders, and some not so fantastic, but I learned at every turn, and hope I was a good leader to those who followed me. Throughout my Navy career, I learned to not give up and to stand up for what I believe to be right and true.

Ross and I are teaching our son, Adam, that there is possibility around every corner and to keep an open mind. When he gets a little older, I'll give him my leather flight jacket. My hope for him is that he remains curious about what is around the corner.

No plan is so set in stone that it cannot be changed; laughter and love of life are what matter.

Rank:	Navy Captain
Years Served:	25
Current Military Status:	Retired
Number of Children:	1

Cynthia (Persinger) Lisa

EA-6B *Prowler*

MY PARENTS ALWAYS ENCOURAGED US TO DO OUR PERSONAL BEST, AND THEY ALWAYS PROVIDED ENDLESS SUPPORT. MY MOM SAYS in jest about my career choice, "We gave our children roots and wings, and Cynthia took us literally."

I fell in love with the Naval Academy and Annapolis the minute I walked onto the academy yard during my junior year of high school. The academy's emphasis on leadership, academics, and athletics was the perfect fit for me. The possibility of flying in the military always interested me but really was just the icing on the cake.

My four years at the academy provided wonderful memories, including meeting Mike Lisa, a fellow academy midshipman. We had an instant friendship and started dating. During my senior year, I was elated to learn I had been selected for Navy flight training.

When my academy experience culminated in throwing my cap in the air at graduation, it was a bittersweet end to four years of hard work, challenges, and lots of fun, but I was ready to become a Navy pilot.

Flight school was incredible! I performed well enough to get selected for my first choice of jets and would ultimately get assigned an aircraft that would be stationed on an aircraft carrier, affectionately called the boat. Since I had first dreamed of becoming a pilot, I'd had one goal—to land on an aircraft carrier.

I finished up flight training learning how to fly the T-45A *Goshawk* at NAS Kingsville, Texas, while Mike, who also selected jets, trained at NAS Meridian, Mississippi. We endured a tough year of being apart, but on Christmas evening 2001, Mike proposed and I happily accepted.

Mike completed his carrier qualifications, graduated from flight training, and transferred to NAS Whidbey Island in Washington to fly the EA-6B *Prowler*, the Navy's four-seat electronic countermeasures jet. Soon after, I headed out to the USS *Harry Truman* to carrier-qualify and to fulfill my dream of landing on the boat—it was every bit as exciting, exhilarating, and scary as I had hoped! One month later, my parents pinned on my wings of gold at my graduation ceremony, and I also was assigned to fly the EA-6B *Prowler* at Whidbey.

Mike and I were married at the Naval Academy Chapel in January 2003, and two days later, I started *Prowler* training. I got my call sign "Chick" as soon as I started the training squadron, since the flight instructors had trouble distinguishing if it were me (Cynthia Lisa) or Mike (Mike Lisa) on the flight schedule. I had a simple solution—I was the "chick" Lisa and Mike was the "male" Lisa. I also happened to be the only female *Prowler* pilot currently flying in the Navy.

After finishing training, Mike and I headed out to different fleet squadrons. Over the next two and a half years, we were often apart, which definitely made it challenging, but through e-mails, phone calls, and making the best of our time home together, we survived.

I loved my time as a *Prowler* pilot, and gained combat experience supporting the ground troops in Iraq during my squadron's six-month deployment in 2005 on the USS *Nimitz* aircraft carrier. Stateside, I also loved flying throughout the United States to different air shows and events, showing off the EA-6B. Invariably, ground crews looked over in shock when my crew pointed to me as the pilot. I did my best to hide my smile, and, someday, I am sure that a petite blonde won't elicit such surprise when piloting a military jet.

LT Cynthia Lisa on the flight deck of the USS Nimitz.

On March 3, 2006, my life changed forever. That day, I led a flight of two *Prowlers* on a low-altitude military-training route at 500 feet and 420 knots. Halfway through the route, we heard a strange whining sound inside our jet. Within seconds, both the front and rear cockpits filled with smoke, and the jet was on fire and uncontrollable.

Approximately twenty seconds after the initial noise, I ejected our crew out of our burning, ballistic *Prowler*. I watched as the jet I had just been flying crashed in a fireball into the side of a hill. Several seconds later, I hit the ground in my parachute. Thankfully, my entire crew escaped with little injury and, more importantly, with our lives.

As I was ejecting, Mike was onboard the aircraft carrier USS *Abraham Lincoln* pulling out of San Diego for a six-month deployment. He learned of my mishap over the satellite phone, but was told that, due to operational necessity, he could not come home.

This was one of the most challenging times in my life. I am extremely grateful that my mother immediately flew out to help me recover physically and emotionally from the crash. During my recovery, I thought a lot about my life priorities. I began to think differently about my career and flying. I realized that I wanted life to be about more than just me and my accomplishments. I wanted to be with Mike, and we wanted to start a family.

Soon after, I had to make a decision on my next assignment, and I decided to take a non-flying job at NAS Patuxent River, Maryland, to be collocated with Mike. He had gotten orders, first to attend the Navy's test pilot school for a year, and afterwards he would be assigned to a squadron at Pax River to fly as a test pilot for a few years.

Walking away from the operational side of the Navy proved to be very tough for me. During the first year of my non-flying job, I questioned if I had made the right decision. I loved being home every night with Mike, having free time, and pursuing other interests, but I longed for the excitement and thrill of flying and being part of a squadron.

All of this doubt and longing quickly disappeared when we found out we were expecting our first child, and, in June 2008, we welcomed our daughter, Julia Mary. From the moment I heard "it's a girl," my heart overflowed with love, hopes, and dreams for everything that she would become and for all of the opportunities she would have. I have enjoyed every minute of being Julia's mother and was ecstatic when our second daughter, Anna Katherine, arrived in September 2009!

I decided to resign from the Navy when my commitment was up in August 2010. Although I have other career opportunities, being a carrier jet pilot will always be a part of who I am. There are days when the clouds beckon me; I hear the roar of a jet and I long to be airborne. I miss the thrill of nothing but open blue ocean beneath me and the satisfaction of bringing my crew home safely after every mission.

I'll always have flying in my veins, but my life has more meaning since Julia and Anna were born. Only another

Mom to Mom:

Being a mom is like being a superhero. The day I became a mom, I got magical superpowers that allow me to get more done, coordinate more schedules, and love more, all on less sleep than ever before.

mother can understand the difficulties of juggling a career, husband, children, and the day-to-day tasks of running a household, but I wouldn't trade any of it. The simple pleasures of seeing my daughters' first smiles and comforting them in my arms make every challenging day worth it.

I hope I will be an inspiration to my children, not simply for being a jet pilot, but for following my dreams, loving my family, serving this great country, and for always giving 100 percent.

I want them to experience life to its fullest, to follow their hearts, and to never give up on their dreams. I want to give them roots and wings and let them decide their own path to fly.

. . . .

"The highest reward for a man's toil is not what he gets for it, but what he becomes by it."

. . . .

—John Ruskin

Rank:	Navy Lieutenant Commander
Years Served:	10
Current Military Status:	Separated
Number of Children:	3

Cynthia has had another child (son Mike) since her original story was written.

Carey (Dunai) Lohrenz

F-14 *Tomcat*, C-12 *Huron*

VERY FEW PEOPLE ARE FORTUNATE ENOUGH TO MAKE IT TO ADULTHOOD AND SAY WITH FIRM CONVICTION THAT THEIR FAMILY HAS ALWAYS stood in their corner. I am one of the lucky ones.

I come from a long line of family members who have served in the Army, Navy, and Marine Corps. My dad flew C-130s in the Marine Corps, and later flew as a test and instructor pilot for Lockheed Martin. He then spent thirty years flying for Delta Air Lines. My mom was also in the aviation business. She worked as a flight attendant for Eastern Air Lines.

When my older brother, Steve, and I were young, we would pretend we were pilots, playing for hours on end with overturned barstools and my dad's silk maps and helmets from the Vietnam era.

My parents were both exceptionally supportive and raised us with no limits or constraints on our dreams, encouraging us to follow whatever career path we wanted. My parents also raised us as equals. When Steve started playing ice hockey, I played. When Dad taught him to change a tire or clean an oil filter, I was right there, too. We were encouraged to be independent and to dream big dreams!

During my senior year in college, I started the application process to join the Navy and fly, but I knew I would be limited in my choice of aircraft, since women were not allowed to fly in combat.

In the fall of 1990, I was accepted into the Navy's aviation officer candidate school. After sixteen weeks of intensive physical and academic training, I received my commission as an ensign in the United States Navy. I headed to Corpus Christi, Texas, to begin primary flight training, where I graduated in the top 10 percent of my class and received my first choice of aircraft—jets!

I transferred to Kingsville, Texas, to start jet training; however, just a few months prior to earning the coveted naval aviators' wings of gold, the Navy announced there were no longer jet slots available for women, since the two support squadrons that women could fly in were being disbanded.

It looked to be the end of my brief career flying jets for the Navy. However, everything changed a few months later, in April 1993, when the combat exclusion law was repealed. This meant I could fly any aircraft in the Navy, including any combat aircraft.

I graduated from flight school in June 1993, and headed to one of the Navy's West Coast F-14 training squadrons in California to learn how to fly the F-14 *Tomcat*. I was the first Navy woman in history to go straight from flight school directly to a combat training squadron.

My assignment to this squadron occurred during a pivotal time in the Navy, and proved to be very challenging. It was in the midst of the infamous Tailhook scandal, a drawdown in naval aviation, and the introduction of women into combat aviation.

The roadblocks and challenges I encountered—being one of the first women to fly a combat fighter aircraft, the excitement of flying the F-14, and the heartbreak of losing several friends to aircraft accidents—were more than I ever could have imagined. I learned to recognize the difference between fantastic leadership and poor leadership, and to understand what a difference having mentors can make. I also saw firsthand the value of truth, integrity, and open communication.

Carey gearing up to fly the F-14 in 1994. Carey was one of the first two women to qualify to fly the F-14 *Tomcat* after Secretary of Defense Les Aspin directed the military services to integrate women aviators into its combat forces.

I enjoyed flying the F-14 immensely and have incredible memories—racing across the desert and ocean at low altitude, participating in large air wing strikes, breaking the sound barrier, dogfighting, and flying around the carrier. Equally exciting were getting shot off the aircraft carrier by the ship's catapult gear and landing on the carrier taking an arrested landing. There is no bigger adrenaline rush out there, guaranteed, and reason enough to go Navy!

After my tour flying the F-14, I transferred to NAS Pensacola and, as a C-12 pilot, flew top Army, Navy, and Marine Corps officers all over the country. This provided me with an opportunity to see much of the United States, mingle with high-ranking officers, perform short-field landings, and more importantly, it gave me the opportunity to start a family.

While my family provided a strong foundation of faith and values, they also raised me to believe in myself enough to trust my instincts. My husband, Doff, is my rock! We met early in my Navy career when Doff was a Marine Corps F/A-18 *Hornet* pilot. After a fantastic career that included flying in the Gulf War and attending the Navy's premier flight school, TOPGUN, he now flies for FedEx.

We had our first child before I started my C-12 tour, just as Doff was getting out of the Marine Corps. Needless to say, we had very busy schedules with both of us flying and having a newborn. We had to develop a work and family balance immediately. I finished my Navy career following the birth of our second child. We have since had two more children, bringing the grand total to four! Although I've taken some time off from flying to raise my family, I've obtained and maintained my professional qualifications, licenses, and ratings, so if I want to fly again, I can.

Today, I am fortunate to be a partner in The Corps Group and work with a great group of former United States Marine Corps officers, many of whom are former fighter pilots. We train Fortune 500 companies with a straightforward process that links leadership to a disciplined approach to execution. Enabling companies to reach their strategic goals is enormously satisfying, and the constant challenges presented and the ever-changing environments make this a fantastic job!

Although at times it can be challenging to raise four kids, it is extremely rewarding. Raised to believe "I could do it all and have it all," as I live more of life and gain more experience, I recognize what was left out of that statement—"but not all at the same time!" Truly, there really is no balancing. You can do your best to blend the different aspects of life, but there are sacrifices that will be made along the way, such as missing the loss of a first tooth, missing out on a school program, not being there to comfort after a scraped knee, and missing those sweet goodnight kisses. But my children also see me as a strong, capable woman, and that strengthens their wings.

The key to my success is a supportive husband who understands that transitioning from Mach 2 to preschool leaves some adrenaline gaps that need to be filled. Doff, I thank you!

We are a generation of women in America whose opportunities and freedoms are unlimited. I'm so humbled by, and grateful to, the women who came before me who were tenacious. They fought for opportunities

Mom to Mom:

The most rewarding thing about being a mom is seeing the world from my kids' perspective—a world filled with unlimited possibilities, opportunities, and laughter. Knowing that, with love and guidance, my children will grow into compassionate people, gives me great satisfaction.

for all of us. We need to recognize that our individual success in the world will matter little if we aren't as focused and as ferocious as our grandmothers and mothers were in making the world better for our children—tomorrow's leaders.

I hope to pass on to my children the value of honor, courage, and commitment. I want them to have strong leadership skills, empathy, the strength to stand up for what they believe in, and to challenge the process. True commitment to a person, a cause, or one's own well-being is the surest way to achieve dreams.

I want my kids to be leaders, to always seek out the truth, and to be authentic. At the end of the day, no matter how difficult a situation, my hope for them is that they will look in the mirror and know they did their best.

I credit my own success in life to the mentors along my way, and also to the support of my family. As I write, it is after the recent passing of my dad. I will do my best to raise my kids in a manner that will honor his memory. To my family—thank you!

Courage is being scared to death but going for it anyway.

Rank:	Navy Lieutenant
Years Served:	9
Current Military Status:	Separated
Number of Children:	4

Linda (Heid) Maloney

EA-7L *Corsair*, EA-6A *Intruder*, EA-6B *Prowler*

I KNEW AS A CHILD GROWING UP THAT LIFE HELD MORE FOR ME THAN STAYING IN MY HOMETOWN, THAT I WOULD DO *SOMETHING*. AFTER HIGH school, my older sister enlisted in the Navy and, since my parents couldn't afford college, I also joined the Navy, hoping to take advantage of the military's educational assistance sometime in the future.

I took the Navy entrance examination and decided to enlist as an air traffic controller. My first duty station—Ford Island, Hawaii. Eight months into my tour, my supervisor encouraged me to apply for an officer program, and I was accepted. I left for an eighteen-month college preparatory program in San Diego, California, then received a Navy ROTC scholarship at the University of Idaho and started college in the fall of 1982.

Four and a half years later, I graduated with a degree in computer science and received my commission as a Navy ensign. I was interested in joining the aviation community, but I had two strikes against me—my eyes weren't 20/20, and since the combat exclusion law was in effect, few aviation positions were available for women.

I was assigned as a public affairs officer at the Navy's aviation training base in Pensacola, Florida, but, shortly after arriving, I was notified that I had been selected for naval flight officer (NFO) training. *Yes!* I did not need perfect vision for an NFO position. NFOs handle an aircraft's communications and navigation gear, the radar and weapon systems. I jumped at the opportunity and started flight school.

In most of my flight school classes, I was the only woman. On one of my very first days of training, a flight instructor directed me to stand up and tell the class a joke. Not a jokester, I failed at this first test and felt very uncomfortable being singled out as the lone female. Regardless,

I enjoyed flight training and did well. Fortunately, my previous time as an air traffic controller had given me added confidence, especially during the communications sections of training.

Even though I went through the same flight training as my male contemporaries, I did not have many choices of where to go once I graduated. The majority of assignments for women aviators were in a support role, not in an operational or combat role.

I was assigned to VAQ-33 in Key West, Florida, to fly the EA-7—a two-seat variant of the single-seat A-7—used to simulate enemy radars and enemy missiles to train Navy ships and combat aviators in electronic countermeasures. The squadron was one of two Navy squadrons that provided this type of training. It wasn't frontline combat and I was frustrated to be relegated to what I thought was a second-rate squadron. I found out later that other female aviator squadron mates felt similarly.

I quickly became bored with the limited NFO role in the A-7 and looked for my next adventure. Our squadron also had EA-6As, an earlier version of the fleet's A-6 *Intruder* aircraft. In a typical fleet combat squadron, the A-6 NFO—called bombardier navigator—had a significant role in the aircraft. Although the mission was modified in our electronic aggressor squadron, the EA-6A offered more of a challenge. My commanding officer approved my request to transition and I left for the A-6 training squadron in Virginia, returning to Key West a few months later.

In February 1991, I flew with a senior pilot in the squadron alongside another EA-6A, providing missile simulations training for the USS *Forrestal* about one hundred miles off the Florida coast. Afterward, we headed

Linda and one of her squadron maintenance crewmembers, February 1991, a few days following her ejection from an EA-6A.

to a nearby Air Force base to refuel, but as we started our climb to 15,000 feet, the plane appeared sluggish, and the pilot grew concerned. One of the hydraulic lights illuminated, indicating a hydraulic failure. I pulled out my pocket checklist, started the emergency procedures with the pilot, and, radioing the air traffic controller, declared an emergency. We changed course and headed to a Navy base so we could make an arrested landing, because we potentially could not slow the aircraft down after landing, due to the hydraulic failure. To make an arrested landing, we would lower our aircraft's tailhook en route to the Navy base, and, after touching down on the runway, the hook would engage the arresting gear (a cable on the runway), causing the aircraft to rapidly decelerate.

However, before we could finish our emergency procedures, the aircraft started to slowly roll to the right, and more hydraulic lights illuminated. The pilot tried to steady the jet, but it continued to roll. The pilot said, "I don't have control; EJECT." Initially stunned to hear those words, I paused. He repeated, "EJECT!"

I pulled the lower ejection handle, and I remember a flurry of yellow papers (from my kneeboard card) flying around, and then my ejection seat exploding through the canopy glass. The pilot ejected seconds later.

I lost consciousness briefly. When I came to, I was hanging in my parachute, descending toward the ocean. In the water, I climbed into my raft. About an hour later, I was rescued by a helicopter search-and-rescue swimmer, AT2 Steven Wishoff. In the helicopter, we traded name patches, and I still have his nametag preserved in a scrapbook with all of my military memorabilia.

I sustained no major injuries following the ejection except for cut and swollen hands since I had not been wearing my gloves (as I should have) during the flight. I was back up flying a few weeks later and felt some trepidation climbing up into the cockpit.

Unbeknownst to me, I was the first woman to eject from the Martin Baker Ejection Seat out of 6,000 previous ejections. Weeks later, I received a call from a Martin Baker representative congratulating me on a successful ejection. He also asked me if I wanted the commemorative Martin Baker tie that they bestowed upon all Martin Baker ejectees, or *something else* since I was their first woman ejectee. Not sure if I wanted a tie, I left it up to the company. Soon after, I received a letter in the mail inviting me to England to officially receive a Martin Baker pewter pin specially designed for the first woman ejectee, to be presented by Diana, Princess of Wales. The Navy denied my request to travel to England for the presentation, stating that military members couldn't be perceived as endorsing a company or product. Interestingly, there were ongoing discussions and debates during this time period regarding women in combat and repealing the combat exclusion law. I was told confidentially by a military official (I never knew if this was, in fact, true) that the Navy didn't want to highlight women aviators during this tumultuous time, because it would show that women could eject from a military jet and survive.

A few months after the accident, I was flying with my squadron mate Lieutenant Kara Hultgreen on a cross-country flight in an EA-6A to Washington, and our canopy popped open at 26,000 feet. We were able to close it immediately, but my blood pressure skyrocketed as I had images of another ejection. Thankfully, we had no other issues, and the flight continued without further problems.

Months later, I was selected to train in the EA-6B *Prowler*, and, in October 1991, I packed up and moved to Whidbey Island, Washington, for the yearlong training program. Although I still would be relegated to a support squadron once I finished the training, I was hopeful the combat exclusion law would soon be rescinded, and, if so, I would transfer immediately to a combat squadron.

Finally, in April 1993, I got my wish—the combat exclusion law was repealed. I quickly joined a combat squadron—VAQ-135, the Black Ravens. I was elated to be part of a combat squadron, and thrilled the Black Raven leadership and aviators welcomed the addition of women aviators. However, within months, all that changed, because a new squadron commander took charge, bringing along several aviators from his previous squadron—VAQ-137, the Rooks. Although the new commander treated the women fairly and was a good leader, the other former Rook aviators changed the environment of the squadron literally overnight to an extremely hostile one toward the women aviators.

In April 1995, the squadron prepared to deploy on the USS *Abraham Lincoln* to cruise to the Arabian Gulf for operations in Iraq and Kuwait. I loved flying off the carrier, and many of my girlfriends, who were previously in support squadrons, were also stationed on the *Lincoln*.

I frequently walked up on the flight deck in pitch-black conditions to preflight the aircraft before a flight. With other aircraft engines turning and the waves splashing high alongside the ship, those nights seemed surreal and dangerous, but equally exciting and challenging.

After my squadron tour was up, I transferred to Washington, D.C., and I spent the next few years trying to decide if I would return to flying—a decision I believed would impact my plans to marry and have a family. As much as I loved my career, my desire to have a family was a higher priority. I knew that if I decided not to return to flying *Prowlers*, my Navy career would potentially be negatively impacted. I wasn't even dating anyone, but after months of prayer and long talks with close friends, I decided to switch to a different career path. I knew I would regret my decision if I had returned to flying. It was as if God whispered to me to trust Him in this decision, and, as scary as it was, I knew I had made the right choice.

The next year, I met my future husband, Dan, and immediately knew he was the man I had been looking for, a man of character who wasn't intimidated by my aviation career. Dan worked in the telecommunications industry, but also was a civilian pilot. He was living in Boston at the time, a single dad of a nineteen-year-old daughter.

We dated for a year, married in 2001, and Dan moved to Maryland where I was stationed. Thankfully, he could telecommute for his company, and, since we lived on the beach, he loved working from home! I became an aerospace engineering duty officer involved in the acquisition and support of Navy aircraft.

We had our son, Ethan, in 2003, a few weeks after I turned 42, and then, three years later, had our second son, Aron. What incredible joy they have brought to our lives! Ethan already loves airplanes, especially fighter jets and helicopters. Aron loves anything Ethan loves, and we plan to introduce them to all aspects of aviation. I have saved my flight gear to pass down to them one day, and, just recently, Ethan has started wearing one of my helmets and pretending he is a fighter pilot.

Since I had my children later in life, I thought I would have loads of patience and that it all would just click. In reality, it has been a tough adjustment after spending years of taking care of just me. Becoming a mom has taught me more about myself than I learned in the previous forty-plus years. I have gotten a crash course on the requirements and benefits of motherhood—pure joy, sacrifice, unconditional love, and forgiveness. It is an incredible dichotomy being a parent, because, as challenging as it can be, it is also the most rewarding and humbling role in life. I truly love being a mom—it fills me up like nothing else can.

Mom to Mom:

The thing that surprised me about being a mom is how instantly I loved my youngest son the moment he was born. I remember thinking before he arrived that I didn't know if I could love another child as much as I loved my first son. My answer came soon enough because, as soon as he was born, my heart was overjoyed and I loved him with all the love a mom could have for her child. He and his brother both continue to fill my life up with immense joy. Being a mom is the best thing I have done in my life.

My husband and I encourage Ethan and Aron to reach for the best in life. We hope to inspire in them a love of learning, an excitement to try new things, and a passion to be men of character who are unafraid to stand up for what is right. I would love for them to join the military and fly, but I want them to do what they love, and I hope to encourage them in whatever paths they pursue.

As much as I enjoyed my Navy and flying career, there is nothing more worthwhile in the world than raising a child.

"Do not follow where the path may lead. Go instead where there is no path and leave a trail."

—Ralph Waldo Emerson

Rank:	Navy Lieutenant Commander
Years Served:	20
Current Military Status:	Retired
Number of Children:	2

Jean (Condie) O'Brien

P-3 *Orion*

MY SISTERS AND I WERE RAISED BY A CAREER MILITARY FATHER WHO SERVED SIX TOURS IN VIETNAM IN COMBAT SEARCH AND RESCUE AND as a mission commander and navigator on C-130s. Though he rarely spoke about Vietnam, he brought home a few audiocassette tapes of live missions. It's definitely eerie to hear a helicopter exploding near the C-130 and listen to the crew reactions.

My father also determined we learn a thing or two about survival, so he brought home Air Force lectures on jungle, arctic, and desert survival training for us to do. While women didn't fly combat aircraft then, my father never discouraged us.

Financially, my parents couldn't put much toward college, so I pursued the college ROTC programs. After interviewing each of the different services' recruiters, I was most impressed by the Navy program. I started college at the University of Wisconsin-Madison in January 1985. I had no scholarship, money for one semester only, and two suitcases and a backpack to my name. I joined the Navy ROTC unit and thankfully received a Navy ROTC scholarship the second semester of my freshman year.

In 1988, I graduated from college with a double major in Russian and biology. My ROTC executive officer recommended I take a job in Washington, D.C., to meet people from all different Navy careers—the best advice I received as a new naval officer, though I always considered flying as an option. My initial designator was as a general unrestricted line officer (Navy lingo for administrative work).

Fortunately, I was assigned to the aviation assignment office, responsible for career progression and personnel management of all naval aviators. One of the first things I learned was that very few women flew in the Navy, and the majority of those flight billets were in a support role due to the combat exclusion law. I spent time speaking with officers from all different professions in the Navy, but it quickly became crystal clear to me that flying was what I wanted to do.

The aviators I worked with showed me what I needed to do to apply to flight school and took me with them to visit squadrons to talk to fleet aviators. Exactly one year after I was commissioned, I was selected for the flight program and headed to Pensacola to start flight school as a naval flight officer. Flight school was both tough and fun, and I was excited to finally graduate and receive my wings of gold in July 1991.

In September 1991, I joined my first squadron, VXN-8, an oceanographic research squadron that flew a modified version of the P-3 *Orion*, known as the RP-3D, at NAS Patuxent River, Maryland, as a newly winged lieutenant junior grade, green in every way a new aviator is.

During my Pax River tour, I met and married the greatest man I have ever known, my husband, Craig. We met at a Navy function at the Navy Yard in Washington, D.C., and sparks immediately flew. He is Long Island born and bred and graduated from the Naval Academy with a degree in systems engineering. We both decided not to be "encumbered" with a spouse early in our careers but love got in the way. We married in April 1992 but didn't actually live together until August 1994. He originally had orders to San Diego, but changed them to Norfolk so we could be stationed closer to each other after I got out of flight school. Since Norfolk and Pax River were about three hours from each other, we did plenty of driving during those two years to spend time together.

Jean in front of her aircraft, 2005, when she was on a detachment performing counter-narcotics operations, Comalapa, El Salvador.

My favorite detachment was an around-the-world VXN-8 mission. We left Pax heading west and kept heading west for fifty-six days until we returned. In the middle of that trip, I found out that the combat exclusion law had been repealed and that combat aviation was now open to women. I was in Atsugi, Japan, when my executive officer called to offer me orders to a VP (patrol aviation) squadron in Florida. These squadrons were previously closed to women. I told him I was interested, but since I was preflighting in just an hour, I would have to delay answering him until I called my husband. We flew to Kadena, Okinawa, that day where I called home and discussed the opportunity with my husband. I accepted the orders on the contingency that my Norfolk-based husband would be given orders to Mayport, Florida.

I reported to VP-16 in April 1994, the third female aviator and first female naval flight officer in a VP squadron. I worked my way through the qualification syllabus and, in December 1995, I became the first woman ever to earn the qualification as tactical coordinator in the P-3C *Orion*. By the summer of 1996, I had accumulated 2,000 P-3 flight hours, which allowed me to join VP International, a group of maritime patrol aviators from forty-four countries around the world; I was the first woman from the United States to qualify.

After our assignments in Florida, Craig and I believed it would be difficult to get future orders together so we decided to leave the Navy. Craig joined a company in New Jersey, and I continued flying with the Navy Reserve in Pennsylvania.

It took us four years to have our son, Joe, and we feel very blessed. He is such a joy and I love staying home with him. I continue to work part-time with the Navy Reserve, originally flying with the P-3 squadron, VP-66, until it was disestablished. I now drill once a month and two weeks every year with a non-flying unit.

There have been so many wonderful people throughout my Navy career. The Navy is a small place, so it is easy to run into people you know anywhere in the fleet. We are all truly shipmates, and our doors are always open to a fellow shipmate.

The highlight of my military career has definitely been flying as part of a crew, with a team of other aviators and aircrewmen. Being the tactical coordinator and mission commander is the best. To make an analogy, the tactical coordinator is the quarterback who drives the rest of the team. You have to be able to receive tactical input from nine different crewmembers, both verbally and electronically; monitor all tactical communications; and devise a course of action.

The running joke in our house is that flying is "women's work," but that we will make an exception for our son, Joe. We try to teach our son the message to not let anyone tell you what you can't do, but prove to them that you can. Of course, given the combination of his dad's engineering brain, my love of aviation, and Joe's new love

Mom to Mom:

Being a mom teaches you so much about yourself, both good and bad! Seeing joy on your child's face while sharing one of your favorite pastimes is fabulous, but having one of your bad habits or sayings reflected back at you is humbling.

for astronomy, he just may be a future astronaut. Whatever he decides to do, all I know is that the sky is definitely NOT the limit!

The best advice I can give to any woman joining the military is to make sure you know who you are. There will be many trying times that are inherent to the job, but there will also be many lonely times inherent to being one of the only women in the squadron. You can and will be accepted by the men in the squadron; you are their professional equal. That said, expect some social exclusion. This is not absolute, just situational. Understand when you are, and when you are not, "one of the guys."

At the end of the day, the respect of the person in the mirror is that which matters most.

Rank:	Navy Captain
Years Served:	21
Current Military Status:	Navy Reserve
Number of Children:	1

Jane (Skiles) O'Dea

C-130 *Hercules,* C-1A *COD*

M Y FATHER WAS A DIVE-BOMBER PILOT IN WORLD WAR II. THAT STARTED MY INITIAL INTEREST IN FLYING. DURING HIGH SCHOOL, I WORKED AT the airport in Des Moines, Iowa. I wanted to work on the flight line, fueling and parking the airplanes, but the manager wouldn't let me because I was a girl, so I worked as the office receptionist.

After graduating from high school in 1968, I attended Iowa State University. Four years later, with degree in hand and a desire to travel and see the world, I decided to join the Navy. Although both of my parents were supportive, my dad was skeptical that I had the "right stuff." My mom, who was a Navy disbursing officer during World War II, was a motivating force right from the beginning. She was extremely supportive and very excited that I decided to join the Navy. Later in my career, my dad became my biggest booster.

In 1973, the Navy announced a test program to train women as naval aviators. However, because of the existing combat exclusion law, women's flying was limited to noncombat missions. Three other women and I reported for flight training on March 2, 1973, to NAS Pensacola, Florida. I knew I would be breaking ground as one of the first women to attend the Navy's flight school, but I was not prepared for the amount of attention and controversy. Overall, flight school was incredible, and the instructors were first-rate.

After the initial phase of classroom training, I flew a variety of Navy training aircraft including the T-34, T-28 and the S-2. One of my favorite memories was flying a cross-country flight into my former employer's airfield in Des Moines, Iowa. I taxied to the parking ramp in my dirty, greasy S-2. My former employer was there to greet me and shake my hand. He rolled out a red carpet usually reserved for wealthy *Learjet* owners. What a sweet moment for a girl who was told she couldn't fuel airplanes on his line!

Another sweet moment was graduation from flight training in April 1974 when my dad became the first naval aviator to pin the coveted wings of gold on his daughter. It was a wonderful day, one of my best.

I went on to train in the Navy's C-130 aircraft at Little Rock Air Force Base in Arkansas, and finally got to my first operational squadron, VR-24, in Rota, Spain. Although the C-130's mission of hauling passengers, mail, and supplies wasn't very exciting, I enjoyed flying all over Europe, North Africa, and the Mediterranean.

My squadron was relatively small with about twenty officers. Although I was not exactly welcomed by the squadron with open arms as their first female aviator, a couple of my fellow squadron mates were very supportive.

I met my husband, Tom, during my tour in Rota. Tom was crew chief on the C-1A *COD* aircraft. Most guys I met were either very impressed or intimidated by my naval aviator status. Tom was neither; he thought it was great, but he appreciated me for me.

We married during this tour, and also had our first child—our daughter, Shannon. I flew the C-130 until I was six months pregnant, and got bigger flight suits to accommodate my growing stomach. The Navy gave me a month of maternity leave, and then I took a month of my own leave after Shannon was born. It was a special time, and I loved being home with my daughter.

In 1978, my next tour of duty was back to Pensacola, Florida, to train student pilots in the T-34 at the training squadron VT-2. I was the first woman instructor pilot

Jane's dad, Paul Skiles (a former World War II dive-bomber pilot), was the first naval aviator in history to pin wings of gold on his daughter, April 1974.

in the squadron. My husband, Tom, left the Navy so he could attend college full-time to finish his degree.

We had our second daughter, Kelly, during this tour, and again I flew while pregnant. I only stopped at six months because I was having a hard time reaching some of the buttons and switches in the T-34. Juggling two young girls, my flying schedule, and Tom's full-time class schedule was tough. Most days, I flew three training flights a day. By the end of each day, Tom and I both were exhausted. I look back on those times now and wonder how we ever did it.

All in all, this was an absolutely wonderful tour with a great group of fellow instructor pilots, both Navy and Marine Corps. However, it was during this time period, in 1982, that fellow female aviator Barbara Rainey died in an aircraft accident. She and I had been quite close during flight training. Barbara was the very first woman to graduate from naval flight school, in 1974. She and her

flight student were practicing touch-and-go landings when the aircraft banked sharply in its approach turn to avoid another plane, lost altitude, and crashed. Both pilots were killed in the crash. The hardest flight I ever flew was the one two days after she died.

The absolute highlight of my military career occurred during my next tour on the aircraft carrier USS *Lexington*, in getting my aircraft carrier qualifications—taking an arrested landing and getting catapulted off the carrier. My orders were actually as the ship's communications officer, but a handful of officers were given the opportunity to fly the ship's C-1A *COD* aircraft hauling supplies on and off the ship. Since joining the Navy and graduating from flight training, I strived to achieve exactly what my male counterparts were achieving. I was frustrated that congressional mandates prevented me and other women from serving in combat because of the no-combat laws, which limited female pilots' opportunities. It was very discouraging to know that the best you could play on was the junior varsity team no matter how good you were.

The tour on the *Lexington* also was very enjoyable because I had the opportunity to work with other women officers—about ten women officers in a wardroom of 120 officers total. I absolutely loved my time on the *Lexington*, which reinforced my belief that naval aviation at sea is what it is all about.

After the *Lexington*, I transferred to Patuxent River, Maryland, to VQ-4, to fly the C-130. I logged many hours flying the VQ mission—in those days, there was always a C-130 flying to provide airborne communications. However, the C-130 missions were long and exhausting—sixteen to eighteen hours—but the camaraderie was terrific. The Pax River community was a wonderful time for our family and some of the happiest in our family memories.

My final flying tour was at Pax. Over the next few years, I was stationed at the Pentagon and also served as the commanding officer of the Navy Recruiting Command in Indianapolis, Indiana. I retired in 1997. Tom and I currently reside in Norfolk, Virginia, where our two grown daughters live nearby with their husbands and children.

Mom to Mom:

The thing that surprised me the most about being a mom is that it is a lifetime commitment. No matter how old your children become—30, 40, etc.—you are their mom. For as long as you live, you will laugh with them, worry about them, celebrate with them, cry with them, be there for them no matter what, and, most of all, love them.

Our granddaughters are the lights of our lives! We love being near them. I am currently a professor at Defense Acquisition University where I teach program management and systems engineering. After thirty-six years of working for the Department of Defense, this is the perfect twilight tour for me. I have the opportunity to pass along the many lessons I have learned. I hope to completely retire in the next few years.

My goal as a mom was to be the best role model for my daughters, and now my granddaughters. I encourage them to pursue their dreams, and to realize that there are no limits to what they can accomplish.

Enjoy the thrill of a truly exciting and rewarding career, but remember, in the end, it is family who are the most important people in one's life.

Rank:	Navy Captain
Years Served:	26
Current Military Status:	Retired
Number of Children:	2

Patsy (Van Bloem) Schumacher

H-2 *Seasprite*, H-3 *Sea King*, H-46 *Sea Knight*, H-1 *Huey*

DUE TO MY FATHER'S DEATH WHILE I WAS IN HIGH SCHOOL, I DIDN'T KNOW HOW I'D PAY FOR COLLEGE. I ATTENDED MY COUSIN'S NAVAL Academy graduation during my sophomore year and thought the academy might be a good option—it was free! Unable to get an academy nomination, I decided on the next best thing—Navy ROTC at Villanova University in Pennsylvania.

A fellow female midshipman who was two years ahead of me entered the Navy's flight program, which had started accepting women in 1973. That sounded very cool, so I decided that's what I'd do as well.

In one fell swoop, I graduated and was commissioned an ensign in May 1983. Checking into the initial phase of flight training, I got my first taste of the real Navy. My luggage had been lost on the flight to Pensacola, Florida, and, having built in no extra time, I checked in wearing my lovely lavender sundress—not my required uniform. The student control lieutenant was flabbergasted and read me the riot act for a good twenty minutes. Ensign Patsy Van Bloem knew she would never get to fly now! But that was only the beginning of an amazing adventure.

I started the flying phase of training in Corpus Christi, Texas, in the single-engine turboprop T-34 *Mentor*. I got sick during every one of my first five flights, which did not endear me to my instructor. Years later, I ran into him on a military transport flight, and I asked him if he had thought I would make it through flight school. His silence gave me the answer. He did say, however, that I was proof positive that someone with pure determination who followed procedures to the letter could make it through.

In January 1985, I finally received my wings of gold and decided to fly helicopters (helos). I joined the helo squadron, HSL-31, in San Diego and flew the H-2 *Sea Sprite* helicopter. Soon after, I deployed with the squadron's helo detachment (det) onboard the USNS *Chauvenet*, a cartographic naval ship run by civilians. At the time, the ship was over in the Philippine Islands. Our det consisted of three pilots and twelve crewmembers whose main job was to transport passengers, mail, and cargo to remote sites in Indonesia. The flying was breathtaking—we could follow rivers and waterfalls on many of the islands, chase mountain goats around the hilltops, and practice instrument training by flying through clouds.

I remember once flying into an Indonesian airfield when I had to have one of my enlisted male crewmembers speak for me, because none of the local maintenance or support personnel would look at or speak to me. I participated in three similar six- to eight-month dets during my squadron tour.

Next, I was selected to be an instructor in the TH-57 training helicopter, and I went back to Florida, this time to NAS Whiting Field, where I became HT-18's first woman instructor pilot. I could tell upon arrival that the male instructors were apprehensive about having a woman IP. I was the only woman instructor in the squadron for the majority of my three-year tour, but I eventually won over most of my colleagues!

I flew more than two thousand hours, and personally trained more than fifty students there. I loved being an instructor pilot and taking students from not knowing anything about flying a helo to seeing the "light bulb" switch on.

Going into the Navy, my life plan included traveling and experiencing the world during my first tour, getting married during my second tour, and finally

Patsy and son, Peter, at Patsy's Navy retirement ceremony, April 2003.

getting out of the Navy and having lots of kids. Well, I didn't find Mr. Right during my instructor tour, so when it was time to transfer again, I went to San Diego to fly the H–3 *Sea King* with HC–1, flying VIP transport, search and rescue, and drone torpedo recovery off San Clemente Island.

Near the end of this tour, two interesting and life-changing events took place. First, the combat exclusion law was rescinded, which meant that women could now fly in combat squadrons. Second, my squadron was closing down and I was to sing in the disestablishment ceremony along with three other officers from my squadron, but we needed another tenor.

A friend knew that fellow aviator Tom Schumacher sang in a large church choir and asked him to be a part of the group. I was prepared for Tom to be a typical jet jock since he was an F–14 *Tomcat* pilot, but was immediately

struck by his humility and civility. And he happened to be really cute! Soon after, Tom, a true traditionalist, asked if he could court me.

Though we had little time until I left for my next job in Washington, D.C., we dated four months until my departure in September 1994. By then I knew he was the right one for me! Tom proposed in December and I excitedly accepted. While he was deployed on the USS *Abraham Lincoln* for almost seven months, I planned our October wedding. After we married, I transferred back to San Diego where Tom was stationed, and I flew the H–46 *Sea Knight*, the helo I had always wanted to fly.

Over the next couple of years, Tom and I managed to get stationed together or near each other most of the time. In 2001, we both got orders to NAS Lemoore, California, where Tom would fly the F/A-18 and I would fly the venerable H-1 *Huey* helicopter as a search-and-rescue pilot. I was delighted to fly the *Huey* and loved being up in the mountains practicing search-and-rescue scenarios; we would then land the helicopter, have a picnic, and fly home following streams and canyons.

Tom and I had been trying to have a baby for a few years when we started talking about adoption. I finally became pregnant at the age of forty—just in time for retiring! I was very excited, but knew my pregnancy was high-risk. My wonderful flight surgeon told me these words of wisdom: "If this baby is not meant to be, there is nothing I can do. But if this baby is meant to be, there is nothing short of you taking up kickboxing that will stop it from being born!" Believe it or not, hearing those words after so many years of trying was therapeutic.

Tom, busy getting ready to deploy on an aircraft carrier, was training at NAS Fallon in Nevada when I went into labor. Tom got to the hospital within hours of our son Peter's birth and was able to spend a few days at home before returning to Nevada.

Since I had put in my twenty years, I decided to retire from the Navy four months after Peter was born. Unfortunately, Tom was deployed so he couldn't be at my retirement ceremony. However, he surprised me by sending a video of himself reading my retirement orders so he could be there in spirit.

Mom to Mom:
Being a mom is the best job in the whole world!

Four months later, he returned and we made our final Navy move to NAS Pax River in Maryland. Tom works at the Navy's test pilot school as an instructor, and I decided to be a stay-at-home mom. To say that has been a difficult adjustment after the career I had is a world of understatement. But God knows what He's doing, and we found a good church home, joined the choir, and I am even a church deacon. Being a mom is the best career I ever could have asked for!

Since Tom and I both are pilots, it's a given that Peter will learn to fly, and we hope he will love it as much as we do. Learning to fly and handling difficult situations, even emergencies, teaches confidence. We know that God has a plan for Peter's life, and we want him to appreciate how beautiful God made the world. And what better way to see the beauty of God's hand than flying overhead and witnessing it firsthand?

. . . .

"As for me and my house, we will serve the Lord."

. . . .

—Joshua 24:15

Rank:	Navy Lieutenant Commander
Years Served:	20
Current Military Status:	Retired
Number of Children:	1

Shari (Pavlik) Scott

MH-53 *Sea Dragon*

BORN AND RAISED IN A TOWN KNOWN FOR ITS LEGENDARY COW TIPPING AND SNIPE HUNTING, I GREW UP THINKING JEFFERSON, IOWA, WAS the land of boundless opportunity. My parents professed that I could do anything I wanted or set my mind to, although I had no idea what that might be.

After high school, I attended the University of Iowa for a year, but then I cut my hair, packed my bags, and headed to Orlando, Florida, for Navy boot camp.

For three years, I worked as a Navy dental technician in San Diego, California, until I realized I was not interested in vesting my future in gum disease and root canals. I applied for an NROTC scholarship, was fortunate enough to be selected the first time around, and started college in August 1986 at the University of Rochester in New York.

Life at the University of Rochester was fun, challenging, and bitterly cold. The campus was small with only 4,000 students, nearly four hundred of them Navy or Marine Corps midshipmen. During my senior year, I had to choose a Navy specialty I would pursue after graduation. I asked, "What are my options?" When offered flight school, I resounded with, "That sounds fun. I'll do that!"

Flight school at Pensacola, Florida, was an amazing experience! I couldn't believe that after only thirteen familiarization flights, they let me solo in the T-34 *Turbo Mentor* trainer. Like all young aviators, I managed to get lost on at least one of my solo flights. On my first precision aerobatics flight, I crammed in as many loops, aileron rolls, and barrel rolls as vertigo would allow, and then realized that my allotted time had quickly approached, and I hadn't done my mandatory five landings at an outlying field. I somehow miraculously stumbled onto an acceptable field, pumped out five quick landings, and returned to home base before they launched the alert.

After primary training, I headed to NAS Whiting Field to train in the Navy's TH-57B *Bell Jet Ranger* helicopter. On my very first flight, I knew my decision to fly helicopters was right. However, learning to hover was humbling, to say the least. I had never worked up such a sweat trying to stay within a box the size of a football field! I earned the coveted wings of gold in February 1993 and received orders to fly the H-53 helicopter.

Shortly after I began H-53 training, my senior leadership approached me about a transition to a different aircraft. It was rumored that the combat exclusion law was about to be repealed, and they wanted to be ahead of the pack and asked if I would consider switching squadrons to HM-14, an airborne mine countermeasures squadron, flying the MH-53E. My response? "*You bet!*"

Being the first female in an aviation wardroom that had been accustomed to the presence of solely male brethren was a bit daunting. I learned early to grow thicker skin, volunteer often, and work extra hard. Gaining the trust of my fellow pilots, the leadership, maintenance crews, and, eventually, the aircrewmembers was an extreme challenge but very rewarding, as was the flying.

I flew low and slow over the water with various mine-hunting or minesweeping devices streaming out the back of the helicopter. Mastering this mission, in all its various configurations, was truly an accomplishment in which I took great pride.

I met my husband during my first flying tour. I remember being extremely intimidated and impressed by

Shay as officer in charge of HM-14 Detachment, June 2003, Bahrain.

his professionalism and his presence. Eventually, I cracked through his tough exterior, and we found ourselves married, and then pregnant, while in Washington, D.C.

During my pregnancy, we learned that our son, Carson, had a rare chromosomal abnormality called DiGeorge Syndrome. The disease manifests itself through various physical and mental challenges, and often requires numerous surgeries. Carson was born in August 1999, and had his first surgery when he was only eight days old. He didn't leave the hospital until nearly two months later.

Between maternity leave and my own personal leave, I didn't return to work until four months after Carson's birth. I reluctantly headed back to my job, leaving Carson in the able hands of my mother-in-law, who was a godsend. Due to the complications with Carson's health, we received orders back to Norfolk, Virginia, where we could get specialized medical care. During this tour, we were blessed with our second son, Harrison. I took six weeks

off for maternity leave, refreshed my flying skills, and then headed back to HM-14 for another flying tour.

Shortly after checking in, I was informed that I would take over the officer-in-charge position of our permanent detachment in Bahrain in a few short months. I was excited by the leadership opportunity, but deeply saddened with the prospect of leaving my family for six months, especially with a baby less than a year old. Regardless, in December 2002, I packed my sea bags, kissed the kids, and headed to Bahrain.

I had barely unpacked and become acclimated to the 120-degree heat, when we were briefed that U.S. forces were starting to build up in anticipation of offensive actions against Iraq in Operation *Iraqi Freedom*. We flew special forces teams into Iraq to set up base camps, flew detainees to makeshift prison camps, completed complex minesweeping operations to allow access for humanitarian aid ships, and flew injured sailors and detainees to hospital ships to receive critical care. I stayed in Bahrain until all major hostilities had ended, and then, in June 2003, I decommissioned the detachment. This tour was, without a doubt, the most challenging and rewarding of my career.

At this point, I had more than seventeen years of active-duty service, and it was time to make a decision about my next career move. I made the tough choice to not pursue squadron command opportunities so that I could transition to a more solid family life.

After transferring to shore duty in Norfolk, I tested and evaluated new helicopters and helicopter weapon systems. My husband completed a major-command sea tour, home-based in Texas, and afterward received orders to the Bureau of Naval Personnel in Tennessee, which has required him to be geographically separated from us for more than four years. This convinced me yet again that when I transferred to shore duty, I had made the right decision for myself and my family.

The Navy has been an adventurous, motivating, and exciting ride. As I finish my military career and begin my transition to civilian life, I know I will always have these amazing friendships and experiences. I have truly learned the value of teamwork, trusting my fellow service members, as well as developing a strong sense of self and knowing how to push myself beyond preconceived limits in order to achieve a goal.

Mom to Mom:

The most rewarding thing about being a mom is experiencing the day-to-day joy that children bring as they encounter new challenges, endure failures, and thrill to successes!
There is nothing that touches a heart and soul like the smiles, hugs, and the love of a child!

I will always be proud and feel fortunate to have served as a naval aviator. I often talk to children, young adults, and especially women about the joy of flying and serving in the Navy, and hope I have inspired many to seek the sapphire skies and indigo seas in their pursuit of happy lives and challenging careers.

I know that my children are pleased with the fact that their momma "wore combat boots." I see their eyes widen with wonder when I tell stories of flying through thunderstorms and searching for mines in foreign waters.

It is their acknowledgement and praise that I seek now. They are my future, and I am blessed to have lived so fully, and to now have more time to watch them grow.

. . . .

"Women who seek to be equal with men lack ambition."

—Timothy Leary

Rank:	Navy Commander
Years Served:	21
Current Military Status:	Retired
Number of Children:	2

Paula (Coleman) Senn

A-4 *Skyhawk,* E-6A *Mercury,* EA-6B *Prowler*

A S A CHILD, I WATCHED AIRPLANES FLYING HIGH IN THE SKY, THE SUN GLINTING OFF STEEL, CONTRAILS FOLLOWING FOR MILES, AND thought flying an airplane would be the most exciting experience in the world. I hadn't really considered the Navy until college, when a blind date my grandma set me up with took me to see the movie *Top Gun.* The aircraft carrier scenes gave me goose bumps, and when I walked out of that movie, I knew I wanted to fly in the Navy.

As fate would have it, only weeks earlier I had sent resumes to several possible employers, including the Navy. The recruiter contacted me, and two months later, in September 1986, I was on my way to the Navy's aviation officer candidate school in Pensacola, Florida. After receiving my commission, my dad and I toured the aircraft carrier USS *Lexington.* As I stood on the wooden deck, I had a strong feeling that I would be there again someday.

In flight school in Corpus Christi, Texas, I learned to fly the T-34C. Primary training complete, I waited on pins and needles for the jet selection results. I made the cut and packed my bags for Beeville, Texas. During intermediate training, I flew the T-2C *Buckeye* and then completed advanced training in the TA-4J *Skyhawk.* Fate stepped in again, and I carrier-qualified in both the T-2C and TA-4J...on the USS *Lexington.*

After graduating from flight school in March 1989, I shipped off to VC-5 at NAS Cubi Point, Republic of the Philippines. There I piloted the A-4E and TA-4J, flying fleet support missions. My time in the Philippines was the most fun flying of my career. Not only did I fly all over the skies of Singapore, Thailand, Malaysia, Korea, and Japan, but I also honed my flying skills and began to appreciate the pure joy of flying.

In the fall of 1991, I received orders to VQ-4 to fly the Navy's E-6A—a derivative of the commercial Boeing 707—involved in the Navy's nuclear contingency communications mission. Although learning to fly a heavy aircraft and operate with a crew was a challenge, the experience paid off greatly in the long run. Nevertheless, my heart yearned to fly a small jet again.

In 1993, when combat flying opened to women, I was offered a transition to a carrier-based jet, and was selected to fly the EA-6B *Prowler,* the Navy's tactical electronic warfare aircraft. Returning to a tactical jet meant learning again how to fly around the aircraft carrier—a daunting task after having not flown in that environment for six years. I also had to deal with the death of my former roommate and good friend, Kara Hultgreen, which happened during an aircraft accident while she was stationed aboard the USS *Abraham Lincoln.* I was so devastated that I nearly quit, but ultimately I realized that Kara wouldn't have wanted that.

During carrier qualifications in the *Prowler,* I was paired with a naval flight officer who flew next to me in the right seat. He and I trained together at our home field for weeks with the intent of developing aircrew coordination and camaraderie, and also to build our skills in preparation to carrier-qualify in takeoffs and landings on the boat (carrier). The night before we were to head to the boat, he pulled me aside and, to my great shock, told me he was uncomfortable flying with me because I was a woman. I told him, "You'd better figure it out, because we're briefing in twelve hours!" How could he do

Paula suited up to fly the A-4 in VC-5, circa 1990, Taegu, Korea.

this to me the night before? At this point, there was no way he could be replaced. I was already nervous because it had been six years since I had been to the boat in flight school, and this added to my anxiety. I slept very little.

The next morning, we launched from the airfield and flew out over the ocean to the boat. When we were cleared to enter the landing pattern, I was so nervous, and now, with what my crewmember had said the night before, I felt all alone. I had no idea what he was going to do, if he would help or just sit there and do the minimum.

The first pass was a touch-and-go, then we were cleared "hook down," which meant we would lower our arresting hook and land the next time around. Though nervous, I managed to land. As I taxied out of the landing area, I felt so overwhelmed and so scared that I promised myself I'd call it quits when it was all over. I felt too much out of my element, too behind. Doubts churned in my

head—maybe the *Prowler* transition was a mistake? But before I knew it, we were taxied over to the catapult and were launched off again.

With each pass, I felt a little better, and even made it through the night qualification period without any problems. That was one of the most difficult things I have ever dealt with, and it would have been less of an ordeal if I hadn't been paired to fly with that person. Despite his comments, which had a great effect on me, I got through it and did well.

Despite these challenges, I successfully completed carrier qualifications and even managed to receive the Top Hook award as the best qualifying pilot for that period. I was very proud, yet somewhat embarrassed to receive the award. I really didn't think I deserved it. I graduated from the *Prowler* training squadron in December 1994, and joined the VAQ-138 Yellow Jackets.

I completed a six-month deployment on the USS *Nimitz* in the Pacific flying with VAQ-138, and was the first woman EA-6B pilot to complete a combat deployment. After this tour, I headed back to the *Prowler* training squadron to instruct student aviators. I loved being an instructor, and I worked for a terrific commanding officer who was a great mentor.

Around this time, I began to realize I was on track to become the first female commanding officer of an EA-6B squadron—the idea excited and terrified me. Fate would play its hand yet again, because that was also when I met and fell in love with my husband-to-be, Matt, a Marine Corps aviator. Shortly after Matt deployed with his squadron to Iwakuni, Japan, he called and asked me to marry him! I said yes! We married after he returned home and before I left on another six-month cruise on the aircraft carrier USS *John C. Stennis.*

Since Matt was a Marine and I was in the Navy, it seemed nearly impossible that we would ever be stationed together. We were at a crossroads in our lives; I could continue an active-duty career, which meant we'd endure long separations from each other, or I could pursue other avenues that would allow us to stay together. It was a difficult decision but I decided to submit my letter of resignation.

After returning home from my cruise, I left active duty, joined the Navy Reserve, and moved to North Carolina where Matt was stationed. It was tough adjusting to my drastically different civilian life. Initially, I thought I missed the Navy, but eventually realized what I truly missed was flying. I was working a desk job for a defense contractor and hating life. One day, Matt said, "Paula, you're going to have to get a flying job, because you're driving me crazy!"

In autumn 2001, I began to work for a commuter airline flying the Canadair regional jet. After four months, FedEx called for an interview. I was hired a short time later. Just after I finished new-hire training, I discovered I was pregnant.

Matt received orders back to Whidbey Island to be an instructor. Shortly after unpacking the last box, in June 2003, our son, Connor, was born. I had no idea I could feel so much love. After seven months, I went back to work for FedEx full-time. I first started at FedEx as a flight engineer, then, after completing upgrade training, I became a first officer on the Airbus 300. The "Bus" is definitely the most sophisticated aircraft that I have flown, and the training was very challenging.

In July 2007, we were blessed with our second child, beautiful little Hanna Michelle. FedEx is a family-oriented company and allowed me to take twenty months of personal leave following Hanna's birth. I missed flying but the time I had with Hanna and Connor was a precious gift! I have since returned to FedEx and back to flying "the line."

Although rife with challenge, I have learned it is possible to have both a flying career and a wonderful, happy family. Balancing the two can be difficult at times—many sacrifices must be made—but when I get to fly and then come home to my beautiful children, it is all worth it.

I am totally devoted to my family. Connor and Hanna give me purpose and keep me grounded and focused on what is important in life. However, pursuing my love for flying provides a different kind of fulfillment, and gives me a sense of individuality and confidence in myself.

I joined the Navy because I wanted to fly. Becoming a patriot was something the Navy taught me. I loved being part of a bigger purpose. The Navy gave me a sense of belonging, as well as stability and security, I had never experienced before. My years in the Navy shaped me as an individual as well as a pilot, and I am so fortunate to have had such incredible experiences and opportunities. I will never forget the day I was sworn into the Navy. As I listened to the words of the oath, my chest swelled with pride, and I had goose bumps all over.

There were many moments throughout my career when I would feel that way again. One was "manning the rails" on the USS *Nimitz* after returning from my first deployment. The ship's flight deck was lined with sailors and officers dressed in their summer whites. We pulled into Pearl Harbor, and I couldn't help thinking about the thousands of sailors who lost their lives when Pearl Harbor was attacked more than fifty years earlier. I was humbled to be a part of their company.

Throughout my career, I was always amazed and inspired by the servicemen and women I worked with. So many made sacrifices, worked long hours, went that extra mile for a fellow sailor, and without a moment's hesitation would put their life on the line. Those people made me proud to serve my country and fostered my feelings of patriotism.

Although there are moments when I really miss the flying and camaraderie in the Navy, I just couldn't bear to be away from Connor and Hanna for six months or longer. Nowadays, I can hardly stand being gone for just a few days. The joy of waking up and seeing my sweet little Hanna's smiling face or hearing Connor's giggles

Mom to Mom:

The thing that surprised me most about being a mom is how much I love my children! The love for a child is unique and powerful. I am so glad they are in my life.

when I tickle him far outweighs what "could have been."

. . . .

"When once you have tasted flight, you will forever walk the earth with your eyes turned skyward, for there you have been, and there you will always long to return."

. . . .

—Leonardo da Vinci

Rank:	Navy Commander
Years Served:	20
Current Military Status:	Retired
Number of Children:	2

Tammie Jo (Bonnell) Shults

EA-7L *Corsair*, F/A-18 *Hornet*

SOME PEOPLE GROW UP AROUND AVIATION. I GREW UP UNDER IT. OUR NEW MEXICO RANCH SAT UNDER THE DOGFIGHTING AIRSPACE OF Holloman AFB. Reading the missionary book, *Jungle Pilot,* by Nate Saint and watching the daily air show cinched it. I just had to fly!

During my senior year of high school in 1979, I attended a vocational day where I heard a retired colonel give a lecture on aviation. He started the class by asking me, the only girl in attendance, if I was lost. I mustered up the courage to assure him I was not and that I was interested in flying. He allowed me to stay but assured me there were no professional women pilots.

I did not say another word. In my heart, I hoped that God had given me an interest in flying for a reason. I had never touched an airplane, but I knew flying was my future. My junior year in college, I met a girl who had just received her Air Force wings. My heart jumped. Girls did fly! I set to work trying to break into the club.

However, the Air Force wasn't interested in talking to me but they wanted to know if my brother wanted to fly. The Navy was a little more charitable and let me take the test and fill out the application for aviation officer candidate school, but there did not seem to be a demand for women pilots. When the military flight program looked like a set of closed, locked doors, I headed back to school, starting a graduate program at Western New Mexico University. I wrestled with modifying my career choice. I did not understand how I could have such an interest in flying, not a passing infatuation but a real desire, and yet have no way of trying out my wings.

Finally, a year after taking the Navy aviation exam, I found a recruiter who would process my application.

Within two months, I was getting my hair buzzed off and doing pushups in aviation officer candidate school in Pensacola, Florida. I had finally broken into the flight club!

After graduation, I started flight training, initially flying the T-34 *Mentor.* It was intense, joyful, and horrible, all depending on the instructor and, ultimately, the leadership. The friendships I made in T-34 training remained a source of fun and encouragement all the way through getting those coveted gold wings at graduation.

Next, I was assigned to one of the training squadrons at NAS Beeville, Texas, as an instructor pilot teaching student aviators how to fly the Navy T-2 trainer. The squadron's commanding officer made his unit a fun place to work and this was a really enjoyable tour. A few years later, I received orders to fly the A-7 *Corsair* and left for the A-7 training squadron—VA-122 in Lemoore, California. I had met my knight in shining airplane—Dean Shults—before I left for Lemoore. We married ten months after we met, and, thankfully, Dean also got orders to Lemoore to fly the A-7.

Until now, being a woman aviator had been no big deal. However, all that changed when I entered VA-122; there was certainly a shift in attitude. The other students were the same guys I had been flying with since flight school but the leadership was not exactly welcoming. Since the combat exclusion law prohibited women from flying in a combat squadron, I had very limited choices where I could fly the A-7 when I finished my training, either VAQ-33 in Key West, Florida, or VAQ-34 in Point Mugu, California. Both were support squadrons that provided electronic warfare training to Navy ships and aircraft. Dean, however, joined a combat A-7

Tammie Jo on the flight line, 1993.

squadron at Lemoore and I chose VAQ-34, two hours from Lemoore.

I was fortunate to work for VAQ-34's first female commanding officer—Commander Rosemary Mariner. Commander Mariner opened my eyes to the incredible influence of leadership. She was a shining example of how to lead. At the time, I was honored to call her my commanding officer. Now, I feel fortunate to count her as a friend.

After flying the A-7 for a couple of years, our squadron transitioned to the Navy's newest fighter, the F/A-18 *Hornet*, but again in a support role with VAQ-34. I went back to Lemoore to learn how to fly the *Hornet*. Women were new to the *Hornet* community, and already there were signs of growing pains. My initial *Hornet* flight instructor, call sign Micro, set the standard for gentlemen in aviation. The flights under

his direction were a dream—the aircraft seemed like magic, mixed with his good company. The euphoria was short-lived, however, because the rest of the training squadron did not share Micro's open-mindedness about flying with women. After completing the training, I went back to VAQ-34 and finished out my tour flying the *Hornet*.

When our squadron tours ended, Dean and I decided to get out of the Navy. We wanted to try our hands at civilian flying and start a family. So, in 1993, I left the Navy, and the following year Dean left active duty as well. We both joined Southwest Airlines—Dean works a full-time schedule, and I typically fly eight to ten days a month. We try to fly the same days so that we are all home together.

There is more to life than flying. Dean and I have a beautiful, darling daughter, now eleven years old, and a handsome son, now ten. They each have sweet yet very opposite personalities, one being "Tarzan Cinderella" and the other "Captain Cautious." We have been blessed with nearby friends and family who provide love and godly council to our children when Dean and I do fly at the same time. We endeavor to teach our children to be leaders, not lemmings. This is especially important when it comes to making the right choice while the crowd is pulling in the other direction.

I recently took a trip with my children and parents to Carlsbad, New Mexico. As we drove, my dad casually mentioned the airfield we were passing. He mused over the time he had soloed at the small airstrip outside the town. I stared at him in amazement. I've been flying for twenty-three years and I never knew he'd soloed. I do have a bit of family history in aviation after all!

Mom to Mom:

The most rewarding thing about being a mom is watching my children grow in their relationship with the Lord. Often, I hear snatches of what is in their hearts and I am very touched——a sweet smile, a word of encouragement, a truth or scripture they share from their own discovery.

I just had to fly!

Rank:	Navy Lieutenant Commander
Years Served:	10
Current Military Status:	Separated
Number of Children:	2

Kerry (Kuykendall) Smith

F-14 *Tomcat,* FA-18 *Hornet*

AS THE OLDEST OF THREE KIDS, I HAVE MEMORIES OF MY DAD REGALING US WITH TALES FROM HIS TIME IN THE MARINE CORPS. "ONCE A MARINE, always a Marine," my dad would say. "There is no such thing as an ex-Marine." My mother is a saint—the most patient and loving woman I have ever known. Only in my adulthood did I begin to realize how very special she is. I have two younger brothers; neither went into the military, but serve in equally noble jobs. Brent is a middle school teacher (a job you could NEVER pay me enough to do) and Craig is a Los Angeles city firefighter.

I decided that I wanted to be a fighter pilot, test pilot, and an astronaut after watching the movie, *The Right Stuff,* in my eighth-grade science class. During high school, I applied to the military service academies, and I discovered that women were prohibited from flying in combat. I wrote President George H.W. Bush to ask why women weren't allowed to fly combat missions. I did receive a response back, stating that he believed it was the feeling of the majority of the nation that women should not be put in harm's way. Though prohibited from entering combat, I attended the Naval Academy in the fall of 1990. Thankfully, during my last semester of school, the combat exclusion law was repealed, and I graduated with a guaranteed flight school spot. After graduating in May 1994 with a degree in astrospace engineering, I headed off to flight school.

I always knew I wanted to fly fighters, and got my wish when I received my wings of gold in November 1996. Much to my delight (and my mother's dismay), my assignment was to fly the F-14 *Tomcat.* My mom actually cried out of fear for me when I got the news, right before the winging ceremony. I was ecstatic because F-14s were my first choice, but it broke my heart to see her so fearful.

After completing F-14 pilot training, I was assigned to fly with VF-32, the Swordsmen. I chuckled when my mom told me she thought the name should be changed to Swordspeople, since there were now women aviators in the squadron. I completed two deployments to the Mediterranean and Arabian Gulf, aboard the aircraft carriers USS *Enterprise* and the USS *Harry S. Truman,* flying twenty-eight combat missions in and around Iraq.

I had been in the squadron six months when I participated in my first deployment and flew in combat. When Saddam Hussein refused to let the inspectors into Iraq, President Clinton ordered Operation *Desert Fox,* a four-day Navy-only campaign in December 1998, to bomb some of Iraq's military installations. I flew on the second round of flights, and remember feeling extremely exhilarated and nervous as we took off from the carrier deck. We could see the neighboring ships launching Tomahawk missiles into the night sky—headed north toward Iraq. As my RIO (radar intercept officer) and I flew into enemy territory, I recall the tracers flying up beneath us. The night-vision goggles were both a blessing and a curse. I could see the other airplanes in my formation, but I could also see the enemy fires from below. Strangely, my concern wasn't for my life—I didn't want to fail in my mission. I remember thinking and praying, "*Please don't &%$* up. Please don't &%$* up.*" As we approached the target, my RIO found it, and I thought, "*Sweet!*" My main job was to get us in the delivery zone at the right time and altitude, and then ensure that we didn't hit any of the other dozens of airplanes in the vicinity. I flipped the master arm switch "on," and bombs away!

After my time at VF-32, I went to the Navy's test pilot school. Though several women had gone before me, I believe

Kerry as F/A-18 test pilot, 2007, VX-31, NAWC China Lake, California.

that I was the first F-14 female pilot to graduate from this elite Navy school. After the yearlong course, I worked as an F-14 test pilot for a few years at one of the Navy's test squadrons in Point Mugu, California, followed by a job as a military aide to a Marine Corps general—much to my father's delight!

Afterward, I had another job as a test pilot, but during this tour, I got the opportunity to work with the Army over in Iraq, working as an electronic warfare officer. It was a very rewarding job, helping the Army train their solders how to use the electronic warfare equipment installed on their vehicles, which would help save lives.

I met my future husband in 2007 after returning from my deployment to Iraq. Matthew Smith was a civilian, and was doing one of the hardest jobs I could ever imagine teaching middle-school science. He didn't care

that I was a fighter pilot. He just knew that he loved me, and said that he would follow me wherever I was stationed. He is funny, loving, great with kids, and patient. I'm a perfectionist, and he's a go-with-the-flow kind of guy. We married in February 2009.

We moved to Monterey, California, where I attended the Naval Postgraduate School and earned a master's degree in astronautical engineering. Since this was a non-flying job, it was the perfect time for us to start a family. We had our first child, a son, in October 2010.

After I was up all night in labor, Tiberius Henry Smith (Ty, for short) was born on a rainy Monterey morning. I was both excited and nervous that he had finally arrived. He had all ten fingers, all ten toes, and a perfect little face. I was exhausted—little did I know that was just the beginning. He had some initial bouts with colic and ear infections, but is a thriving active boy, almost a year old, and is the light of my life! I am constantly amazed and joyful at how quickly he grows and learns new things. We recently moved to Virginia for my next military assignment. As with any new job, I was coming home feeling overwhelmed and anxious. But with one smile, Ty took away all the worries and stresses of my tough day. A hug and slobbery kiss from my little boy was more powerful than my 1000-pound bombs. Although he can't say it yet, I'm anticipating his first words and finally hearing the sweet sounds of "Mama."

What amazes me is how insecure I felt at becoming a mother. I have flown a multi-million-dollar fighter plane in combat, but I am afraid of failing at the most important job I will probably ever have—motherhood. In an airplane, I am in control. I am the one who flies her, who executes the emergency procedures, and ultimately lands the crippled bird. With children, all bets are off. You can't will a baby to stop crying. You can't just press a button and have your children be honest, successful, joyful beings. It's a labor of love, and I only hope that I am up to the task. If I could be just half—no, just a quarter—of the mother my mom was, I will be a huge success.

I have always been a believer in hard work and dreaming big. It also doesn't hurt to have a little good

Mom to Mom:

I think the most rewarding thing about being a mom will be watching my children learn and discover new things.

luck. As one of my old bosses used to say, "Better lucky than good." I feel so blessed to have had the opportunity to serve my country and fly my first love, the *Tomcat*. I hope to pass on to my kids a sense of pride, honor, commitment, and pure joy. I want them to know that they can do anything they set their minds to.

In my military jobs, I have had amazing friendships and seen the true meaning of loyalty. Nothing makes you closer than trusting your fellow aviator to have your back, whether in the air, in the bar, when you've screwed up, or when you are feeling low. My career has been incredibly rewarding, and I just hope that my children have the opportunity to feel the same way.

. . . .

"The best and most beautiful things in the world cannot be seen or even touched. They must be felt with the heart."

. . . .

—Helen Keller

Rank:	Navy Commander
Years Served:	16
Current Military Status:	Active Duty
Number of Children:	1

Jenny (Merrill) Tinjum

UH-3H *Sea King*, UH-1 *Huey*, MH-53 *Sea Dragon*, MH-60S *Seahawk*

I WAS BORN FUELED WITH DETERMINATION AND ENERGY. ALWAYS ACTIVE, I INVOLVED MYSELF IN SPORTS, CLUBS, AND STUDENT GOVERNMENT. AS far back as junior high school, I knew I was going to be a pilot; the question was when and how.

With a few bucks saved up from my minimum-wage job and also help from my parents, I sought private pilot lessons. Once my wheels lifted off the ground for the first time, my fate was confirmed.

Unlike most teenage girls, my walls were plastered with photos of *Spitfires* and P-51s rather than *Teen Beat* hunks. I attended every air show within a day's drive and memorized aircraft facts as if I were auditioning for *Jeopardy*.

Flying in junior high was scary as well as exciting. I soloed an aircraft before I ever got my driver's permit. My parents listened on a hand-held radio as I flew around one of the busiest airspaces in the country—Los Angeles.

About that time, I also joined the Civil Air Patrol, which taught me about military bearing, uniforms, pride, and, most of all, the service academies. I applied to all three—West Point, the Air Force Academy, and the Naval Academy—and was accepted to all three. I fell in love with the Naval Academy after visiting the campus and, upon high school graduation, officially became a member of the U.S. Naval Academy class of 1996. I enjoyed my time at the academy, and four years later graduated with a degree in aerospace engineering.

Next, I started flight school. It was challenging, but becoming a helicopter pilot and flying "low and slow" was more exciting than I ever imagined. If I had selected jets rather than helicopters, I would not have met my husband, Lee, a Marine Corps aviator also going through helicopter flight training.

Receiving my wings of gold marked a milestone in my life—I had finally accomplished what I had dreamed of and worked so hard for. Lee and I married right after we graduated from flight school, and we both received orders to San Diego. I would be flying the Navy's UH-3H at HC-11, and Lee would be flying the Marine Corps CH-46.

I checked into my squadron with my new name and a new career waiting. My job was to be a search-and-rescue pilot and also fly VIP flights for the commander, Third Fleet. Wherever the admiral went, we went—a great tour.

My second tour was even more exciting. I was going to be a *Huey* helicopter instructor pilot for the Marine Corps in San Diego. Talk about being given the keys to Dad's sports car! I felt like I could do anything in the zippy little *Huey* and was thrilled to teach tactical flying. The duty kept me in San Diego, which was great because my husband was still flying the CH-46 helicopter at a local Marine Corps squadron.

About eight months into my second tour, and after four years of trying, I finally became pregnant. I was a little nervous about breaking the news to my squadron, because I was a flight instructor and I was also working with Marines in a very female-limited environment. Not only did they appear truly happy for me, but they also let me fly until I was seven months pregnant. Our son, Maddox, was born in April 2003 at Camp Pendleton, and several of the squadron officers came to my hospital room to welcome him.

Shortly after, Lee left on his second eight-month deployment to Iraq for Operation *Iraqi Freedom*. It was a

Jenny and her kids--Maddox, Rylan, Rogan, and Murphy, 2009.

difficult time for me. Runny noses, fevers, and sniffles that are expected with kids are hard to factor into a demanding flight schedule when you are a single mom in the military. I also missed my husband and was concerned about him overseas. Thankfully, I had incredible support from my squadron leadership.

After this tour, Lee received orders for flight instructor duty at Corpus Christi, Texas. I was up for sea duty orders, and there was nothing in Corpus that would qualify as sea duty. It was difficult to coordinate orders between two active-duty individuals, and even more difficult to be separated as a family...especially now that we had our son. It was a really agonizing decision, but I felt it was best to leave active duty.

I wasn't ready to say good-bye, but I felt guilty that Maddox had spent his first year in daycare, and part of me was really looking forward to be able to greet Lee at the door each night when he came home. Leaving active

duty wasn't such a terrible idea—at first. I left during my second pregnancy, this time with twins. I had visions of stay-at-home-mom life with cookies, play dates, and family life, and was ready to embrace this next step in my life! I left the Navy in March 2005, and the twins were born just a couple of months later.

As a stay-at-home mom with three kids under the age of three, I did my best, but after eight months of being out of the Navy, I realized I was no Martha Stewart. I was exhausted and missed flying. I also really missed being surrounded and supported by other people who had similar experiences. Being a full-time stay-at-home mom is the toughest job there is.

I found myself in the recruiter's office signing up to fly part-time in the Navy Reserve. My new squadron, HM-15, an active-duty/reserve MH-53 squadron in Corpus Christi, Texas, welcomed me without hesitation. I had the best of both worlds—I flew a couple of days per week *and* I was still a stay-at-home mom! I realized that I was a better wife and mom when I got my feet off the ground and a little whiff of JP-5 airplane fuel.

After a year at HM-15 in Corpus Christi, my husband received orders to the Navy's postgraduate school in Monterey, California. I decided that I'd have a better future as a reserve pilot if I transitioned to the Navy's new helicopter, the MH-60. I was selected by HSC-85, an MH-60 squadron based out of NAS North Island in San Diego.

I hit the ground running, and completed all of the ground requirements before having our fourth child, our daughter Murphy Rae, then I quickly climbed back into the cockpit.

The commute down to San Diego wasn't too difficult from Monterey, especially since I drilled for a few days at a time. However, when we moved to Virginia the next year, the cross-country commute became too difficult on my family.

I decided to leave HSC-85, but spent an incredible final week with the squadron flying firefighting missions, recovering torpedo targets (used in Navy training missions), and having the opportunity to fly with some of my closest aviator girlfriends.

Transferring to a reserve squadron closer to home was a welcome break from the long commute from Virginia to California every month. I made a huge transition from rotary-wing to fixed-wing aircraft as I switched into VR-56, a C-9 reserve squadron, transporting people and supplies. What a challenge to re-learn how to fly something with wings!

As a mom, every thought and every breath has a purpose now, one that must include the safety and welfare of these four tiny people. It has definitely been challenging, but the rewards of being a parent make the journey worthwhile. No one but a parent can understand the overwhelming love you feel for your child, even though, at times, it is the hardest and most frustrating of jobs.

I am proud to serve my country, and I hope that my husband and I will create the same patriotism and respect in our children. I want to pass on to my kids that they can accomplish anything with faith in God and determination in their hearts. Like any parent, I want them to have the world, pursue their dreams, and not let minor setbacks or failures keep them from reaching their goals.

Life is nothing without the love and support of friends and family, and you only get that by genuinely caring for both.

Mom to Mom:

The thing that surprised me most about being a mom was how much more challenging it was than being a military pilot. For years, I have trained and retrained to maintain the skills to be a professional aviator. So, how hard can it be to be a mom of a tiny little infant? I found out really quickly that being a mom is so much more challenging, both physically and emotionally, but also so much more rewarding. With my type-A personality, I am used to being good at everything, being efficient at everything. I am used to schedules, punctuality, and commands both given and executed. I quickly realized kids don't necessarily like to follow those rules we moms establish. Learning to accept that I will have exceptionally good days and exceptionally lousy days has been my biggest challenge as a type-A mom! My level of greatness is no longer determined by grades or medals, but by how much time and love I choose to give.

Nothing will get you farther in life than a genuine smile.

Rank:	Navy Lieutenant Commander
Years Served:	14
Current Military Status:	Naval Reserve
Number of Children:	4

Linda (Evans) Wackerman

H-46 *Sea Knight,* C-12 *Huron,* C-9 *Skytrain,* T-34C *Mentor*

MY BROTHER AND I BOTH CAUGHT THE FLYING BUG FROM OUR DAD—A BRITISH ROYAL AIR FORCE ORDNANCE MAN. WE GREW UP IN CANADA AND Mexico City and then, finally, in Miami, Florida. As a teenager, my brother got his commercial and certified flight instructor pilot's licenses, and then, after college, he joined the Navy and became a pilot. He gave me my first flying lesson from an instructor friend as a birthday gift when I turned thirteen. I fell in love with flying and took a half-dozen more lessons. However, my fifty-cent allowance couldn't pay for the cost of flying lessons, so I put the dream of flying on hold.

After graduating from high school in Miami, I attended Hawthorne College in New Hampshire for two years, and then completed my degree in aerospace science at the Metropolitan College in Colorado in May 1986. During college, I flew and received my pilot's license and worked full-time to support my flying habit. I was in the process of becoming an American citizen, and decided to join the Navy. It seemed like a great way to give back to my new country and also to continue my dream of flying.

One month after college graduation, I started the Navy's aviation officer candidate school in Pensacola, Florida—it was challenging, but nothing was going to stop me from finishing! Next was primary flight training in the T-34 *Mentor.* I definitely had an advantage during flight school because of the civilian commercial and instrument flight ratings I had gotten during college.

I met my future husband, Dean, before primary flight training. I was moving into the same apartment complex that he lived in and he offered to help me move my things in. A few weeks later, we started dating. He, too, was in flight training but soon graduated and transferred to San Diego to fly the H-46 helicopter.

I originally requested to fly jets, but due to changes in anthropometric (body) measurement requirements, I needed a height waiver since I was only five-foot-two. While I waited on the waiver, the Navy suggested I start training to fly helicopters (helos), and once the waiver was approved, I could switch to jets. I was almost completely done with helo training when my waiver was approved.

However, Dean and I had recently married, and I opted not to start jet training but to finish up with helos, also selecting the H-46 helicopter so that we would have a better chance of getting stationed together. Also, at that time, this was the only naval aviation community where women could do exactly what the men were doing, including going to sea, and I wanted to go do the real mission.

Upon graduation from flight school in October 1987, I received orders to HC-11 in San Diego, the same squadron Dean was in. The commanding officer actually had requested me to join his squadron, although married people weren't typically stationed in the same unit. Since there were no other married couples present, I was very conscientious not to promote any perception of favoritism or special treatment. The squadron leadership was great! There were about ten women aviators out of ninety pilots. It was a healthy and positive environment, and I always felt like I was around a bunch of brothers and sisters.

As part of the H-46 squadron's mission, we participated in combat logistics support, vertical replenishments of other ships, search-and-rescue missions, and special forces operations. My first deployment was a 1988 Western Pacific cruise, flying off of the USS *Mount Hood,* part of the USS *Enterprise* carrier battle group.

Linda and her husband, Dean, July 1987. They had been married about a year and Linda was just preparing to join helicopter squadron HC-11 and fly H-46s (the same squadron as her husband).

Sadly, while on this tour, one of my best friends was killed in an aircraft accident. Jane Paradeis and I went through flight school together, and she also flew H-46s, though on the East Coast. I was at my squadron and heard of an H-46 crash back on the East Coast. A shiver rippled through me, and I thought, "I hope it's not Jane," but unfortunately it was. I immediately flew back to be with her family.

As much as I always knew I would fly, I also knew I wanted to be a mom. I had my daughter, Carly Jane (named after my aviator friend who had died), in March 1991, and soon after, Dean and I both got orders to NAS Whiting Field as instructor pilots teaching naval student aviators. This was one of the most rewarding tours of my career. I loved taking a student pilot who had no concept of flying and seeing him or her blossom into a new and confident pilot. We had our second daughter, Madeleine

Kristina, in March 1994, during my last year at Whiting Field.

After this tour we moved to Quakertown, Pennsylvania, and bought a house on twelve acres near Dean's family. Dean decided to leave the military and flying for a while and took a management job nearby. I decided to fly for a Navy reserve squadron at NAS Willow Grove, Pennsylvania, where I would be a full-time active-duty member. I flew the C-12 for the next two years, and then flew the C-9 aircraft for three years. Both aircraft provided passenger and cargo transportation for all the military services.

I loved the squadron and the people I worked with. In addition, I got to fly all over the world. However, I knew that if I stayed in the active-duty Navy and pursued senior leadership opportunities, I would have to move my family several more times over the next few years. Therefore,

I made the decision to join the Naval Reserve in 1999, still fly C-9s in the same squadron, but on a part-time status. I also joined American Airlines, flying full-time. I couldn't ask for a better airline. It has been a great fit for me, and I have enjoyed flying the MD-80 and the Boeing 757 and 767.

We have had two more kids, Benjamin in 1999 and Jacob in 2004. I am still in the Navy Reserve, and between my airline schedule, reserve schedule, Dean's flying schedule (he flies the C-12 for the Navy Reserve), plus the kids' busy schedules, we constantly work to make everything fit.

The highlight of my military career was serving as the commanding officer of VR-52 from 2005 to 2007, but my highlight in life has been being a mom. Interestingly enough, being a leader in the military has helped me to be a good mom, and the qualities of a good parent have helped me to be a good leader—listening and making the hard (not always the popular) decisions. I could die today and be happy with what I have achieved in life.

Mom to Mom:

The most rewarding thing about being a mom is the joy of watching my children grow and learn. They have taught me everything I know about the gift of life. Being a mom is better than I ever thought it would be!

My hope for my kids is that they each find their passion in life and pursue it. Success isn't about money; it is about finding something you love. Success will then follow. I hope to pass down to my children that family is the most important priority. I have never made a decision without considering my family first. I also hope to encourage them to go out and make a difference, and to leave their mark in life.

Life is not about the destination; it is about the journey.

—paraphrased from Ralph Waldo Emerson

Rank:	Navy Captain
Years Served:	24
Current Military Status:	Naval Reserve
Number of Children:	4

air force/air national guard

Tammy (Ward) Barlette

T-37 *Tweet,* A-10 *Thunderbolt II,* MQ-1 *Predator,* MQ-9 *Reaper*

AS A CHILD, THE IDEA OF TAKING TO THE SKIES EXHILARATED ME, BUT I NEVER THOUGHT OF IT AS A CAREER POSSIBILITY—MAYBE BECAUSE IT seemed like so much fun.

Despite my constant interest in being in the military, the thought of military training made me apprehensive. Even so, I was extremely impressed with the high-caliber, motivated people in the Air Force ROTC program at the University of Minnesota, and knew it was where I wanted to be.

As an ROTC cadet, I attended a career briefing with hundreds of other cadets, and the only pilot at the event singled me out. Pointing to me, he asked, "Are you going to be a pilot?" I responded that I thought I would be disqualified due to a previous knee surgery. When he replied, "There's a waiver for everything," my last obstacle disappeared, and the new idea materialized into a reachable goal. I was off and running, and later found out the surgery was so common that I didn't even need a waiver!

In 1997, I was chosen to participate in a program for cadets called Operation Air Force, and spent three weeks at Spangdahlem Air Base (AB) in Germany. Since I had been awarded a pilot slot the previous year, I shadowed an F-16 pilot. During a backseat ride in an F-16, I was really sick from all the yanking and banking, and became nervous about attending flight school. However, the pilot I was shadowing encouraged me, saying, "Don't worry about it. You'll get over it—everyone does."

In 1998, I graduated from college and started pilot training at Laughlin AFB in Del Rio, Texas. The Air Force's basic trainer, the T-37 *Tweet,* was the first jet I ever flew—I learned the basics of takeoffs, landings, aerobatics, stalls,

spins, and instruments, and fell in love with the challenge of flying formation.

Upon completion of the T-37 program, I was selected for the fighter/bomber track, and moved on to learn to fly the T-38 *Talon* trainer. After honing my formation skills, breaking the sound barrier, and practicing low-level tactics at 500 mph in this high-performance jet, I graduated from pilot training in April 2000.

I spent the next few years as a T-37 instructor pilot. Teaching students the basics of flying was absolutely the most rewarding job I have ever had.

For my next challenge, I hoped to fly the A-10 *Thunderbolt II,* more commonly known as the *Warthog.* My dream came true and, a few months later, I moved to Davis-Monthan AFB in Tucson, Arizona, for training. The A-10's primary mission is close air support, and I learned to employ the 30mm Gatling gun, use various techniques to drop bombs, shoot the Maverick missile, and fire rockets. It was very challenging, but the best training I have ever received.

In November 2004, I left Tucson to complete a one-year remote tour in the 25th Fighter Squadron at Osan AB in South Korea. My time in Korea was amazing, and I had some of my best flying experiences there. During my first in-country flight, after not flying for more than three months, I experienced an in-flight emergency. I first noticed the airplane's oil pressure jumping around more than normal. After monitoring it for several minutes, it became apparent that I would have to shut down the engine. The intense training I received on aircraft emergencies just naturally kicked in, and I ran through the procedures from memory, following up with the checklist. I looked for a runway close by—Kunsan AB was a

Tammy and A-10, October 2004, Davis-Monthan AFB, Arizona.

few miles on the nose. I shut down the malfunctioning engine, "blew" the landing gear down (alternate gear extension), and successfully landed with a single engine.

Near the end of my tour, I was given the opportunity to fly the A-10 to an air show in Tokyo, Japan—something I will never forget. The people there were very friendly and enthusiastic about aviation and loved taking our photos. Months later, several of the photos were published in Japanese aviation magazines.

After returning home from South Korea, I was assigned to an A-10 squadron back at Davis-Monthan. However, I only flew one flight with the squadron. A persistent and increasingly painful neck problem was diagnosed as a herniated disc in my cervical spine.

After a serious spinal surgery, I chose to separate from active duty in 2006, and joined the Arizona Air National Guard, flying the MQ-1 *Predator*, a remotely piloted aircraft used by the Air Force. The aircraft, located in either Iraq or Afghanistan, is operated from right here in the United States from a ground control station. The

pilot controls the aircraft, while the sensor operator controls the targeting pod. The aircraft's current mission is to support our ground troops by utilizing the targeting pod for intelligence, surveillance, and reconnaissance, but it is also armed with one or two Hellfire missiles to provide close air support.

I have held a full-time position with the Arizona Guard since separating from the Air Force, and have found it to be a perfect transition for my life. Although I miss the exhilarating feeling of being in the air, the *Predator* allows me to utilize my flying skills, including much of my tactical training gained from the A-10, especially shooting the *Predator's* Hellfire missiles. I hope to continue full-time with the Guard until I retire.

In February 2004, I had met Bob, a Buffalo, New York, native who had moved to Tucson to begin his new career—a U.S. Border Patrol agent who tracked the Arizona desert in search of illegal immigrants. Despite my countless hours studying and his crazy work hours, we found time to spend together.

After I returned home from the one-year remote tour in South Korea, Bob and I picked up where we left off and then married in the spring of 2007. The following year, we welcomed our first child, Rose Grace. A short four months later, we found out our second child was on the way.

When I was five months pregnant, I was offered an incredible opportunity to attend Air Force Weapons School in Nevada. I was very honored, but at the same time unsure of the way forward. I asked for some time to talk to my husband. As soon as the words came out of my mouth, my husband said, "You have to do it!" I couldn't figure out how it would work with two young children and a husband with a demanding job, but Bob was supportive and said we would find a way to make it happen. And that is exactly what we did. That July, I left my family for the six-month intensive course. My daughter was eighteen months old, and my infant son had just turned three months old. Although we figured out the logistics of me being gone, the emotional side of it was the most difficult. Thankfully, my mother and stepfather (who live nearby) stepped in and provided help and support. I returned home once a month during training, but it was challenging for both my husband and me. We made it through successfully, and now I have returned to my squadron as the chief of weapons and tactics.

Mom to Mom:

The most rewarding thing about being a mom is being reminded how simple love really is.

I encourage other young people, especially young women who want to fly, that as long as your heart is in the right place and flying is what you want to do, aim straight for that goal and let nothing stand in your way. Don't look for potential discrimination, because you will either find it or think you have found it, and that belief may slow your progress or make you bitter. Push forward with your eyes on your goal, and become the best you can be.

I want to pass down to my children that they can do whatever they set their minds to. All they need is determination and dedication! I want Rose and Bobby to enjoy a happy life and to always know they are loved, and to also realize that a person is not defined by their accomplishments, but by who they are as a person.

"What would you attempt to do if you knew you could not fail?"

—Dr. Robert Schuller

Rank:	Air Force Major
Years Served:	11
Current Military Status:	Air National Guard (Active Duty)
Number of Children:	2

Lisa (Willman) Berente

KC-135 *Stratotanker*

I NEVER MEANT TO BE A PILOT. I WANTED TO BE A MOM, AND, ALONG THE WAY, DO THE BEST AT WHATEVER I SET OUT TO ACCOMPLISH. I ALSO wanted to attend college but, as one of seven children, I realized I needed a scholarship. Thankfully, the Air Force Academy accepted my application.

I played several sports there, including basketball, track and field, soccer, and the national champion handball team. *Glamour* magazine also honored me as one of the "Top Ten College Women in America."

During my senior year at the academy, I had to decide which career field to pursue in the Air Force. My roommate and I both passed the initial qualifications to receive pilot slots but we interviewed for many non-pilot positions to give us more options. When the night came to sign the paperwork, we said to each other, "I guess we'll try being pilots."

Pilot training was initially very challenging. In fact, had I failed one more event, I would've washed out. However, everything clicked during my T-37 formation flight. After the flight, the other jet's instructor pilot raved about what a fantastic job I did, and my flying life changed. I finished strong in the next trainer, the T-38, and moved from the bottom to the top half of my class. I graduated in August 1991, and selected the KC-135 tanker aircraft at Grand Forks AFB, North Dakota.

My tour at the 905th Air Refueling Squadron at Grand Forks was incredible, both professionally and personally. Several of my squadron mates were newly returned *Desert Storm* veterans and provided outstanding mentoring. They helped me to grow into a seasoned tanker pilot, and to command worldwide air-refueling and airlift missions in challenging conditions.

Personally, this was a very significant tour, because I met and married my husband, Istvan, and we had our first baby. Originally from a small town in Hungary, Istvan had defected and immigrated to Canada. My young sister, Suzy, met him during a training event for a church mission. After the training, he planned to go back to Budapest for a two-year mission. Suzy thought he and I would make the perfect match and tried to encourage Istvan to write to me.

Since I wasn't interested in being set up by my baby sister, I had no intention of writing him. She, however, told Istvan that he should write me because I was lonely in North Dakota. Eventually, Istvan wrote me because he felt sorry for me. However, he was taken aback when he learned I wasn't lonely at all but loved my job and the opportunity to fly all over the world. Still, we kept writing.

After six months of writing and three months of phone calls, we finally agreed to meet. When we look back on it now, we see God's hand at work, leading us to get married in 1994. Istvan moved from Canada to Grand Forks and finished his undergraduate degree at the University of North Dakota.

Istvan and I waited two years for me to get pregnant, and when I did, I was nervous about the reaction of my male squadron mates. My concerns were unfounded, because the guys and their spouses were magnificent. It seemed to us that our daughter, Courtney, was the most anticipated baby in April 1996 and, when she arrived, our world instantly changed. We looked at her big blue eyes and beautiful porcelain skin with gratitude and amazement and announced to her, "Little girl, this is the world."

Three months after Courtney's birth, we transferred to Mountain Home AFB, Idaho, where I flew the

Lisa with children, Courtney and Zoli, in Salt Lake City, Utah, before Lisa left
for a deployment in March 2003.

KC–135 tanker with the Gunfighters of 22nd Air Refueling Squadron. Istvan took this opportunity to obtain his master's degree at nearby Boise State.

We typically don't go by call signs in the tanker community, but all Gunfighters had call signs. I still remember getting mine. One of my squadron mates asked me if I was named yet. Not really sure what he was saying, I just looked at him. Taking that for a "no," he looked me up and down and stated, "Bear...that'll do." From then on, I was "Bear." When my strong, four-month-old baby weighed in heavier than his ultra-petite eighteen-month-old, he murmured, "Bear makes big cubs." And from then on, there were a variety of bear-isms.

A year after I joined the squadron, I found out I was pregnant with our second child, our son, Zoltan, "Zoli." Again, my squadron mates were fantastic. Though my husband was a phenomenal stay-at-home dad, it just got

to be too hard having two little kids seventeen months apart in age while I was flying all over the world.

At the end of my tour in 1999, I left the active-duty Air Force and joined the Utah Air National Guard, flying a few days each month. I also started flying full-time for United Airlines. Life was busy for a while because we were still living in Idaho so I would commute to Utah each month to fly for the Guard but, finally, in 2001, we moved to Utah.

Shortly after we moved, the events of September 11, 2001, transpired, and I was furloughed by United Airlines. However, I was very fortunate to get a full-time position with the Utah Guard and have been working full-time since and will continue until I retire. Thanks to United Airline's strong support of military service, I can return to flying with United after my military service.

We had our third child—Hannah, our little surprise—in 2005. Istvan again pitched in as a stay-at-home dad. A few years after Hannah was born, however, Istvan received an opportunity to work in his master's field at our children's school. This caused a dilemma because, although he enjoys teaching and is proud of the strong impact he has on schoolchildren, we had our wonderful Hannah at home to consider. The miracle answer came in the form of an amazing neighbor and surrogate grandmother, Grammy Southwick, who has become part of our family.

One of my flying career highlights occurred during a deployment to Turkey in support of Operation *Northern Watch*. After finishing a routine tanking mission, we were on our way back to our home base when we got a call on the radio asking if we had any extra gas. Before we knew it, an F-16 and F-4 strike package showed up on our wing. We figured it must be an emergency and, after we gave them as much gas as we could, they peeled off and quickly disappeared. We used every fuel conservation trick we knew, but still landed with little fuel in our tanks. We didn't know if we were heroes or in trouble for giving away so much gas.

The crew and I quietly got out of the airplane and went to complete our post-mission paperwork. The wing commander walked in during our debrief and said, "I can't give you all the details, but you did an unbelievably good

Mom to Mom:
I love being a mom because I cannot be fired. No matter what happens, no matter how great or poor I am, I am Mom and will always be Mom.

thing today and ultimately saved the lives of an entire convoy." We were relieved to be heroes! As we finished the paperwork, tears welled up in my eyes when I realized it was Christmas Eve. I was thankful there were people out there who could celebrate another Christmas. The Lord is great and mindful of us all.

It's amazing to see how my priorities in life have strengthened over the years, since getting married and having children. I am crazy about my kids and want the best for them. It is beautiful to watch the three of them interact, laugh, and play together.

I hope they are strong and valiant in their lives, and I encourage them to be what Abraham Lincoln described: "Whatever you are, be a good one." It is important for me to help guide them in discerning truth and distinguishing the right path. I believe if I do that, it will keep them safe and honorable and provide a solid foundation.

Being a mom is both humbling and self-inflating.

Rank:	Air Force Lieutenant Colonel
Years Served:	19
Current Military Status:	Air National Guard (Active Duty)
Number of Children:	3

Shannon Cary

F-16 *Fighting Falcon*

'VE BEEN SURROUNDED BY AVIATION MY WHOLE LIFE. WITH NO ROADS LEADING INTO OR OUT OF JUNEAU, ALASKA, WHERE I GREW UP, WE HAD TO travel by boat or plane to get anywhere. That also meant that many people owned their own boat or plane. While we didn't have a plane, plenty of my parents' friends did, and I bummed as many rides from them as I possibly could. Only much later did I learn that my parents paid for all those flights.

I remember my very first flight. It was in a Stearman and we flew up over the Mendenhall Glacier and did aerobatics until it was time to come home. That was all it took—my future had been born!

In 1993, I graduated from high school and entered the Air Force Academy, not really knowing anything about the military at that point except that the academy was free and I could fly there. Obviously, I was in for an abrupt awakening but, after a rocky start, the academy was definitely the launching pad to reach my flying goal. While there, I earned my private pilot's license and became a soaring (glider) instructor pilot. During my junior year, I went through the first phase of Air Force pilot training—initial flight-testing in a T–3, a fun little aerobatic single-engine turboprop.

After graduating from the academy in May 1997, I packed my possessions into my jeep and moved to Enid, Oklahoma, for undergraduate pilot training. I stayed on after receiving my wings to be an instructor pilot and spent three more years in Oklahoma. While it wasn't the most glamorous way to start, I wouldn't trade my experiences there for anything, because it opened my eyes to all aspects of military aviation. In addition to learning about the different military aircraft, I learned to truly appreciate each mission and what every pilot and airframe brought to the fight.

After my stint as an instructor, I moved to Luke AFB in Phoenix, Arizona, and began F-16 *Viper* training. Nine months later, I graduated and transferred to Kunsan AB, South Korea, joining the 35th Fighter Squadron—the Pantons. Kunsan was very remote, cut off from everything, but it was the perfect place for my first fighter assignment. In Korea, I learned firsthand the importance of camaraderie and what it was like to work with a group of outstanding professionals for whom I would give my life.

I stayed with the 35th for nineteen months until I was reassigned to Misawa AB, Japan, to the 13th Fighter Squadron—the Panthers. The pace grew faster and more hectic, and I loved it. New, sophisticated technologies made the F-16 an incredible aircraft to fly. I loved being on the cutting edge!

While in Korea and Japan, I had the opportunity to travel quite a bit, including a couple of trips back to the States and home to Alaska. We also flew to various parts of Southeast Asia, but the most memorable trip for me was our deployment to India, the first time American F-16s had flown in an exercise with the Indian Air Force, and I was the first female fighter pilot ever to fly with the Indians. It was an amazing experience, culminating in my leading a section of four fighters, American and Indian, in engagement against several other fighters.

The highlight of my aviation career so far has been the friendships forged. I have great friends all over the world. Flying taught me to take nothing for granted, as things can change in a heartbeat. You never know what's in store for you, and your only option is to take what life gives you and make it work.

After two years in Japan and more than nine years in the Air Force, I decided to separate from active duty and

Shannon with her squadron mates from the 35th Fighter Squadron, May 2003.

concentrate on starting a family. The hopes of a family came to fruition in February 2008 when I welcomed my son, Jaime, into the world. He is perfect, and I truly feel blessed. Every day he amazes me and does something new. His life is a clean slate, and anything is possible for him. Who knew something so small could become my entire world? Having a child makes me look at life differently—makes me slow down and appreciate the details.

I recently started flying under the general aviation umbrella again and got my certified flight instructor qualifications. It has been great fun to teach again. The planes are definitely slower than the F-16, but flying is flying, and it is great just to get airborne. Flying has been and will always be a part of my life. It's been quite a life so far and it's only getting better!

Another fantastic event that happened was the creation of the Chick Fighter Pilot Association, an organization open to female fighter pilots from all branches of the military. While unofficial, it is an amazing group of women who share the same interests. Our organization has been a backdrop for women fighter pilots to meet one another, share stories

Mom to Mom:

The most rewarding thing about being a mom is the pure joy I see on my son's face when he discovers something new, something amazing.

and experiences, provide motivation, and encourage others. These are friends that I will have for my lifetime, and even though I am no longer in the Air Force, I will be a part of the Chick Fighter Pilot Association forever.

My hopes for the future revolve around my son. I can only hope to be a positive role model and pass down to him a love for life and the belief that anything is possible. I can't wait to play catch, watch as he sheds his training wheels, cheer him on, and, of course, teach him to fly.

"The most difficult thing is the decision to act, the rest is merely tenacity."

—Amelia Earhart

Rank:	Air Force Captain
Years Served:	9
Current Military Status:	Separated
Number of Children:	1

99

Elisa (Romano) D'Antonio

KC-135 *Stratotanker*, C-21 *Learjet*

WHEN I WAS ONLY TWO, MY MOM AND I TOOK A CROSS-COUNTRY AIRPLANE TRIP TO VISIT MY GRANDMOTHER. I DON'T REMEMBER MUCH, other than being on a big airliner. I guess that trip made a big impression, though, because I still have a clear image in my head of walking up and down the aisle of that airplane.

In seventh grade, I rediscovered airplanes and decided I wanted to fly when I grew up. However, I really didn't know how to go about it. No one in my immediate family was remotely associated with aviation, and I didn't live near an airport or military base.

While in my first year at San Jose State University, I met two Air Force ROTC cadets whose enthusiasm for ROTC inspired me to start the program the next fall. Within a couple of days of joining, I was captivated—I had found my niche and my path—and, from then on, I couldn't imagine doing anything else.

My first military challenge was acquiring a pilot slot. Back in 1983, there were very few women Air Force pilots and it was extremely competitive for women to obtain pilot billets. To improve my chances, I became actively involved in the ROTC program, attacked my academics with passion, and also earned my private pilot's license.

I could barely afford to pay for college, let alone a private pilot's license, and so it seemed to be an impossible hurdle. But my mom was my biggest supporter, living on a shoestring for a year to send me extra money. I took her up as my first passenger after passing my Federal Aviation Administration flight test.

Prior to graduation in May 1987, I was ecstatic to find out that I had received one of the coveted pilot slots. My college graduation, with commissioning ceremony, was a very special day, and I was excited to have all of my family and friends at the ceremony, including my older sister (an Army captain) and my younger brother (a private first class in the Army). My sister commissioned me, and my brother gave me my first salute.

Flight training was extremely stressful, a lot tougher than I anticipated, though I was thrilled to be there and loved the flying. My biggest shock was struggling with airsickness during the initial phase of flight school, flying the T-37. I eventually conquered airsickness, graduated, and was assigned to fly the KC-135 tanker at Grissom AFB in Indiana.

The KC-135 wasn't my first choice or my second—it was number fourteen on my list. My first choice was to fly fighters, but women were not allowed to fly combat aircraft for the Air Force then. Ironically, flying the KC-135 at Grissom turned out to be my best assignment in the Air Force. I loved the airplane, the mission, the people—everything about it.

After my Grissom tour, my next assignment was to Loring AFB in Maine, where I met my future husband, Rob D'Antonio. For the first year, he was just another pilot in the squadron. What I didn't know was that he had his eye on me for a few months but was hesitant to ask me out. Finally, he called me one evening and asked if I wanted to have dinner, not really a date, but a casual meal with a fellow squadron mate. I had already eaten that evening, but for some reason I said yes. We had a great time, and the rest, as they say, is history.

We married in 1996. A few years later, our son was born. Since I had been selected for Air Command and Staff College in Alabama, and Rob had been selected to fly for the 89th Airlift Wing (used by the president of

Elisa's retirement ceremony, Aug 10, 2007. From left to right: LT Richard D'Antonio, USN, Ret. (father-in-law); Lt. Col. Robert D'Antonio, USAF, Ret. (husband); Ryan (son, age 7); Elisa; Denise (daughter, age 5); Anne Romano (mom); and Maria D'Antonio (mother-in-law).

the United States) at Andrews AFB, Maryland, I went to Alabama with our infant son, and Rob went to Maryland. Although we managed to get together fourteen times, the yearlong separation was one of our biggest challenges as a dual-military couple.

After graduating from school, I moved back to Maryland and flew the C-21 *Learjet* at Andrews AFB as part of the Air Force Flight Standards Agency, involved in developing policy and procedures for operations and air traffic control.

Nine months later, our daughter was born. Juggling two small kids and two pilot schedules became quite a challenge. I had seriously considered leaving the Air Force at the fifteen-year mark when I was pregnant the

second time, but with the support of family, friends, and a wonderful nanny, we were able to manage the kids and careers until Rob retired in 2005. A few years later, I also retired.

Rob and I have infected our kids with our love of aviation since they were babies. We own our own airplane, and our son's first flight took place when he was six weeks old. The kids love flying and my husband keeps a logbook for each of the kids, detailing all their flights.

We now live at an airport, in a residential airpark, and the kids run excitedly to the window to watch the airplanes take off and land. They both knew the difference between a jet and a propeller before they were two years old. Our son is now the family expert on a computer simulator game and, as a true aviator, he regales us with his "there I was" stories.

Although I truly enjoyed my career, I am enjoying a less hectic lifestyle with more time to devote to my kids. As I look back on my career and the challenge of being a mom and a military pilot, there is a lot I have learned about life and myself. I think the biggest lesson I have learned is that it would have been easier to manage the dual challenge when I was younger. I was thirty-five when my son was born, and thirty-eight when my daughter was born. The extra energy required to chase two small kids around—as well as endure the late nights and early mornings, the early show times, and long flying days—would have been easier to handle in my twenties rather than late thirties or early forties.

Mom to Mom:

The most rewarding thing about being a mom is when your kids finally repeat back something, or demonstrate a behavior, that you've been trying to teach them seemingly forever.

However, I can't complain. Whenever I spent six hours slipping the surly bonds in a *Learjet* and then came home to two little kids running to the door to jump into my arms, I knew that all the hard work was worth it, and I really had the best of two worlds.

The best part of my day is spending time with my kids!

Rank:	Air Force Lieutenant Colonel
Years Served:	20
Current Military Status:	Retired
Number of Children:	2

Celeste (Sanders) Dryjanski

C-141B *Starlifter*, C-130H-3 *Hercules*

M Y CHILDHOOD WAS THE CLOSEST THING TO A SMALL-TOWN EXPERIENCE AS YOU COULD GET, GROWING UP IN A SUBURB OF DETROIT. MY younger brother and I played stickball in the street with the neighborhood kids, clearing out whenever anyone yelled, "Car!"

Our stay-at-home mom instilled in us that you can do anything if you give it your best shot. Looking back, her staying at home was such a gift and taught me far more about a work ethic than had she gone to work outside the home.

Our dad was brilliant, and finished his college degree at night school as we were growing up, which further emphasized the value my parents put on education. Going to college was an assumption I never questioned.

When I was thirteen, we moved to the suburbs of St. Louis where my high school years consisted of honors classes and marching band—the highlight of my youth. I led the band during my senior year as the head drum major. I hadn't given the military a moment's thought until I learned that some other band members had received full ROTC scholarships for college—tuition, books, and spending money. It sounded like a fortune! So, on a whim, I applied and won an Air Force scholarship.

The funny thing is, until I was a second lieutenant headed to a plum assignment at Charleston AFB in South Carolina as a logistics officer, I didn't realize that I might want to fly. A year later, I won a slot to navigator training, and soon transitioned into a new world of flying and being a distinct minority. There was only one other woman in my navigator training class, and we graduated first and third in our class.

It was a tough but rewarding year, both personally and academically. Finishing as the distinguished graduate and receiving my choice of assignments—flying the C-141 at Charleston—proved to be one of my career highlights. I spent the next seven years flying low-level airdrop missions and, on occasion, flying missions to countries around the world.

One of the most unique cultural experiences occurred in Saudi Arabia, shortly after the first Gulf War, during crew rest. Back then, women could travel off base with their crew if they were in uniform, so our crew decided to go to dinner in town. As I walked down the street, the local men looked away since my face was not covered and I was wearing a flight suit, then they secretly stared once I passed by. I quickly realized how out of the ordinary my appearance was in their country, and my heart raced as the "religious police" looked on from across the street. Once at the restaurant, we were quickly shown to a family table in the back of the restaurant, where the curtain was drawn in order to shield me from the men dining in the rest of the establishment.

During my Charleston assignment, the restrictions barring women from flying certain special operations were lifted, and I became the first woman in Air Mobility Command to fly special operations. At one point, I was the only woman flying in a unit of more than two hundred men, and, during joint exercises, the female aircrew tent consisted of me and a C-130 loadmaster from another base sleeping at one end of a tent, with a blanket strung up to section off our quarters.

I absolutely loved flying the special operations mission, and I have many fond memories, but none as

Celeste and Family, September 2009, Provence, France.

great as meeting Jim. Handsome, smart, and kind, he was the new guy on the crew. I invited him to the annual Thanksgiving dinner at my home, to which I always invited several single friends to share the holiday with me and my visiting family. As a result, Jim became acquainted with my family before our first date, which soon followed, and, by the next June, we were engaged, and, thankfully, on different crews—I never wanted to fly with someone I was dating. We married in January 1999, and our marriage has been a life-changing blessing ever since.

My career raced ahead fast and furious, as I was promoted early to both major and lieutenant colonel. I flew the C-141 and the C-130, but my flying time slowed down considerably as our family grew. (Only another nursing mom can truly know the challenge of hurriedly using a breast pump in the tiny bathroom of an aircraft.) I completed my final active-duty tour in 2003 as the commander of the 321st Training Squadron at Lackland AFB, Texas.

My squadron command tour was an incredible experience, since I got to see the best in people. I took over command while seven months pregnant with my second daughter, Alexis. Sixteen months later, I gave up command while eight months pregnant with my third daughter, Zoë. I was a sight to behold in the midst of this lean-and-mean culture!

After Zoë's birth, I decided to leave the active-duty Air Force, because Jim and I both felt strongly that God was leading me home to be with our children. People thought we were crazy—I had sixteen years active duty, and getting out meant giving up an active-duty retirement unless I could stick it out four more years. To us, four more years meant separations for our family with a high likelihood of deployments away from our children, and definitely an outsourced life of nannies and daycare. The value of giving up those costs was priceless.

And so, with peace in our hearts, I transitioned to the Air Force Reserve. We still are fortunate to serve the country as an Air Force family since Jim is still active duty and he now has the newfound freedom to take the assignments that will best use his professional gifts.

Transitioning from a squadron commander to full-time mom, now of six children, has been an incredible spiritual journey. I went from a world of "yes ma'am" and sharp salutes to small children who often say "no!" I didn't know how different it would be to be with them every minute instead of getting the hero's welcome at the end of each workday. I didn't know I had a temper. I didn't know I was so lousy at keeping a clean house. I thought when I decided to stay home with my kids that I'd have time to write to friends, work on crafts and scrapbooks, lead a Bible study, write in my journal, and do a host of other activities. I quickly realized it was futile with little kids at home. But I also didn't know what I had been missing before.

I hadn't known how much closer we'd be. I hadn't known how sweet it would be to hear their questions about God, about the world, about people, and what a privilege it would be to provide those answers. I hadn't known how many hugs, sloppy kisses, skinned knees, books read together, and bird-watching walks I'd been missing out on. I hadn't known my daily love, encouragement, discipline, and presence would change our family the way it has.

Mom to Mom:
The most rewarding thing about being a mom is knowing that I am taking part in something that will last through eternity.

Do I miss flying? Yes, at times. Do I miss working? Yes, and I miss the world's measure of accomplishment and respect that comes with success in the workplace. But I wouldn't trade this time at home, this chapter in my life, for anything.

To my six little blessings—whatever you do in life, look past a merely good life. Instead, seek God's best for your life, which means you will need to be strong and courageous, and, most certainly, that you will each be required to follow a different path.

"Be strong and courageous. Do not be terrified; do not be discouraged, for the Lord your God will be with you wherever you go."

—Joshua 1:9

Rank:	Air Force Colonel
Years Served:	20
Current Military Status:	Retired
Number of Children:	6

Laurie (McLean) Farris

KC-135 *Stratotanker*

I GREW UP IN MASSACHUSETTS WHERE MY DAD WORKED AS A CARPENTER AND ALSO SERVED IN THE MASSACHUSETTS NATIONAL GUARD. WHEN I was twelve, my mom and dad took me on a scenic flight, and I decided afterwards that I wanted to be a flight attendant. My mother asked, "Why don't you become a pilot?"

Her simple words profoundly affected my life—I became focused on attending the Air Force Academy. The Air Force prep school offered me a nomination, so I jumped at the opportunity. Following the yearlong prep school, I attended the Air Force Academy.

My time there was the most difficult of my life. I was not a good student, and was a little too rebellious. One ray of hope I could count on was the letters my dad wrote to me every single week, not missing one week until I graduated. No matter how hard the week was, I knew my dad's letter would be in the mailbox encouraging me—it would lift my spirits enough to get me through another week.

After graduation, I started flight training at Vance AFB, Oklahoma. I looked around the room the first day—there were fifty men, and me. Since this would be my family for the next year, I realized I needed to fit in to make it work.

How would I describe flight school? Awesome! After my first flight in the T-37 jet trainer, I realized this all was going to be worth it! When my instructor let me fly solo, I couldn't stop smiling and yelling "Yahoo!" for the hour-long flight.

Next, I trained in the T-38, another amazingly cool jet. I couldn't believe the Air Force was letting me take this supersonic jet out for a ride. "Finally," I thought, "this is where I belong!" When I received an assignment to fly the KC-135 *Stratotanker* at Loring AFB in Maine, I was

devastated. Although my first choice wasn't the KC-135 and I didn't want to move to Maine, it turned out to be a great five years. I flew all over the world, transitioning upward from copilot to aircraft commander to instructor pilot. I also met Len, a navigator in my squadron, who became one of my best friends—we both loved sports and the outdoors. Our friendship turned to a romance, and we married soon after.

In 1993, we moved to Robins AFB in Georgia, where life changed forever as we became parents. With all the deployments facing me, I knew I couldn't stay in the Air Force and be the kind of mom I wanted to be, so I left active duty.

After our daughter, Taylor, was born a year later, I began to feel as though I had given up everything for her and Len. Len had always supported my aviation career, and he knew how much I loved the Air Force and flying. We came up with the idea that I would fly part-time for the Air National Guard. I could stay home with Taylor and still fly once a week.

So I joined the New Hampshire Air National Guard, excited beyond words. The first time I took the controls of the aircraft, I knew I was home again. Being an aviator is entrenched in who I am. It's not just a job. After a few years of flying for the Guard, our son, Drew, was born, and our family was complete.

I still actively fly in the National Guard, and since the Global War on Terror began, I've had to be away from my family more than ever. I'm fortunate that my husband was a military aviator, because he understands my obligations. We also have two sets of supportive grandparents, along with great friends and neighbors, who pitch in when we need help. Knowing that I balance being a full-time mom

Memorial Day, 2003. Laurie with her dad, Mac; daughter, Taylor; husband, Len; son, Drew; and mom, Mary Lou.

and a part-time pilot, my Guard unit has always been very supportive.

Sometimes I feel like two different people, with one not quite understanding the other. One day I am planning one of my kid's school parties with other moms, and then the next day I am flying a night mission leading a flight of five aircraft across the ocean.

I am currently serving as the New Hampshire 133rd Air Refueling Squadron commander, and just like I do with my family, I do my best to take care of my squadron personnel. I enjoy finding out what their talents are, and try to inspire each of them for continued success. I feel if I listen to them, believe in them, and empower them, they will make a positive contribution.

I love being an aviator and a commander, but at the end of the day, nothing is better than having my children

still give me a hug and kiss goodnight. I see the kind of caring and loving adults they are growing into, and I realize being a parent is the most important job there is.

My sixteen-year-old daughter, Taylor, told me once that she couldn't understand why there has never been a woman president because "the girls are the smart ones." I laughed and realized how fortunate her generation is, seeing themselves with limitless possibilities.

My thirteen-year-old son, Drew, loves baseball, and we share a passion for the Red Sox. Together we watch ESPN SportsCenter every morning. Whenever I deploy, he keeps me posted on all the New England sports I miss.

When asked about my potential legacy, it's a very easy answer for me. I want my family to know I love them—they come first—and that I am here to help them reach their potential. I also want my colleagues to know that I believe in them and that I want what is best for our country, our unit, and them as individuals.

I am very grateful to my parents for encouraging me to pursue my dreams—to my mom for inspiring me to believe I could do anything I wanted, and to my dad for his love of our country and the patriotism he passed on to me. I also thank my husband and children for understanding why I love to fly, and for letting me serve our country. I couldn't do it without them!

My children understand sacrifices firsthand, and they know what Memorial Day and Veteran's Day are all about. They understand the meaning of freedom, and how lucky they are to live in this great country.

I would love it if my children chose to go into the military, as I believe it is a great start for young people, but it has to be their choice. Most of all, I want them to be happy, and I hope their life dreams come true.

Mom to Mom:

Flying airplanes is great, and it's a lot of fun, but being a good mom is the most important job of all.

"A hundred years from now it will not matter what my bank account was, the sort of house I lived in, or the kind of car I drove...but the world may be different because I was important in the life of a child."

—Forest E. Witcraft

Rank:	Air National Guard Lieutenant Colonel
Years Served:	22
Current Military Status:	Air National Guard
Number of Children:	2

Susan (Rank) Foy

C-141B *Starlifter*, C-9A *Nightingale*, C-21A *Learjet*, C-32A

BORN IN NEW JERSEY IN 1969, I GREW UP AS THE ONLY CHILD OF GERMAN IMMIGRANTS. MY PARENTS CAME TO THE UNITED STATES IN 1964 right after their wedding, not speaking a word of English. Throughout my childhood, we traveled to Germany every couple of years to visit family.

My grandfather, Opa Martin, a pilot in the German *Luftwaffe* in World War II, was my inspiration to become a pilot. I remember visits to Germany as a young girl, back when fighters were still allowed to fly super low, right over the villages—everyone ducked and covered their ears. But not Opa Martin and me! We gleefully watched the jets scream across the sky, pointing and shouting, in German, of course, "There he goes! Did you see he had a white helmet?" Those memories, and Opa's stories, sparked my yearning to fly.

During a career day in high school, I walked past the military representative's display and picked up a brochure about the Air Force Academy. While I had heard of West Point and Annapolis, I had no idea there was an Air Force Academy. That very day, I decided that's where I would go.

My mind was made up so strongly that my parents had to literally force me to sit down and fill out applications to other schools. I became enthralled by the Air Force Academy and everything it stood for, and wanted so badly to be a pilot in the U.S. Air Force. Luckily, I was accepted!

After graduation in 1991, I went to pilot training at Reese AFB, Texas. Although tough, the training was awesome. What a feeling to take a T-37 in the air solo for the first time, and then getting to fly the T-38—what a kick in the pants! Ranked number four in my graduation class of thirty student pilots, I got my first choice of available

assignments—the C-9A *Nightingale* at Ramstein AB, Germany.

That first assignment to the 75th Airlift Squadron was fabulous! As a young lieutenant, I flew all over Europe and even to Saudi Arabia. Just when the regularly scheduled missions began to feel mundane, I'd launch on an urgent air-evacuation mission dedicated for immediate transport of someone in danger of losing life, limb, or eyesight.

Those missions were truly humbling and rewarding. Also, not only was the flying and living in Europe fascinating, but I got to live within an hour's drive of my grandparents and other relatives for the first time in my life. What a blessing!

After my tour ended, I transferred to the 8th Airlift Squadron at McChord AFB in Washington to fly the mighty C-141B *Starlifter*, which became my favorite airplane. I flew to every continent on the globe, including Antarctica, and I refueled in flight from tankers, flew low-level formation airdrops, occasionally flew air-evacuation missions, and hauled cargo to more places than I ever dreamed of going.

I flew the C-141 for almost six years, and was truly sad to take one to the boneyard just before my next assignment. What a moving experience it is for a pilot to bring an aircraft there, knowing it is the very last time that particular aircraft will fly.

The McChord assignment was special to me for another reason as well—that is where I met Scott, an Air Force intelligence officer. One of my Air Force Academy roommates and I were training together to run a marathon, and she invited Scott to train with us. After many long runs together and a successful marathon, Scott and I married in August 2001. We returned from our

Colonel Susan Foy and her daughter, Martina, sitting in the front seats of the C-32, the plane Susan currently flies, during a family day on Thanksgiving weekend, 2009.

honeymoon the night before the September 2001 terrorist attacks.

After McChord, Scott and I both transferred to Scott AFB in Illinois, where I flew the C-21 *Learjet* at the 458th Airlift Squadron, transporting distinguished visitors. I found out I was pregnant shortly after arriving, and our daughter, Martina Morgen Foy, was born in March 2003, bringing unimaginable joy to our lives. She is named after my Opa Martin. Martina's first word after Ma-Ma and Da-Da was "airplane," although she pronounced it "bairplane!" as she pointed to the sky.

For our next assignments, Scott and I were both selected to attend the Joint Military Intelligence College at the Defense Intelligence Agency in Washington. D.C. The program involved earning an eighteen-month master's degree in ten months, including writing a thesis. After

graduation, we were both assigned to the Pentagon. We also had our second child, our son, Aiden, in July 2008.

In 2009, I interviewed and was hired to fly C-32s at the 89th Airlift Wing at Andrews AFB in Maryland near Washington, D.C. The C-32 is a B-757 modified for VIP support and our primary customers are the vice president (using the "Air Force Two" call sign), first lady, secretary of state, secretary of defense, and chairman of the joint chiefs of staff. This assignment has definitely been my dream flying job so far. Not only am I getting to fly a fantastic aircraft, but I am part of a team that enables our nation's leaders to execute domestic and foreign policy on every mission.

Being a dual active-duty family does pose challenges, especially making sure at least one of us gets out of work in time to drive to daycare before it closes. Of course, we also have to plan for the potentiality that we could both have to travel or deploy at the same time. Luckily, our parents are very supportive and able to help out, even though they do not live in the local area. We also accept the fact that, in order for both of us to continue serving and to keep our family together, we will probably have to make some tough choices regarding assignments and other opportunities. Fortunately, in the seven years that Scott and I have been married, we have had caring and supportive senior commanders who have gone out of their way to keep us stationed together.

As a first-generation American, I have always been very patriotic, even while still keeping close ties to my German roots. At age three, I had one of those little desks with the attached chair where the writing surface lifts up for storage. After learning the Pledge of Allegiance in preschool (where I also learned English), I attached an American flag to that little desk and practiced saying the pledge with my hand over my heart. When my Oma (grandmother) came from Germany to visit, I taught her the pledge too, and made her say it with me! To this day, I still get excited about Fourth of July parades, get goose bumps when I hear the national anthem, and feel a lump in my throat when former military members march by proudly wearing the uniforms of their younger days.

While I would naturally be excited if Martina decides to become a pilot like her mom, I will be so proud of her regardless of what she chooses to do in life, and will give her my unwavering love and support. Ever since she was about three years old, she has been telling me that she is going to fly a rocket ship to the moon when she grows up, and asks me if I will come with her. She even drew me a picture of herself as an astronaut, complete with a bubble helmet and a space suit. It melts my heart when she says, "Mommy, when I grow up, I want to be a pilot because I want to be just like you. Will you teach me how?"

Mom to Mom:

The thing that surprised me the most about being a mom was how intense and unconditional a mother's love is, and how hard a job motherhood can be sometimes. Every day, I realize how blessed I am to be a mom to such wonderful children.

What I want Martina and Aiden to learn from my career as a pilot and Air Force officer is that girls (and boys) can grow up to be *anything* they want to be. Moreover, I want them both to appreciate the freedoms, opportunities, and choices they have due to the sheer fact that they are Americans.

Much of the world still has a long way to go in providing equal opportunities for women. This hit home for me when I gave a tour of the C-9 to some German military medical personnel during my Ramstein assignment. One of the young women told me how lucky I was to be a pilot, because in the German military women could only be in the medical corps or the band. That has since changed, but I realized I would not be where I am today had my parents stayed in Germany or moved back while I was still very young.

Although I did the majority of my flying before becoming a mom, I can still share my stories and pictures with my children, and show them that there are exciting careers in aviation regardless of gender. Hopefully, I can get back into the cockpit again and share the experience with them more directly.

In the end, I've realized that becoming a mom really brings life into perspective, and no matter how much I love flying, nothing in the world compares to the love a mother feels for her children.

Girls can grow up to be anything they want to be.

Rank:	Air Force Lieutenant Colonel
Years Served:	18
Current Military Status:	Active Duty
Number of Children:	2

Barbara (Brumme) Garwood

T-38A *Talon*, KC-135E *Stratotanker*, TG-7A Motorglider, Schweitzer 2-33 Glider

MY FATHER EMIGRATED WITH HIS PARENTS AS A FIVE-YEAR-OLD BOY FROM GERMANY TO THE UNITED STATES IN 1929. LATER, WHILE SERVING in postwar Germany as a U.S. Army artillery officer, he met my mother, a tailor, who became his war bride. In all, my father served thirty-four years and participated in World War II, Korea, and Vietnam, retiring as the most senior Army colonel in Europe. My older brother and I moved with our parents almost every three years, all across the United States. As a result, my entire childhood revolved around the military.

After high school, I attended the music college at Willamette University, Oregon, and quickly realized my piano and organ skills would make me a good piano teacher and church organist, but nothing more. I quit college after two years and moved with my parents to Stuttgart, Germany, for my father's next assignment. After spending almost a year working in Germany, I left to attend the University of Miami to major in English.

There were daily anti-war rallies on campus protesting the Vietnam War, and the Air Force ROTC building had been set on fire the year prior. I clearly remember one student with an extremely powerful stereo in our dorm who kept blasting the song with the lyrics: "And it's one, two, three, what are we fighting for?" out the window each night. Not only was I confused as to why so much hatred was directed at our military, I felt angry at the way our Vietnam vets were being treated.

In my junior year of college, I decided to join the Air Force ROTC program, and I got my first military jet ride in a T-33 during summer camp. Women could not fly in the Air Force at this time, so after graduating from college in 1974 as a distinguished ROTC graduate, I became a public affairs officer at Seymour Johnson AFB in North Carolina for the 4th Tactical Fighter Wing.

Working on the base newspaper, I wrote stories about the fighter wing's history, and of the men who flew and maintained the F-4E *Phantom* aircraft. I photographed the F-4E many times on the flight line and loved the way it looked and sounded. I helped to coordinate the base's open-house events, arranged billets for the U.S. Air Force Thunderbird team, helped with aircraft static displays, and put together itineraries for distinguished visitors. In exchange for arranging one P-51 *Man O' War* to come to our base during the open house, I managed to convince the pilot/owner to take me for a ride in it. I sat in the back, on a seat over a fuel barrel, and I loved it! I also wrote a newspaper article about the base commander who flew F-86s in Korea, and he took me on my very first Cessna plane ride.

The flight line was a fascinating place to me, so when the Air Force opened a test program for women pilots in 1976, I was in the personnel office the next day to apply, thinking I could get right in. Although two thousand men were accepted to flight school each year, only ten slots were available for women, so it was very competitive. After three years of applying, I was finally accepted in 1979, and attended flight screening school in Hondo, Texas, at an old Army Air Corps field, training in the T-41B (a modified Cessna 172).

Then I left for Williams AFB in Arizona for undergraduate pilot training. None of the flight gear fit any of the five women in my class of 61 students, but we made it work. Pilot training was very demanding, and I put all my effort into it every day. I got my first choice upon graduation, becoming the third female T-38 instructor in the Air Force. I secretly wanted an F-4E, but at that time,

American Airlines DC-10 Flight Engineer Barb Garwood getting ready to leave for New York City with daughter, Erika, September 1987, from Colorado Springs, Colorado.

women could only get trainer, transport, or tanker aircraft assignments.

I instructed for five years, and will never forget each student I had, and the look of despair on their faces when they first met me and realized they had a female instructor! Later, when we started flying, my students realized I was as committed and demanding as any man in getting them through the program, and that their dreams were my dreams too.

One day, during my instructor-pilot assignment, I was jogging along the old canals in Arizona, and got the idea of forming a women's pilot group. I sent surveys to all seventy Air Force women pilots back then, and sixty-four surveys came back with a big "Yes, I want to join." With help from former Women Airforce Service Pilots (WASP) and other active-duty women Air Force pilots, we formed the Women's Military Pilots Association (now the Women Military Aviators), an organization to help mentor and support women pilots, and to assist in expanding flying opportunities for women in the military.

For our first Women Military Pilots' convention in 1983, I gathered women T-38 pilots from two bases in order to have enough (eight) for an all-female T-38 four-ship flyby of the Indianapolis Motor Speedway. It really was the very first all-female T-38 four-ship, and took six months to get approval from headquarters. People never believe me when I tell them it really happened. The pilots were Captains Barb Brumme, Jane Logan, Gwen Linde, and Karen Daneu; First Lieutenants Olga Custodio and Dee Hornbostel; and Second Lieutenants Mee Mee Crane and Kathi Durst. I remember my operations officer had said to me, "If anything goes wrong, don't bother coming back."

Helping to establish the Women Military Aviators organization was one of the best things I've done in my life. I also became their first active-duty president. Now the organization is open to women in all types of aviation careers, and all military services.

My husband-to-be, Tracy, was one of my students when I was a T-38 instructor. We started dating after he graduated from pilot training and became a T-38 instructor pilot. After we married, I got my first choice of assignments to Randolph AFB, Texas, to train pilots to be instructors in the T-38. My husband's assignment was blocked by a general there who did not want a dual-military couple. I had just found out I was pregnant with our daughter when faced with the dilemma of trying to get orders together. We applied for and got special duty assignments to the Air Force Academy, teaching cadets how to fly. I was in charge of the "Soar for All" program, and taught cadets to fly the TG-7A motor-glider and the Schweitzer 2-33 glider, while my husband taught the cadets to fly the T-41 trainer aircraft.

After this academy tour, in 1986, I decided to get out of the Air Force, because my choice of flying jobs was limited, and I realized it would be difficult to get assignments in the same location as my husband. After leaving the Air Force, I was hired by American Airlines in 1987 and I also continued to fly in the Air Force Reserve, piloting the KC-135E tanker at Grissom AFB in Indiana, where my husband was flying the EC-135 on active duty.

Our son was born soon after we moved to Indiana. A year later, *Desert Storm* began, and my reserve unit prepared to mobilize to go overseas. I remember sitting in a top-secret briefing—the operations officer told us thirty tankers would possibly be lost in the first night of the war. There was a long silence. I was afraid that my two very young children would have no mother. Volunteers for the first deployment were ample; after they left, I became afraid for the crews I knew so well. During the five-month

Mom to Mom:

The most rewarding thing about being a mom is that I never knew I could love my children so unconditionally, so deeply, and so much; the kind of love that makes you put yourself second in everything. It is the most powerful and encompassing love I have ever known, and I am so thankful I chose to have that experience in my life.

mobilization (I deployed twice but did not fly in the actual air war), I realized that this is what it really means to serve, and I gained a whole new respect for all previous soldiers in all earlier wars. During my deployments, my biggest fear was not seeing my children grow up. I would spend my evenings looking at their photos, reading the small Bible we were given in the immunization and vaccine line, and I spent a lot of time praying!

After my reserve unit demobilized, I made the difficult decision to give up sixteen years of active and reserve duty in order to care for our two children and still fly for American. My husband left the military in 1991, and was also hired by American Airlines. We have flown together on the 727 and DC-10, he as flight engineer and me as copilot.

I never really took much of a break during my entire career, because the flexibility was simply not there. Since the terrorist attacks on September 11, 2001, the airline industry has experienced a lot of changes, which certainly affected my airline career. Although I had been an S-80 captain for seven years and have more than 10,000 flight hours, I recently decided to return to being a first officer on the B-767/757, due to the airline's downsizing and my lack of seniority as a captain. I now fly only to Hawaii, and I have super schedules.

Raising two children with both parents as airline pilots has been very challenging, especially trying to arrange all of our schedules. Now that my daughter is on her own and my son is in college, I hope to return soon to the position of captain. Bottom line, the ups and downs are definitely there when mixing two aviation careers and two children, but it can be done. You just have to really want it.

Today, military aviation holds so many more opportunities for women. I love seeing women fighter pilots, women flying in combat roles, and women involved in almost every military job. I am so proud of them! For those contemplating aviation, whether military or civilian, pursue your dreams, get strong, and just go after it!

I am so glad that I had children, and that my husband and I have learned how important it is to nurture them, teach them to have faith in God, guide them with what we've learned, and then to cut them loose to solo in this world to do what they want.

I am very proud of my daughter and son. They both are quite independent, stubborn at times, and also excellent students. My dream for them is that they can find something they love to do, do it well, and never get discouraged or give up.

My children are the highlight of my life.

Rank:	Air Force Major
Years Served:	16
Current Military Status:	Separated
Number of Children:	2

Kelly (Neal) Goggin

KC-135 *Stratotanker*

"AIM HIGH, AIM FAR, YOUR GOAL THE SKY, YOUR AIM THE STARS" WAS A POEM THAT A BABYSITTER WROTE DOWN FOR ME WHEN I was in fifth grade. I posted the poem on my bedroom mirror, and the words became etched in my mind.

As I reached junior high, I decided I wanted to become an astronaut. It seemed to impress people, even though I had no idea how I was going to make it happen. I knew that military flying was one path to becoming an astronaut, so I joined the Air Force ROTC program at Central Washington University, Washington, and graduated with shiny Air Force second lieutenant bars and a degree in physics.

My less-than-perfect eyesight kept me from a pilot slot, so I went to navigator training at Mather AFB, California. Since it was 1989, not many aircraft were available to women due to the combat exclusion law prohibiting women from flying in combat squadrons. So I selected the KC-135 tanker and started my first flying tour with the 407th Air Refueling Squadron at Loring AFB, Maine. The 407th was a great squadron and the command climate extremely positive. Out of eighty pilots and navigators, there were a total of four women. The women's bathroom had four stalls, and the four of us each had our name posted on our own door. My flying crew was fantastic, and the aviation team camaraderie provided encouragement and support. I still keep in touch with some of my crew and consider them close friends. Some of the experiences we shared still make me laugh.

During this tour, I deployed on and off for four months to the islands of the Azores in the Atlantic and to Diego Garcia in the Indian Ocean in support of Operations *Desert Shield* and *Desert Storm*. Our squadron's mission was to refuel aircraft from all the different branches of the military, and my job as a KC-135 navigator was to know the exact location of our plane at all times. Flying during these conflicts was both challenging and an incredible opportunity to put our training to work. Several of our missions involved refueling large formations of fighters across the ocean during bad weather, and dropping them off at certain key locations in the Arabian Gulf so they could conduct their combat missions.

My first child, Courtney, was born during my time at Loring and then, a few years later, my son, Cameron, arrived. In 1996, I transferred to Kadena AB in Okinawa, Japan. I absolutely loved this tour, and it was a wonderful place for a family. However, shortly after moving to Kadena, my first marriage of nine years ended. It was a difficult family transition when I became a single mom of two young children with a busy career. Two years later, I met my future husband, Jeff, who was also stationed there flying the KC-135. I remember thinking he had the biggest personality I had ever encountered, and an enthusiasm and gift for flying that were very inspiring. Once we realized we were on the path to marriage, I introduced him to my kids, and, although it wasn't a job interview, it was important to me how he would fold into our family.

Prior to leaving Kadena, the Air Force decided to upgrade the KC-135 navigation system with a global positioning system (GPS), eliminating the need for navigators during most missions. That meant I would be out of a flying job, but, fortunately, it was the right time in my career for a non-flying staff job.

Jeff and I married toward the end of our Kadena tour, and transferred together to Scott AFB, Illinois, where our daughter, Caitlyn, was born. I was a major when I had

Kelly serving as a KC-135 squadron commander during a deployment in support of Operations Iraqi Freedom/Enduring Freedom, 2007.

Caitlyn, and remember getting quite a few stares as an older mom. Nowadays, it is more common to see senior-ranking women having kids. On the flip side, since I am a more senior-ranking officer now, it is a tougher challenge to balance my job and family, since my current job comes with a great deal more responsibility than when, as a younger officer, I had only Courtney and Cameron.

Although I didn't fly for the next seven years, I was still involved in career-enhancing assignments. During my tour at the Pentagon, my son, Colton, was born and afterwards I was senior enough to be eligible to command a squadron. However, since my navigator job was eliminated for the majority of KC-135 missions, senior leaders and mentors advised me that I most likely would never be selected as an operational squadron commander. Never one to take no for an answer, I kept pursuing my dreams, remembering that childhood poem to keep

reaching for the stars, and I was selected to command the 319th Operations Support Squadron in Grand Forks, North Dakota, where I led one hundred sixty Air Force personnel. I took command in November 2006, and spent the next two years leading the squadron, including deploying to the Arabian Gulf to provide air-refueling support in both Iraq and Afghanistan. This tour turned out to be one of the highlights of my career! I loved the operational tempo, and leading such a fine group of service members.

After Grand Forks, I found myself back at the Pentagon, this time on the air staff working mobility requirements and then as the division chief for Air Force congressional inquiries. I pinned on colonel and I hope to be selected for command again.

Frequent moves and deployments are hard on military families. Our most recent move from North Dakota back to the Washington, D.C., area was difficult on our older kids, as they didn't want to leave their school and friends. I hope in the future that my children will understand my love for our country, and realize that without a strong military they would not enjoy the freedoms they have—even the freedom to be mad at their parents because they have to move when they don't want to.

My experience as a mom was invaluable in my role as a leader and mentor during my squadron commander tour. Being a mom gave me the unique perspective and understanding to encourage and support both the people who worked for me, as well as their families. Many times, the doors of communication opened for squadron family members once they realized I had a family of my own and understood what they were going through.

I could never have made it this far in my career without my children to ground me and to show me what was

Mom to Mom:

I love being a mom because my kids have shown me more than I could possibly have shown them.

really important. Interestingly, though, if I had not had a family, I would have gone even further in my career. Even so, I have never doubted for a moment that I have made the best choice.

I feel very fortunate knowing I have set my kids on a path to happy and prosperous lives.

"This is our mom and she flies airplanes."

—Kelly's kids

Rank:	Air Force Colonel
Years Served:	22
Current Military Status:	Active Duty
Number of Children:	4

Ann (Bunton) Halle

C-17A *Globemaster*

I GREW UP IN WHITTIER, CALIFORNIA, AND ENJOYED RAISING ARABIAN HORSES WITH MY FAMILY. TRAINING AND SHOWING HORSES AND PLAYING school sports prepared me for the on-demand performance needed later in my Air Force career as a pilot.

During my senior year in high school, my sister applied to the Air Force Academy in hopes of becoming a pilot. The idea of becoming a pilot intrigued me, and I began to research different aviation careers. My parents surprised me with flying lessons for my seventeenth birthday. I was hooked.

After high school, I enlisted in the Air Force and spent more than three years as an air traffic controller. Taking college classes in my off-duty time, I completed most of my bachelor's degree. Toward the end of my first enlistment in 1993, I decided to join the Army's warrant officer helicopter pilot program, since Air Force pilot slots were incredibly hard to obtain during this time period. When the Army offered me an opportunity to fly, I jumped at the chance.

I attended the Army's warrant officer school at Fort Rucker, Alabama. Shortly after starting, however, I realized the Army wasn't for me, and that I would give anything to get back to my precious Air Force, even if it meant not flying. If there was a way to gain an Air Force flying billet, that would be the icing on my cake.

After some research, I found that I could transfer to an Air Force ROTC commissioning program and leave the Army, so I did. I finished both my bachelor's degree and a master's degree in professional aeronautics at Embry-Riddle Aeronautical University in Daytona Beach, Florida. Then I gained my commission as a second lieutenant in the Air Force, and garnered a pilot slot.

Pilot training at Columbus AFB, Mississippi, was fifty-two weeks of stress. Of twenty-six student pilots in my class, only two were women. About one-third of the total class didn't make it. I graduated first in my class, receiving my choice of aircraft. I picked the glorious C-17A *Globemaster III*, not only for its combat airlift mission, but also because of its great crew rest and lavatory facilities.

My first flying job was piloting the C-17 at the 14th Airlift Squadron, Charleston AFB, South Carolina. During this tour, I flew mainly Pacific Rim missions, as well as many stateside missions, and I learned that the C-17 is the military's worldwide truck.

Two years later, I received orders to the 7th Airlift Squadron at McChord AFB, Washington. During this tour at McChord, I routinely flew combat missions all over the world. One of the big highlights of my career was piloting a C-17 in a two-ship formation at the start of the Iraqi war in 2003, inbound to northern Iraq. We wore night-vision goggles during the flight and could see ground fire below us.

I met my husband, Greg, at the gym while we were both in the Army, during my time at Fort Rucker. Greg was an infantry lieutenant at Fort Campbell, Kentucky. Both of us on Nordic Tracks, we skied away, smiling and flirting with each other. Within ten minutes, he asked me out, and from there, our relationship blossomed and led to marriage.

While at McChord, Greg and I decided to start a family. During my first combat deployment in Iraq, I realized I might be pregnant. When my crew and I ferried a C-17 back to the States the next week, I went to the clinic for a pregnancy test and learned I was right. A few months

Ann with son, Beau (one year old), in C-17 simulator, 2006.

later, I transferred to the Pentagon in Washington, D.C., for the Air Force Intern Program.

This program provides a unique opportunity for junior officers to increase their leadership knowledge and the application of air and space power. A fast-paced program, it combines hands-on experience in several different high-level military settings with graduate courses in leadership and management at George Washington University. Our daughter, Brooke, arrived shortly after our move east.

About a year later, I became pregnant again. Soon after, we moved to Altus AFB, Oklahoma, where I worked as a C-17A instructor pilot. This tour was the best and worst of my career! The exceptional parts included the birth of our son, Beau; selection as chief of wing flight safety; and then the honor of being selected to attend the School of Advanced Air and Space Studies. I also had a rewarding overseas deployment to the Republic of Kyrgyzstan at Manas AB. On the flip side, this tour had its share of challenging and stressful times, both at work and at home.

The rigors of a flight commander position—along with requalifying as a C-17 instructor and flying in the most dynamic environment—resulted in a hectic work schedule and challenged my family/work balance.

The School of Advanced Air and Space Studies at Maxwell AFB, Alabama, was an incredible opportunity, for which I thank God every day. The most selective of all Air Force schools, only five percent of those eligible are selected. After this fifty-week course, I hope to continue serving the Air Force and my country.

My best friend is a CH-58D *Sea Stallion* helicopter pilot in the Marine Corps. She and I met in college, and have been each other's strong girlfriend to rely on ever since. The importance of friendships with other military women is key to a great life in military aviation, where there are so few women. They can support you in ways that no one else can. If you make these connections, they are golden.

For other women who decide to go into the military, especially in flight-related areas, I encourage you to find the military service that is the best for you. Do this by researching the different military careers available, talk to as many people as possible, and pray and search your heart. I believe all these efforts will result in a right decision and a satisfying career, one that will fulfill your wildest dreams.

It is an incredible feeling to enjoy what you are doing and to serve your country, all at once. I encourage young women to always be true to themselves to allow the greatest opportunity for happiness and success.

Since our children are still young, I don't yet know what their dreams are. I see my job as a mother to be a great example for them to follow, to provide an environment where they can explore life to the fullest, and to help them learn how to make their dreams come true. I want my legacy to be their successful and happy futures.

Mom to Mom:

The thing that surprised me the most about being a mom is how hard it is. However, as hard as it is, it is incredibly rewarding.

My hopes and dreams for my own career are to go as far in the Air Force as possible, and then become a successful chief operations officer of a major airline. My goals are important, but even more important is being a devoted mother and wife.

I would not have been able to do anything in this life if it weren't for the love of the Lord, my God. He is my Savior, and all things can be done through Him.

Rank:	Air Force Major
Years Served:	17
Current Military Status:	Active Duty
Number of Children:	2

Kelly (Waltmire) Hamilton

KC-135 *Stratotanker*, T-38 *Talon*, T-41 *Mescalero*

A VIATION WAS ALWAYS A BIG PART OF MY LIFE. MY DAD WAS A CAREER MILITARY OFFICER WHO SERVED IN THE ARMY AIR CORPS, AND THEN the Air Force, as a command pilot, and flew more than fifty different types of aircraft. My mom, a gracious lady, exemplified the characteristics of the supportive military wife and mom.

At nineteen years old, after I had a disastrous flight attendant interview with United Airlines, my father suggested I could be a pilot. I set out to become one.

In 1973, two years after graduating from college, I joined the Air Force. Although women were still prohibited from flying in the Air Force, my first assignment was aviation-related at the Avionics Maintenance Squadron at Nellis AFB, Nevada. My job included testing and evaluating avionics systems on high-performance jets, as well as flying in the back of some of the jets.

My first flight in the backseat of an F-4 was unforgettable. The exhilarating air-combat training with a couple of F-5s reinforced my beliefs that I should be flying, not riding. Also, I decided to begin a campaign to change both the policies and the laws that prohibited women from flying.

In 1975, I met and married two fine men—Captain Linn Hamilton and his son, Jeff, who was in kindergarten. Back then, military women were not encouraged to balance family and career, so the Air Force immediately gave me the option to leave and be a stay-at-home mom.

When we discussed our options as a family, my husband understood that I wanted to be a career military officer and pilot. I decided to stay in the Air Force on active duty and, within months of our marriage, news came that the Air Force would accept women to pilot training. I applied and was among the first twenty women to attend. While all of life is a balancing act, being a wife, mom, and test case under the watchful eyes of the media and Air Force during flight training made life interesting.

Since my son wanted to learn to play the violin, and his dad was not at all musical, I spent evenings teaching him to read music and to refine his musical ear. At the same time, I also practiced my aerobatic maneuvers using the stick-and-rudder simulator my husband built. So each evening, the two of us, mother and son, did our homework together. To this day, I believe he can recite my T-37 single-spin recovery sequence by heart, because I said it in rhythm with his violin scales.

In 1978, I graduated from flight school and received two sets of wings—my father gave me his original Army Air Corps wings, and Mike Brazelton, a friend and former POW in Vietnam, gave me my first set of Air Force wings. I was very proud to wear both! Years later, my dad and I attended the Women Airforce Service Pilots and Women Military Aviators conventions together. He dressed in his "pinks and greens" (Army Air Corps uniform) and swapped tales of flying with all the women pilots. Those were very special times.

After flight school, I flew the KC-135 tanker and the T-38 trainer at Fairchild AFB in Washington. For about eight months, I was the only woman pilot in the squadron. Prior to my arrival, the commander called all the crews together to ask, "Who would be willing to fly with the woman?" Needless to say, there were some growing pains from the top down. Not everyone was thrilled to have a woman aboard.

Throughout my career as an aviator, I found there were 98 percent professionals and 2 percent jerks. I say

Kelly and her father, Lt. Col. Don Waltmire, USAF, Ret., dressed in his WWII Army Air Corps uniform (popularly known as "pinks and greens"), attending the Women Military Aviators Convention, 1988, San Antonio, Texas.

jerks because no matter how well you flew or what your background was, they refused to accept a woman as a peer. They would say, "I have a problem with a woman in the cockpit." Then I would say, "I understand *you* have the problem. I am just a pilot here to fly."

When Jeff was in fourth grade, current events were a daily part of my son's lessons. One day, he arrived home and asked me, "Is what you do unusual?" I said, "No, not really. Why do you ask?" It seems the teacher had held up a newspaper article with a photo of me and my aircraft and the title, "Mom Flies." A classmate immediately volunteered that this could not be a real story, because there were no women pilots. Jeff, a little confused by this, wanted to be certain before he corrected his classmates.

Throughout my career, I was very protective of my family. I did many interviews, considering it part of my job as a military officer and pilot; participated in opening and expanding career opportunities for women; and petitioned for changes to legislation concerning women in combat. But not until my deployment during the Gulf War in 1999, to fly the KC-135R air-refueling missions, did I give my son the option to be interviewed. I felt quite odd when I was contacted by *People* magazine, which was doing an interview on moms going to war. My first reaction was to protect my family from the press, but I left the decision up to Jeff, since he was now an adult.

Even though I knew and understood the risks of deploying to the Gulf, I felt compelled to sit down and write each member of my family a letter, letting each one of them know they were loved, and that it was my choice to serve my country while proudly flying the refueling missions.

I encourage young men and women interested in flying and/or the military to go for it. If flying is your passion, then just make up your mind and do it. Take control of your destiny.

Understand clearly that you have the power to make dreams a reality, but you need to research your dream so that you can understand everything about it. If you want to be a pilot, tell a pilot—the next one you see! Want to be an astronaut? Write to one. Ask questions, lots of them. Don't be shy about your dreams. If you need information, get it from friends, family, the Internet, and teachers. The sources are endless. Then make a plan by writing down your goals and giving yourself tasks and dates to achieve them. The more you say it out loud, the closer it is to being reality. Soon, others will see your vision, too. Finally, every night when you close your eyes, and every morning when you rise, see yourself achieving your goal.

I had a great career and really enjoyed it. I also loved being a mom. I taught my son impeccable manners and how to be a gentleman—to hold the door for ladies, speak with respect to his elders, not interrupt a conversation, and proper table manners. Now, I see him passing these lessons in manners on to his children. More

Mom to Mom:

The most rewarding thing about being a mom is seeing the wonders of the world through your child's eyes.

importantly, he always finds time in his busy schedule for his family.

I now have four grandchildren who know I am a pilot. To them it seems quite natural. The only confusion in their minds comes from seeing an airplane overhead and gleefully shouting "Grandma, Grandma!" instead of "airplane, airplane!" My legacy to them is to never lose sight of their dreams, and to never keep their dreams a secret.

· ·

You need to know it was never about me. All the successes I achieved were about opening doors for you and others. I never wanted you to hear the words, "Women can't fly jets."

· ·

Rank:	Air Force Colonel
Years Served:	25
Current Military Status:	Retired
Number of Children:	1

Casey (Legler) Hinds

C-130 *Hercules*

WAS BORN AT THE DAWN OF THE AGE OF AQUARIUS IN CALIFORNIA IN 1970. MY PARENTS WERE AN UNLIKELY MATCH—MY FATHER, A HIPPIE and peace activist; my mother, the daughter of a career Air Force officer. In a rather remarkable display of responsibility, my parents elected, because of my mother's pregnancy, not to make the cross-country road trip to Woodstock in the summer of 1969.

With those counter-culture beginnings, how did I end up nearly a quarter-century later flying military missions into war-torn Sarajevo? How did I, coming of age under the influence of women's lib, end up ten years after that, living my grandmother's life as a stay-at-home mom in Lexington, Kentucky?

A number of factors shaped my interest in flying. My parents divorced when I was very young, and I always looked forward to the airline flights to visit my father. I loved looking at the world from 30,000 feet. Also, my maternal grandfather—a World War II bombardier and later a navigator and flight test engineer—often regaled the family with his flying adventures.

Most significantly, while I was in middle school, my mother married an Air Force colonel whose career included astronaut training, flying F-4s during Vietnam, and flying everything else as a test pilot. After retiring from the Air Force, he worked as flight test manager for Martin Marietta, resulting in a family move to California where life revolved around flying, space shuttle landings, and the aerospace industry. My stepfather's enthusiasm for flying was contagious, and I was bitten hard by the flying bug.

As determined as I was to become a pilot, I was not single-minded. On the first day of high school, a cute boy on the bus caught my attention—Bruce Hinds. No one knew if I joined the cross-country team to help get into the Air Force Academy or because Bruce was also on the team. We became high school sweethearts, but I left California for Colorado and the Air Force Academy, to pursue my flying dreams.

I survived the academy's basic cadet training by visualizing myself throwing my hat into the air on graduation day. I called my family every weekend during my freshman year to tell them I would be quitting that week, but their unwavering support and encouragement always got me back on track. After four years, I crossed the podium to shake hands with President George H.W. Bush and tossed my hat into the air with the rest of the graduating class of 1991. The next stop—Phoenix, Arizona, for undergraduate pilot training as a member of the last class at Williams AFB.

During flight school, I flew both the T-37 *Tweet* and T-38 *Talon* trainers. After growing up listening to sonic booms and tales of Chuck Yeager, I was somewhat disappointed when I went supersonic in the T-38 and found there wasn't much more to it than watching the dial hit Mach 1. Nevertheless, flying the T-38 cross-country solo to Edwards AFB in California to have lunch with my family is one of my favorite memories. After graduation, I trained to fly the C-130 *Hercules*, which performs low-level formation flying, airdrops, and assault landings on short, dirt airstrips.

My first assignment was Pope AFB in North Carolina, and I flew missions all over the world, including Bosnia, Haiti, Thailand, and Saudi Arabia. I flew into Sarajevo's airport during the Kosovo conflict to deliver relief supplies after previous United Nations aircraft received debilitating anti-aircraft fire. Seeing the shell-damaged apartment buildings on final approach highlighted why I'd been

Casey attending pilot training at Williams AFB, Arizona, 1993.

prepared with so much training. We landed, kept our engines running during the offload of the humanitarian supplies, and got out of there ASAP!

The first Thanksgiving following my grandmother's death, my grandfather came to North Carolina to spend the holiday with me. I was scheduled to deploy to Hawaii the following week and managed to convince my grandpa to take advantage of his retirement benefits and fly Space-A on my C-130. He impressed my navigator with his skill at celestial navigation en route, kept up with the aircrew as we wined and dined, and regaled us with stories of his World War II and Korea exploits. I fondly remember that week I spent with Grandpa Al as one of the most memorable highlights of my flying career.

I formed lasting friendships during this first assignment and benefitted from being mentored by a handful of more senior women aviators, who are still great friends. Even now, we get together on occasion and enjoy wonderful reunions with our growing families, and I continue to rely on their wisdom, especially now that we are all mothers.

During my Pope tour, my high school sweetheart, Bruce, finished graduate school, secured a post-doctoral research job at North Carolina State, and asked me to marry him. We returned to California for our wedding, ending years of long-distance dating. In a memorable toast, Bruce's father told our guests that, as his children grew, he had diligently warned his daughter about the ways of Air Force pilots, and she very wisely married a fellow with a good job at Microsoft. Never in his wildest dreams did he imagine he should have been warning his son of the challenges that came with marriage to an Air Force pilot! Bruce's father, also a test pilot, had flown the first flight of the B-2 bomber for Northrop. The number of aviators in the family continued to grow.

Now married, Bruce and I faced a geographical puzzle to make my next assignment work with his career as a research scientist. An interesting solution emerged—a move to Japan would support both of our careers. Bruce could work at Tokyo Institute of Technology, and I could fly at Yokota AB. Since Bruce also had a private pilot's license, we often rented airplanes from the aero club and made aerial sightseeing trips together. Flying around Mount Fuji must be one of the most breathtakingly beautiful sights anywhere.

The end of my tour in Japan brought me to a crucial decision about whether to remain in the military. Numerous deployments had taken their toll on my hope to successfully juggle the professional demands of an Air Force career with the personal demands of raising a family. In the end, I left the Air Force in order to fulfill my dream of becoming a mother.

My training and experiences as a C–130 aircraft commander provided great preparation for motherhood. For relief supply missions into Sarajevo, I carried all the necessities—flak vest, helmet, gun, pubs, checklists, flashlights, secrets, and charts. As a mom, I carry all the necessities—diapers, wipes, drinks, snacks, books, sunscreen, and toys. When I flew transport missions in Thailand, I helped the loadmaster fit all the cargo into the back of the C–130. Now I help my husband fit all our luggage and car seats into the back of a Subaru. In the Middle East, I had to deal effectively with different personalities, including men whose culture didn't allow women to drive, let alone fly airplanes. As a mom, I have to deal with the personalities of my toddlers and occasionally pull out my "command voice." As a pilot with a failed engine en route to Haiti, I relied on my training to deal with emergencies by maintaining control, analyzing the situation, and taking proper action. As a mother, I do the same, only now the emergencies come on a daily basis.

Being a mom is a wonderful study in contradictions—depleting yet totally fulfilling, complex but simple, full of

Mom to Mom:

The thing that surprised me the most about being a mom is the immense responsibility of it all.

long days leading to short years, mundane and compelling. Every day presents a new challenge and there's always something to learn. It is incredibly rewarding to see your children display the values and character you've worked so hard to instill.

When my stepfather, Dick, passed away, I was given his 1963 Mooney M20C. Our daughters ride along for our family flying trips just like I used to as a girl. We carry a picture of Grandpa Dick smiling down on us as we fly along. Our daughters, Katherine and Natalie, aren't as enthusiastic about family trips in the Mooney, though, as Bruce and I are. They've discovered commercial flights have much better amenities than Mom and Dad provide. When we tell them about an upcoming Mooney trip, they usually ask, "Can't we go in a jet instead?!"

Several years ago, my husband and I took our daughters to the Air Force Museum in Dayton, Ohio. We showed them their great–grandfather's airplanes, their grandfathers' airplanes, and their mother's airplanes. Our daughter, Katherine asked, "Where's my airplane, Mommy?" Looks like the family tradition may carry on into the next generation.

Whatever paths they choose, I hope to pass on to my daughters the same kind of love and support I received so that they can follow their own dreams.

. . . .

"Every version of the present moment that is not dominated by a calm, kind attitude is devoid of real meaning and doomed to be unsatisfying."

. . . .

—Hugh Prather

Rank:	Air Force Captain
Years Served:	10
Current Military Status:	Separated
Number of Children:	2

Christina (Allick) Hopper

F-16 *Fighting Falcon*

THREE THINGS INFLUENCED MY INSPIRATION TO FLY IN THE MILITARY: MY PARENTS' EXAMPLE, MY ROTC COMMANDER'S ENCOURAGEMENT, AND my relationship with God.

Both of my parents served in the Air Force, so I learned about discipline and diligence at a young age. In college, I joined Air Force ROTC and, during my junior year, my ROTC commander encouraged me to apply for a pilot slot. Because I had never considered a flying career, I spent much time in prayer regarding the decision. Two weeks later, I applied, and later that year found out I was selected to attend pilot training.

After college graduation in 1998, I received my Air Force commission, and several months later started pilot training at Vance AFB, Oklahoma. My first year of training proved very demanding, as I battled airsickness, sleep deprivation, and other new stressors. In spite of these challenges, I earned my wings in 2000, and was selected to fly the F-16 *Fighting Falcon*, a single-seat, single-engine, multi-role, air-to-air and air-to-ground fighter jet, also affectionately known as the *Viper*.

As I prepared to leave for my F-16 training at Luke AFB in Arizona, I met a man named Aaron who was standing behind me in line at Subway getting lunch. I noticed he was wearing the familiar Air Force flight suit, so I struck up a conversation with him about flying, and found out he had just begun pilot training. Later that week, we ran into each other again, and our new friendship grew and culminated in marriage eight months later.

When we married, I was in the middle of F-16 training, and Aaron was in undergraduate pilot training, so we had no idea if we would even fly the same aircraft or be stationed together at any time in our careers. There was

so much to be anxious about for our future together, but we trusted that if God brought us together in the unique way that He did, then He would also make a way for us to have a life together. God was faithful, just as we had trusted—Aaron was selected for F-16 training and, after living in different states for more than a year, we were finally reunited at Cannon AFB, New Mexico, flying F-16s.

My first operational squadron was with the 524th Fighter Squadron at Cannon—when I arrived, I was the only female pilot in my squadron, and one of only three female pilots on the entire base. In December 2002, my squadron deployed to Kuwait for three months, flying in support of Operation *Southern Watch*. However, as tensions heightened in the region, our tour was extended for two additional months, to support the beginnings of Operation *Iraqi Freedom*. Within the first few days of the war, I flew multiple combat missions, but one mission stands out—a two-ship night mission during one of the worst recorded sandstorms in Iraqi history.

We flew to the tanker at night wearing night-vision goggles, conducted air-to-air refueling amid violent turbulence, and then pressed on to our target carrying 2,000-pound GPS-guided munitions. As we proceeded north toward a point just twenty miles outside of Baghdad, my F-16 was struck by lightning. Though I wasn't hurt, the lightning destroyed my threat warning system that would notify me if my aircraft was targeted by anti-aircraft munitions.

At that point, my flight lead and I had a decision to make—return home or continue with the mission. We decided that we wanted to finish what we started. I know we made the right decision, because when we arrived at our destination, the coalition forces were engaged in a violent firefight with the Iraqi Republican Guard. Our

Christina with her first child, son Asher, February 2007.

mission was to destroy a major Iraqi supply line. When we dropped our bombs, we not only destroyed the supply line, but the explosions frightened the Iraqis so greatly that they stopped fighting.

We were able to return home from that mission with a deep sense of satisfaction from accomplishing our job. Throughout my time in Iraq, I flew more than fifty combat missions, and earned four Air Medals and an Aerial Achievement Medal.

When our initial tours in New Mexico ended, Aaron and I transferred back to Luke to be F-16 instructor pilots. After seven months, I became pregnant with our first child, and was immediately grounded due to the F-16 high-G environment and the ejection seat.

I was pleasantly surprised that my squadron commander and the other members of my squadron were so supportive, especially since it meant the squadron had one less instructor pilot. I found it difficult to be out of the cockpit so long, and to work a desk job during my pregnancy, but it was worth it when my son, Asher Michael, was born in October 2005. He was and continues to be such a blessing in my life, and I can't imagine not having him.

I took six weeks off for maternity leave before returning to work. Though the transition was difficult, it was eased when my mother moved in with us to take care of Asher. At work, I spent another four months at a desk job while I was nursing, before returning to fly.

In late 2006, just before Asher's first birthday, we found out my husband would deploy to Iraq for a year. We worried that Asher wouldn't remember him when he returned home. I also worried for Aaron's safety, because the conditions in Iraq were so volatile with the unpredictability of the insurgents and the constant mortar attacks.

In spite of all this, God protected Aaron, and midway through his deployment he returned home for a few weeks.

When Aaron returned to Iraq, the last three months of his deployment were the most stressful, because I found out I was pregnant with our second child, and we were anxious about Aaron making it home alive. Thankfully, he returned home safely again.

Following Aaron's homecoming, in February 2008, we welcomed our precious daughter, Aaliyah Linn, into the world. Her birth was the first link in a chain of rapid changes. In June 2008, I separated from the active-duty Air Force to become a stay-at-home mom. Shortly after, we moved to Iquique, Chile, in South America because Aaron received orders to fly F-16s with the Chilean Air Force. And finally, after nineteen months of being in Chile, we received an additional blessing when our third child, Judah Benjamin, was born.

In the last few years, life changes have caused me to reflect on my career as a military officer and aviator. The most important lesson learned in my ten years of service is that I never know where God is taking me, so I have to be open to His plans for me. While it is important to set goals and seek to achieve them, it is also important to be flexible with those goals and willing to proceed down a

Mom to Mom:

The thing that surprised me the most about being a mom was how hard it is. There is a saying that "everyone is the perfect parent until they become one." It looks so easy from the outside looking in, but when it's your child throwing the tantrum in a public forum, it's truly humbling.

different path than the one originally set out on.

I think about this lesson often, and couple it with the legacy that I want to pass on to my children. I want them to know God and His son, Jesus Christ. I want them to be flexible to God's plans for them, and to know that they don't have to have all of the details worked out, but they do have to constantly trust that God is working them out. If I pass that legacy on to them, then I will have fulfilled my purpose as a mom and woman of God.

. . . .

"Those who hope in the Lord will renew their strength. They will soar on wings like eagles; they will run and not grow weary, they will walk and not be faint."

. . . .

—Isaiah 40:31

Rank:	Air Force Major
Years Served:	10
Current Military Status:	Separated
Number of Children:	3

Valerie (Perkins) Kester

C-130 *Hercules*

FLYING MUST BE IN MY GENES—BOTH OF MY PARENTS WORKED FOR UNITED AIRLINES, MY DAD AS A PILOT, AND MY MOM AS A FLIGHT attendant. It wasn't until college, though, that I considered aviation as a career for myself.

I had been a competitive figure skater all through my youth, but after spending one particular summer training with Olympic coaches, I came home and decided the skating chapter of my life would end and the flying one would start. I wanted to join the ranks of those fascinating, high-spirited daredevils known the world over as pilots.

Unsure of how to proceed, I enrolled in ground school at a local community college and relished every moment of learning about the miracle of flight. Before I knew it, I was flying the *Tomahawk*, a Piper two-seat airplane, solo over the beaches of Malibu, California.

While working at the flight school to help pay for lessons, I joined the 99s, a women's aviation club, and even entered a couple of air races—an exciting time of flying low and fast and exploring the Pacific Northwest coastline. I also attended several Women in Aviation, International conferences, and was inspired by women breaking the mold in every aspect of aviation. I will never forget Shuttle Commander Eileen Collins who, at one conference, shared her personal photos from space, as though she had just attended a family picnic.

By the time I graduated from college, I had earned all my civilian aviation ratings and was teaching at a flight school at John Wayne Airport. I was also involved in Civil Air Patrol and several friends encouraged me to join the Air Force as a reservist or to join the Air National Guard. Being the kind of girl who considers roughing it to be a morning without a blow-dryer, I felt perhaps the military

was not a good fit for me. But my curiosity and patriotism got the better of me, and next thing I knew, I had secured a C-130 aircraft pilot slot with the California Air National Guard.

Pilot training was one of the toughest and most exhilarating events of my life. I made lifelong friends, flew night and day, memorized regulations, practiced emergency procedures, parasailed in the desert for ejection-seat training, attended combat survival and resistance training, and will never forget water survival and the infamous dunker training. One of my proudest moments was earning my Air Force wings in 1998. After flight school, I trained to fly the C-130 *Hercules*.

While in C-130 training at Little Rock, Arkansas, I met my future husband, Dave, and we dated for several months. After my training ended, I returned to California to fly for the Air National Guard on a part-time reserve status. We agreed to date long-distance, since Dave flew for the Ohio Air National Guard.

A year into our courtship, I received a job offer to fly for United Airlines. I had always dreamed of flying for United and following in my dad's footsteps, and I felt so proud to wear those United wings! My father passed away before I ever started flying, but I think he knew I had joined his ranks. In fact, after a time, I started wearing his wings on my coat, in lieu of my own. I was trained initially as a flight engineer on the Boeing 727, and later as a first officer on the Airbus A319/320.

In the meantime, Dave proposed, and we decided he would move to California and join my Guard unit. Two weeks before we married, the terrorists attacked the World Trade Center, and by the time we returned home from our honeymoon, we both were activated by our

Val, wearing night-vision goggles, piloting the C-130E into a combat zone in Bagram, Afghanistan, while on deployment in 2004 in support of Operation *Iraqi Freedom*

Guard unit to fly Operation *Noble Eagle* missions in support of homeland defense.

The next couple of years were a whirlwind, with family and military duty. My career with United was initially short-lived because, after 9-11, I was furloughed. However, I spent the next eight months on active duty flying for the Guard and enjoyed flying a variety of missions. I flew military personnel and equipment all over the United States, and I even had the opportunity to fly special airlift missions for the Secret Service in support of the vice president. One of my favorite missions was providing airlifts for Navy SEALs in training doing high-altitude low-opening drops, where we flew all night long on oxygen as the SEALs jumped out of our airplane at 20,000 feet.

During this active-duty period, I found out I was pregnant with my first son, Nicholas, and flew until I was six months pregnant. Shortly after Nicholas was born, Dave deployed to Qatar, flying in support of Operation *Iraqi Freedom*. Once he returned home, I then deployed to Qatar, also flying similar missions. Our second son, Anthony, arrived a year later, following my deployment and, with great sadness, I resigned from the military after nearly ten years of service. There simply was no way to provide any kind of family stability without one of us getting out of the military. Furloughed from United for five years, I took the time to stay at home with my sons, watching them grow, knowing those days would quickly slip by.

In 2007, I returned to the line at United, again flying the Airbus A319/320 out of Los Angeles. I enjoyed the short work trips away from home—mini-vacations from motherhood and the opportunity to sleep uninterrupted in a quiet room and read a good book or magazine. My being home more also relieved my mom, the "Granny Nanny," of her full-time obligation to us, as she is the third parent in our family and has helped us tremendously in juggling both of our flying careers.

Though my husband and I both loved the camaraderie and spirit of the Air National Guard, as well as the amazing flying we both experienced, we have each retired our military flight suits. Dave completed his twenty years with the Guard and is now a full-time Southwest pilot. I was furloughed again by United in 2009 but I hope to be recalled soon. For the time being, I plan to stay home with my kids and continue volunteering for their different activities. I am enjoying a lifestyle where I am home every night. It's a nice change of pace! These sabbaticals from work allow me the diversity to enjoy the stay-at-home-mom experience, knowing I have a career to return to sooner or later.

I love being a mom, because I have the opportunity to experience childhood all over again with a new and fresh perspective. I love my boys' innocence, their amazement with even the most mundane things. However, the thing that surprised me the most about being a mom is the amount of work it is, 24/7, and how much patience is often required! I can truly say, though, that being a mom is the ultimate career, and has tested every skill I ever learned in the air and on the ground.

Flying has brought so much to my life—friendships, my husband, and traveling all over the world. I have watched the sun rise and set in thirty different countries. I have seen children at air shows squeal with delight as we dropped paratroopers, and I have seen the face of war, when our lives depended upon precision flying and skill. I have flown over the Pacific Ocean, watching whales frolic in the blue, and I have seen the mountains of Afghanistan

Mom to Mom:

The most rewarding thing about being a mom is the unconditional love and wonder my boys have for me. I am simply a goddess to them!

and Pakistan in the dazzling green hue of my night-vision goggles. I've watched flight students fly alone for the first time, and I've met young pilots, old pilots, and even Chuck Yeager.

I have served my country, and I garner a pride, that I can't fully describe, in all my accomplishments. Flying has vigorously reinforced my belief that hard work and believing in oneself make a dream become reality. I want my children to understand how important it is to have a dream and believe in it. I will be there to cheer them on as they discover that they can forge a path to whatever it is they aspire to do and be.

My husband and I will expose them to all that flying has to offer. I want them to learn the lesson I did from flying, that life is a magical experience that can be lived in so many ways. I will encourage and support them in anything they do, and perhaps they, too, will enjoy life's best, once they discover their little corner of the sky.

Pilots, by nature, seek out the most life has to offer and want each experience to be had in its fullest.

Rank:	Air Force Captain
Years Served:	10
Current Military Status:	Separated
Number of Children:	2

Michele (Meyer) Kilgore

F-16C *Fighting Falcon*, KC-10A *Extender*, C-12J *Huron*, EA-6B *Prowler*

AS MY EIGHTEENTH BIRTHDAY GIFT FROM MY PARENTS, I FLEW THE MIGHTY CESSNA 172 WITH AN INSTRUCTOR LOW OVER THE PACIFIC shoreline, sea salt spraying on the cockpit windows, snow-white seagulls rising alongside us. In that moment, I knew flying was in my future—not a matter of *if* but *when*.

The Air Force Academy seemed a natural gateway to my goals, so, five days after high school graduation, off I went. Four years later, as a new Air Force officer, I went to pilot training at Columbus AFB, Mississippi. After graduating in 1993, I flew the KC-10A tanker aircraft and deployed all over the world.

About this time, the combat exclusion law was repealed, and women could now fly in combat squadrons. Interestingly also, due to the overzealous defense cuts in the early 1990s, the Air Force was experiencing fighter pilot shortages. In a once-in-a-career opportunity, fighter cockpits were opened to 150 pilots who had been flying other aircraft.

I applied but wasn't initially selected, and knew those slots would evaporate unless I could get into a job that garnered higher visibility and recognition. I requested to fly the C-12J at Osan AB, Korea, a one-year remote assignment, flying high-ranking military officers around the Korean peninsula. On each mission, I eyed the F-16s sitting on the Osan ramp, and reminded myself to stay focused on my goal to fly fighters.

When it was again time to apply for an open fighter slot, I approached my boss, an Air Force three-star general, boldly stating, "Sir, I would really like to apply to this board. If you don't think I'm qualified, I won't waste your time." He emphatically agreed to support my request, to the point of writing his recommendation by hand. Months later, I found myself at Luke AFB, Arizona, transitioning to the F-16.

I thoroughly enjoyed the training and, with more than two thousand flight hours and three desert deployments under my belt, found it to be relatively easy. I went on to fly F-16CJs at Misawa AB, Japan, and then did an exchange tour with the Navy, flying EA-6B *Prowlers*.

After my exchange tour with the Navy, I left active duty to fly the F-16C+ for the New York Air National Guard in Syracuse, New York. The decision to leave active duty was actually a matter of logistics—my future husband, also a pilot, was stationed in New York.

Since my transition to fighters, I have logged more than 1,300 fighter hours, made three combat deployments to Operations *Northern Watch* and *Iraqi Freedom*, and have flown more than fifty combat sorties in the F-16. With more than 3,200 total flying hours, it's difficult to pick the flights that stand out from the rest. The most rewarding sorties were the close-air-support missions over Iraq in the F-16, protecting Army troops on the ground, often in close proximity to advancing insurgent forces. The most dangerous flights were those flown over Iraq, getting shot at while flying in a single-engine aircraft. The most humbling flight was carrying back the human remains of a pilot. He'd survived an ejection, tried to haul his severely injured body into his life raft, managed to make a final radio call with a message to his fiancée, yet ultimately succumbed to his injuries. Each of these flights is more than just an entry in my logbook. They are experiences woven together in the tapestry of my life, and a career dedicated to the service of my country.

Michelle as an F-16 student pilot, 1999, Luke AFB, Arizona.

I always thought that if I did marry, it would have to be to another pilot who understood what it takes to be a military pilot. My husband, Bob, pilots the C-130 for the Niagara Falls Air Reserve Base and, although we fly at different New York bases, we live under one roof and get to do what we love.

Sometimes our schedules pose a three-ring circus of adjustments, but, thankfully, we've never deployed at the same time. My stepdaughter, Erica, was unfazed when a news story featured us as a husband-and-wife team of military pilots. I love that she will never remember a time when women didn't run for president, pilot the space shuttle, or fly in combat. Our house mantra is "Girls rule!"

After my last deployment, we were delighted to find out I was expecting a baby girl, Abby, who was born in July 2009, much to Erica's delight. This also solves any question of what I am going to do with my free time once I close out my flying career.

As I approach my twenty years in the military, I am ready to pass the reins, salute smartly, and hang up the G-suit. I love the dichotomy that being in the Air National Guard as a part-time pilot has allowed me. One day I'm driving Erica to swim lessons and making hot dogs, and the next day I'm dropping bombs. I can go to Iraq for a month and focus 100 percent on flying combat sorties, then I can spend a month at home swimming in a pool full of little girls who know nothing about politics or war, only thinking it's cool I'm the only woman in the whole state who flies F-16s. I often tell them, "I'm living the dream," because when I

Mom to Mom:

The thing that surprised me the most about being a mom is that despite complete sleep deprivation and exhaustion, a little smile, hug, or laugh can energize and keep you going all day.

was their age, women flying fighters was just that—only a dream.

Part of my legacy is my family history. My grandfather earned a Purple Heart in World War II, and my father, a Marine Corps F-4 pilot in Vietnam, earned twenty-three Air Medals and ejected over Vietnam.

I tell my girls, "In life you can have anything you want, but you can't have everything." Figure out what it is you want to accomplish, surround yourself with people who have similar interests, and just go do it. Never, *ever*, take no for an answer. When the helmet goes on and the visor goes down, it doesn't matter what color your skin is or what gender you are. Everyone is equal and a member of a team, with people on the ground

and in the air depending on you to make the mission a success.

After every flight, when I step down out of the jet and shake the crew chief's hand, I thank him or her for the great jet I just flew. When they ask how my flight was, my response is always the same: "It was awesome—I'm living the dream."

. . . .
Girls Rule!
. . . .

Rank:	Air National Guard Lieutenant Colonel
Years Served:	18
Current Military Status:	Air National Guard
Number of Children:	3

Christi (Falavolito) Legawiec

C-130 *Hercules*

MY MOTHER'S FATHER, PAPAW, A B-29 PILOT IN THE 1940S AND 1950S, PASSED AWAY WHEN I WAS SIX YEARS OLD, BUT I REMEMBER MY Nanaw telling stories of his flying experiences, full of adventure and romance.

My own fascination with aviation started as a teenager when my Nanaw bought me a pair of silver Air Force pilot wings. I wore them as a reminder to myself and to others what I intended to accomplish one day.

Although my parents divorced when I was quite young, my mom remarried a wonderful man I've called Dad for as long as I can remember. He was, and continues to be, a perfect example of a great dad. While my mom was the cautious one, my dad always encouraged me to take risks and try new things. He encouraged my interest in aviation, and even sent me to a summer camp specializing in space travel.

I wanted a traditional college experience, so I attended Tulane University on an Army scholarship. It didn't take long for me to realize I wasn't a good fit for the Army, and I transitioned to the Air Force ROTC program in 1993. I was on my way to those silver wings.

During my senior year of college, I was selected to attend Air Force pilot training upon graduation. One of my college roommates had already graduated, received a commission in the Navy, and was attending the Navy's pilot training at NAS Whiting Field in Florida. She mentioned that a few Air Force pilots were being offered the opportunity to attend Navy flight school. Living near the beach in Florida while learning how to fly sounded like the perfect life to me. So I applied, and soon found myself headed to Navy flight training.

After training in the T-34, I moved to Corpus Christi, Texas, to train in the Navy T-44. At my winging, my fellow aviator friends teased me, saying I should be given Navy wings of gold instead of Air Force silver since I had never actually trained in an Air Force jet.

After graduating, I selected the Air Force C-130 *Hercules* to fly, because I loved the concept of a multi-person crew, and the C-130 offered just enough of an in-the-dirt military mission mixed with hauling cargo. Finally, in 1999, I arrived at my first operational squadron—the 2nd Airlift Squadron at Pope AFB in North Carolina.

I joined the squadron eagerly anticipating my first deployment to Ramstein AB, Germany, where the squadron would support peacekeeping operations in the Balkans. From Germany, we further deployed to Operation *Southern Watch* in Saudi Arabia and Kuwait. I loved the camaraderie of an entire squadron deployed together overseas to conduct real-world missions. It brought me great satisfaction to know that what I was doing made a difference. I met my husband, Joel, during that tour—he also was in the Air Force, working as a C-130 loadmaster, but decided to leave the Air Force to pursue his college degree.

In 2002, shortly after marrying, I received my next assignment—the 37th Airlift Squadron at Ramstein, Germany. This was our dream assignment! Joel worked as a mechanic at the base auto skills center and continued to attend college. The excitement of living in Germany, however, faded after I had deployed 300 of the first 360 days. Trying to start a family was quite challenging with my busy deployment schedule. One of our squadron deployments was to Romania. "Romania?" I thought, "Why

Christine and her family sitting in the back of a C-130, 2007.

are we going to Romania?" My squadron mates and I packed our bags, got our immunizations, kissed our families goodbye and headed out. We were staying in a hotel in Constanta that catered to Eastern European tourists in the summer, but was closed for the season. We were paired two to a room and my roommate was my navigator, Jo Dible, who also was a good friend. That first night we nearly froze—there was no thermostat in our room, and it never warmed up. Later, we discovered an eight-inch hole in the wall that led directly to the outside. No wonder we were freezing! But aircrew had it better than most. The special forces troops we were carrying in our C-130 slept on the floor in the airport.

On the morning of our first mission into Iraq, we walked through the makeshift operations center set up in the Constanta airport. We got our intelligence briefing and made our survival and evasion plans in the event we had to make an unscheduled landing (crash) in hostile

territory. Even though I knew we had done everything by the book, covered all our bases, I still felt a twinge of "there's something I'm forgetting." But there wasn't. We had done this drill so many times before in training that it had become automatic. Our leadership, the ones who had gone to war before us over a decade earlier, trained us well. We were ready. We had flown in the Balkans, in Operation *Southern Watch*, and into less-than-friendly airstrips in Africa. But this was the first time any of us were flying into a country that we were at war with. In January of 2003, Iraq was still a dangerous place for U.S. and allied aircraft. And in a slick C-130, we didn't have any offensive weapons at our disposal. We had to rely on our situational awareness and mission planning to avoid the threats, because we were not in a position to confront them.

It was on that day that I understood the definition of the word brave. Brave doesn't mean you're not scared.

It means that you go anyway. And I went. With a crew I trusted with my life and my best friend navigating our way, we headed out over the Black Sea toward Iraq. Initially, the flight was calm and perhaps a little boring. We all made jokes to ease our nerves. As we approached the entry point into hostile airspace, the entire crew got quiet. Serious. Focused. We donned our helmets and body armor, reviewed our route into and out of Iraq, and put our game faces on. "Crew, we are in Iraqi airspace," Jo announced over the intercom.

The stress of combat flying had its intended and positive effect of sharpening our senses. We executed our mission flawlessly. Exiting Iraqi airspace was a great relief, and my proudest moment as an aircraft commander. Every member of my crew played a vital role that day. I've flown into Iraq many more times since, but nothing compares to that first mission, where I learned that I have what it takes to fly in combat, to get the beans and bullets to the ground troops that need them. My courage was tested that day, and I was proud that I passed.

Joel and I finally realized we were expecting our first child during our tour in Ramstein. We were scared and excited all at once! Nine months later, we welcomed our daughter, Genevieve, "Genna." I remember knowing that my life would change once my daughter arrived, but I had no idea how much. I had just gotten the hang of balancing a husband and a career, and now I had a child. This was going to be a challenge! We decided it made sense for Joel to quit working and stay home with Genna. Having him home with her made it much easier for me to go back to work.

In August 2005, we transferred to Dyess AFB near Abilene, Texas, for my next assignment, the 39th Airlift Squadron. Joel's job as a motorcycle-builder and mechanic enabled him to drop off and pick up Genna from daycare if I was flying odd hours. The next year, we happily discovered I was pregnant again. But on November 10, 2006, our lives were changed forever

when Joel, while on his motorcycle, was hit by a car whose driver failed to yield the right-of-way. He suffered severe, unrecoverable trauma to his left foot, and it had to be amputated. After his initial hospital stay, he transferred to Wilford Hall Medical Center in San Antonio, four hours away from our home in Abilene. Thankfully, the Air Force approved my request to transfer to nearby Randolph AFB, but the next two months were extremely difficult.

After our son Cael's birth, I took six weeks of maternity leave, and then returned to work and to flying. During this tour, I flew the C-130J, the newest generation of tactical airlifter. Cael was only three months old when I had to leave to attend two months of C-130J training at Little Rock AFB, Arkansas. I flew home every weekend so I could continue nursing Cael.

It was certainly inconvenient to travel with frozen or refrigerated breast milk and a breast pump every weekend. It was also a challenge to schedule my necessary pumping sessions, four times a day, around my academic and flight simulator schedule. It was absolutely worth it, though. Joel is an excellent father, and I knew my babies were in good hands while I was away. That, combined with my ability to continue nursing, made the time away from my family more bearable.

I used to feel like I had to be doing something productive every waking moment. I would stress out because the laundry wasn't done or the mail wasn't sorted and filed. Then one day, I realized that my daughter loves me and thinks I'm super cool, and that I am my baby son's entire world at this stage in his life.

It dawned on me that it won't always be like this. They will grow more independent and figure out I don't know everything. I want to build memories with my kids, not of mom filing bills or folding clothes, but of mom playing with them from the moment she got home from work until they went to bed. More than anything in the world, I want them to know how much they are loved.

Mom to Mom: The thing that surprised me most about being a mom is that I never knew it was possible to love someone as much as I do my children, and I'd be so willing to give up anything and everything for them.

I also want to teach my children how to deal with adversity—it is normal for life to be challenging. What matters most is your response to those challenges. My dad never let me say "I can't." Joel and I don't let Genna say those words either. We've taught her it is okay to say "I need help" or "I don't know how." We will do the same with Cael. I want them both to know that when life is hard or doesn't go the way they're expecting, they can handle it and be better for it.

"Life is a journey, not a destination."

Ralph Waldo Emerson

Rank:	Air Force Lieutenant Colonel
Years Served:	14
Current Military Status:	Active Duty
Number of Children:	2

Kate (Wildasin) Lowe

F-16 *Fighting Falcon*

'VE OFTEN LOOKED AT MYSELF IN THE MIRROR AND WONDERED, "HOW DID I GET HERE?" "HERE" IS A GREAT PLACE TO BE, THOUGH IT'S NOT ONE I imagined as a kid.

I grew up in Lancaster County, Pennsylvania. From my dad, a high school guidance counselor and football coach, I learned loyalty and a strong work ethic. From my mom, a dental hygienist, I learned personal responsibility and enthusiasm. My younger siblings, Greta and Mark, taught me about teamwork and fun. For some reason, the military always appealed to me, though I had no connections to it besides my grandfathers who fought in World War II.

In 1993, I decided to attend the University of Notre Dame on an Air Force ROTC scholarship. Impressed with the pilots I met through the ROTC program, I decided to try flying as a career. During my junior year, I submitted a package for pilot training, and I celebrated my twenty-first birthday the same week I found out I got a pilot slot. During my senior year, I finished my ROTC career as the cadet wing commander, the leader of all the cadets in my ROTC unit, and prepared to start life as a second lieutenant in the Air Force.

Before starting flight training, I ran into a guy I met at ROTC field training—Greg Lowe. Also in the Air Force, he served as an aircraft maintenance officer. Within a few weeks, we started dating, and when I started pilot training, I knew I'd marry him someday.

Flight school was a significant challenge, and I was overwhelmed right from the beginning, but I had never failed in anything, and I was not about to start there. Hard work, my determination to successfully finish, and help from great friends and instructors were the reasons I graduated and earned an F-16 *Viper* slot.

In 2000, Greg and I married and moved to Hill AFB, Utah, to start our life together. I was the first female pilot in the 34th Fighter Squadron, known as the Rude Rams, but my gender didn't matter. I was just like every other new fighter pilot in the squadron.

I had a lot to learn about flying, about being a fighter pilot, and about myself. Typically, fighter pilots go by call signs and are assigned them during naming ceremonies. My naming ceremony was one of the highlights of my time at Hill. The guys had a great time naming the first "chick" in the squadron. At the end of the evening, my call sign was officially "Jiga," and she's been part of me since.

Life was good that first year in the squadron. We trained in hopes of supporting no-fly operations over Iraq. Then, the events of September 11, 2001, occurred, and life in the fighter squadron suddenly changed. Within days, I was sitting alert duty at Hill, and within weeks, we were sitting alert duty in other states and flying missions over several major cities. Those missions weren't glamorous, but we knew they were important, especially when we flew missions protecting the 2002 Winter Olympics.

In 2003, Greg and I received an assignment together to Luke AFB, Arizona. I joined the 62nd Fighter Squadron as an instructor pilot. As an instructor, I had my dream Air Force job—flight commander, where I was responsible for training students and scheduling instructor pilot flights. I loved teaching my students and working with my fellow instructors, and I loved working for my mentor and squadron commander, Skip, who to this day was the best boss I ever had.

Two years later, in August 2005, Greg and I once again had to think about our next assignment. As always, our priority was an assignment together. This time,

Kate and her husband, Greg, at their wedding, 2000.

however, we had one more consideration. We wanted to start a family. We were both thirty years old, had been married for five years, and we were ready for a baby.

I approached the assignment gurus and told them honestly that I was planning to get pregnant at my next assignment. I thought it was in everyone's best interest for me not to be assigned to a cockpit, as I would be unable to fly in the F-16 while pregnant because of its ejection seat. We found a staff job for me, and a maintenance job for Greg, at Nellis AFB, Nevada. We arrived in Las Vegas with our dog, Lager, and when we had unpacked, we knew that a baby was on the way. My staff job was not as exciting as my flying assignments, but that was okay. I knew that our baby was worth it. We spent most of 2006 getting ready for the baby. I took the same approach to preparing for a baby that I did to flying. I studied, organized, and visualized.

Our baby girl, Becca Elizabeth, arrived on December 20, 2006, and changed our lives instantly. It was the best Christmas we ever had. Between my maternity leave and personal leave, I got to spend nine weeks at home with her. Knowing that I would have to return to work allowed me to savor each moment, and Greg's support throughout the entire experience was unlimited and uplifting. I knew that soon enough I would be back to work, and my afternoons spent watching her in wonder would end too quickly. She would only be this small for a brief moment, and I didn't want to miss any of it.

With sadness in my heart, I returned to work at the end of February 2007. As heartbroken as I was, I knew that I had to determine what I wanted now. I didn't want to quit the Air Force or give up flying, but I also had a baby girl. I took a break from flying, yet stuck with the Air Force to see how I liked being a working mom. Only time will tell what is best for me, for Becca, and for our family. Whatever happens, though, I know that we'll be okay.

I hope that my children have a wonderful childhood filled with love and adventure. I want them to know that they can be anything they want to be. I also hope to teach them to do their best, treat people with respect, and that determination and teamwork will always bring success.

Now when I look at myself in the mirror, I realize that "here" is a place I have arrived at through the encouragement of my family, the love of a wonderful man, the mentoring of my outstanding leaders, the support of my peers, and my own hard work and determination. I am

an Air Force officer, a pilot, a wife, a daughter, a sister, a friend, and now, a mother. Whatever happens, "here" is an amazing place to be.

Mom to Mom:
The most rewarding thing about being a mom is seeing a smile of pure joy on your child's face, followed up by a big hug.

"Nothing great was ever achieved without enthusiasm."

—Ralph Waldo Emerson

Rank:	Air Force Major
Years Served:	13
Current Military Status:	Air Force Reserve
Number of Children:	1

Juli (Dahnke) Mansfield

KC-135R *Stratotanker,* T-37 *Tweet*

TWO CHILDHOOD EVENTS INSPIRED ME TO JOIN THE AIR FORCE AND BECOME A PILOT. FIRST, BEFORE I WAS BORN, MY MOM SERVED AS ONE of the first women Air Force officers; she always encouraged me to pursue any career that I wanted. Second, I grew up near a military base in California and our family often attended spectacular air shows. One year, the Thunderbirds were flying in the air show. They performed incredible aerial maneuvers and were captivating to watch. Although still young, I began to wonder if I too could become a pilot.

While in high school, I met a couple of women officers who had just graduated from the Air Force Academy. They encouraged me to apply and, after graduation, I was on my way to the academy and an Air Force career.

My four years at the academy greatly impacted my life—I developed lifelong friendships, got an excellent education, and became even more motivated to attend pilot training. I majored in aeronautical engineering, and, although the academic curriculum was challenging, I still participated in other activities—soccer, rugby, and parachuting. I also had the opportunity to fly in gliders and the T-41 *Mescalero*, a military version of the Cessna 172, used by the Air Force as a pilot-training aircraft.

The summer before my senior year, I received a couple of flights in the T-33, a two-seat jet trainer, at Elmendorf AFB in Alaska. What an incredible experience I couldn't wait to get to graduate and start flying! My sister, Lida Munz, also an Air Force officer and pilot, commissioned me a second lieutenant in the Air Force after I graduated from the academy in 1986. Next, I headed to flight training at Williams AFB in Phoenix, Arizona.

I loved every day of flight school and enjoyed flying up among the clouds. I rented a house close to the training base with three other women I knew from the academy. The house was pretty well worn, but we cleaned it up enough to make it habitable for a year. However, that house did have one essential to the Phoenix area—a pool! Our pilot training classes routinely held parties at our house, and I think everyone was thrown into, or fell into, our pool. That year I also fell in love, marrying a great guy from my pilot training class who had also been in my academy class—Bob Mansfield.

After we married, Bob and I were lucky enough to be stationed in the same state, Georgia, for our first assignment. I flew the KC-135R *Stratotanker* at Robins AFB and Bob flew the F-16 *Viper* at Moody AFB. We bought a house in between and both drove quite a ways to work. Although we put in long days, we were happy we could live in the same house.

I enjoyed flying the tanker, because it had a great mission and every day was different. I probably refueled every plane in the Air Force and Navy inventories. In 1991, *Desert Storm* was in full swing, and for most of the war I sat alert duty back at Robins. However, I did deploy for a short time to Saudi Arabia.

After my three years flying the tanker, Bob and I got a joint assignment to Laughlin AFB in Del Rio, Texas. I instructed in the T-37 trainer, the first jet a student learns to fly in pilot training, and Bob instructed in the T-38, another trainer.

I had wanted to be an instructor pilot since flight school, so this was a dream assignment. I loved teaching students how to fly their first jet, and after three years of

Family photograph of Juli, husband Bob, and children, 2005.

flying straight and level in the KC–135R, I was happy to be spinning and doing acrobatics again. I enjoyed watching my students solo and build their skills and confidence. Much of what I learned as an instructor, I have applied to raising my own kids—like lots of patience!

We had several great friends in Del Rio and spent time with them and their kids. That motivated us to start our own family. While pregnant with my first child in 1993, I wasn't sure if I would stay home or continue flying the Air Force T-37. However, after holding my daughter in my arms, I knew I couldn't leave her in the care of someone else, even for the workday. Shortly after she was born, I separated from the active-duty military. Bob also left the Air Force and was hired by United Airlines, and we moved to the Denver, Colorado, area. Soon after, we had our second child.

However, after five years at home, with a 5-year old daughter and 3-year old son, I decided I wanted to fly

again. I missed the flying and being part of a squadron. I returned to the cockpit to instruct in the T-37 for the Air Force Reserve in Del Rio, Texas. There was a catch though—we lived in Denver. Although it was a long commute each month, I loved flying again and my skills came back very quickly. It was so good to be back spinning and doing acrobatics again!

Bob and I traded off with the kids, but after a year of not seeing much of each other, I decided the commute was too much. I needed and wanted to spend more time at home with my family. I also wanted to have another baby, and we had one more son in 2000.

I've heard it said many times, and it proved to be true for me—you can have it all, just not all at the same time. I loved being an Air Force pilot, and I love being a mom. I just couldn't do justice to both jobs at the same time. As I look at my kids now, ages 17, 15, and 10, and see what great people they are and the fun memories we share, I wouldn't change a thing.

I don't know what my kids will pursue for their own careers, and right now they seem to change their minds every day! All three of them have said at one time or another that they would like to be a pilot...or a teacher, soccer player, or rock star. I just hope they find something they love doing as much as I have loved flying.

Mom to Mom:

Being a mom is the best thing that has ever happened to me. I love just being with my kids and doing things with them and watching them grow into amazing people.

There is no better job than flying in the Air Force, except for being a mom. I am blessed to have gotten to do both!

Rank:	Air Force Lieutenant Colonel
Years Served:	23
Current Military Status:	Retired
Number of Children:	3

Kelley (Sloan) Marcell

F-15E *Strike Eagle*

'VE WANTED TO FLY FOR AS LONG AS I CAN REMEMBER. IN HIGH SCHOOL, I JOINED THE CIVIL AIR PATROL AND LEARNED ABOUT AIRPLANES, aviation history, and how to wear a uniform. Extremely driven, I focused on everything it took to get into the Naval Academy. However, after graduating from high school, I decided to join the Air Force instead, and received an Air Force ROTC scholarship to Embry-Riddle Aeronautical University in Daytona Beach.

I enjoyed college, pursued a degree in aerospace engineering, and also earned my private pilot's license. I set goals to make 1993 a significant year for me—I would graduate from college, receive my Air Force commission, and hopefully get a coveted pilot slot and start flight training. Another significant event took place in 1993 with the repeal of the combat exclusion law, previously prohibiting women from flying in combat. I always wanted to fly fighters and now it was a possibility!

However, there was a glitch to my carefully laid plans— the Air Force decided to reduce the number of pilots, so there were no pilot slots available. I received a navigator slot instead. Navigators are aviators, but typically manage an aircraft's weapon systems, communications, and navigation equipment. It wasn't a pilot slot but I'd still be flying!

Then another unexpected and disappointing change to my career plans occurred when the Air Force reduced the number of navigators and closed navigator training. I lost my navigator slot, forcing me to pick another career field. I chose ground-controlled intercept (controlling our aircraft to intercept enemy targets), a career field associated with aviation, just a momentary delay to my carefully laid plans. I remained determined to work as a controller for a year and then apply for pilot training. After completing the controller training, I transferred to Korea for my first operational assignment, which turned out to be a fantastic adventure. I worked with the F-16 squadron at Osan AB and also worked with the A-10s and F-16s at Kunsan AB, controlling all kinds of missions and exercises.

Ten months into my tour, I had my pilot training application all ready to go, when I got an order to report to navigator training immediately. Unbelievably, the Air Force had let too many navigators get out, and now there was a shortage. I'm a firm believer that everything happens for a reason.

Basic navigator training complete, I received my wings and found out I was the very first woman selected to train as a weapon system operator in the F-15E *Strike Eagle*. My first F-15E flight was amazing. I still remember the rush of the afterburner takeoff and the amazing view as we climbed during the high-performance vertical takeoff. I couldn't believe I had finally made it!

After completing *Strike Eagle* training, I joined my first operational flying squadron—the 494th Fighter Squadron, Lakenheath, England. I loved being part of the squadron, even though it was very challenging at first to get mission-qualified and to prove myself, but that goes with the territory. For the most part, fitting into the squadron was seamless. It was an outstanding squadron with great leadership. The squadron commander and his wife, also a lieutenant colonel, were wonderful, inspirational mentors. After this tour, I transferred to the 336th Fighter Squadron at Seymour Johnson AFB in North Carolina.

I initially met my future husband, Chris, during my Lakenheath tour. He was an F-15E pilot in the squadron. We worked together and even flew together once. He

147

Kelley, husband Chris, and son Ian, circa 2009, Pensacola, Florida.

was married and had children and I was dating someone who was stationed in Germany. Months after I returned to Seymour Johnson, in 1999, Chris received orders to the North Carolina area. I came home one day to find a message from him on my answering machine, saying he was now living nearby and wanted to get together. I thought nothing of it, since we had been squadron mates and friends from our time in England. After meeting up with him, however, he told me he had gotten divorced. What I thought was just going out with a "bud" was actually him asking me on a date! We started spending some time together as friends. Our friendship grew into a dating relationship, and two and a half years later, we married. I am also truly blessed to have three wonderful stepchildren, Michael, Katie, and Mandy.

Chris and I spent a few years at Seymour Johnson, and then, in 2003, we both were selected for Air Officer Commanding billets at the Air Force Academy. We would be cadet squadron commanders, guiding, mentoring, and leading cadets at the academy. I looked forward to this

awesome opportunity to impact young cadets' lives. I really wanted to make a difference, share my operational experiences with them, and prepare them to become Air Force officers. I also wanted to provide a female perspective to the women students, and my husband and I offered the unique perspective of being a dual-military couple.

I thought I had a lot to impart, but I soon realized I had a lot to learn. As squadron commander to 130 college students, my job had many different descriptions—commander, mentor, role model, parent, and disciplinarian. Filling all these different roles was challenging and difficult at times, but it is very gratifying now to run into a former cadet who is an Air Force officer and hear a "thank you" for helping him or her along their journey at the academy

Several months before we left Colorado, we learned we were expecting our first child together. Chris received a unique opportunity to command a Navy training squadron at NAS Whiting Field near Pensacola, Florida, and to teach pilot training. My orders were also to Navy flight school, but to a different base, NAS Pensacola, Florida, to teach naval flight officer and weapon system officer students.

We welcomed our son, Ian, in August 2006, shortly after we moved to Pensacola. Having our son brought new meaning to the word love, and that deep feeling comes from a place that I never knew existed. It is indescribable to know that I am responsible for another life, for his development and nurturing. Ian is an incredibly happy little guy—all dimples and smiles.

Going back to work after maternity leave proved to be one of the hardest things I've done. My priorities have changed since having Ian, since, before his birth, I was a consummate workaholic and always stayed late at work to complete tasks. Now, I realize that the paperwork will always be there. I can have the worst day, feel frustrated, or have a headache, but the moment I walk into daycare and see his smiling little face, it all goes away. Most days, I'm home before my husband, and as soon as Ian hears his daddy open the door, he squeals with delight, and we all enjoy the ritual of our family hug.

The Air Force has provided me awesome opportunities. It has been a challenging but rewarding life. I've

Mom to Mom:

The thing that surprised me the most about being a mom was how hard it was to go back to work seven weeks after I had my son, Ian, and also realizing how much my priorities changed once Ian arrived. Truthfully, I was always a workaholic. However, after learning that I was pregnant with my son, I realized that the work would always be there...no matter how late I stayed. Finding a balance is tough, but I understand the importance of taking time for my family, and I wouldn't trade it for the world!

met truly wonderful people, and have had many great experiences. The military aviation training I received has taught me that I can overcome any obstacle and move forward, that I can do anything.

Wearing my military uniform means something special to me. They are not just clothes I wear to work. The uniform represents our country and freedom, everything I work for and support. I want my children to understand the importance of serving our country, even when it is not always the easiest or popular thing to do.

My hopes for my kids are that they will find their passion in life and go for it, and hopefully have a good time along the way. I also want them to be trustworthy people of character, who do the right thing, even when no one is looking.

. . . .

Be happy, because life is too short not to be.

. . . .

Rank:	Air Force Lieutenant Colonel
Years Served:	17
Current Military Status:	Active Duty
Number of Children:	4

Christine (Callahan) Mau

F-15 Strike Eagle

AS A LITTLE GIRL IN CALIFORNIA, I LOVED WATCHING FIGHTER JETS ZIPPING AROUND EL TORO MARINE CORPS AIR STATION (MCAS). ONE day, I looked up toward the sky and told my mom that I wanted to fly one of those jets when I grew up. She responded, "Oh no, honey, women can't fly those." And she was right; at that time, they couldn't.

I grew up around pilots. My dad flew C-130s in the Air Force, and then flew for both Continental Airlines and the California Air National Guard. My grandfather flew the B-24 in the Army Air Corps during World War II.

When I was in high school, I decided that I wanted to be a military fighter pilot, and from that point on, everything I did was geared toward achieving that goal. My dad convinced me that the Air Force was the way to go, so I applied and was accepted into the Air Force Academy class of 1997. The academy was a rewarding experience, but also something I'm glad is behind me.

After graduating with a bachelor of science in biology, and getting commissioned in May 1997, I went to flight training at Sheppard AFB, Texas. This was an awesome experience because several students and instructors were from different NATO countries. I felt blessed to get my first choice of aircraft, the F-15E *Strike Eagle*! I loved the two-seater F-15E, because it has a dual role of both air-to-air and air-to-ground missions.

Following the initial pilot training, I moved to Seymour Johnson AFB in Goldsboro, North Carolina, to learn how to fly the F-15E. I'll never forget my first flight and the "kick in the pants" I felt as the afterburners lit on take-off. Eight months later in July 2000, I officially started my first operational assignment with the 492nd Fighter Squadron at Lakenheath, England. This was the best first assignment I could have hoped for. Our squadron deployed to Kuwait and Turkey and trained all over Europe.

When I arrived at the 492nd, there were two other female aviators in the squadron. Overall, the squadron attitude was very professional and welcoming toward female aircrew. But, there were still a few old, crusty guys who made things a little more challenging; however, the squadron leadership was great, and I enjoyed this tour.

I met my future husband, Steve, in England. He was an F-15E crew chief in my squadron, and we got to know each other as friends while deployed to Kuwait. We both played on the local military volleyball team and competed in tournaments against other European teams. He separated from the Air Force after his time in England, so that he could be closer to his son and pursue his college degree in earnest.

My follow-on assignment was back to the 333rd Fighter Squadron at Seymour Johnson AFB, North Carolina, to teach. I loved teaching the basics of fighter fundamentals to student pilots and student weapon system operators.

Steve had also moved back to North Carolina, and after six months of dating, we married and I became an insta-mom because we gained custody of his then four-year-old son, Marcus. Getting married and becoming a mom during my flight instructor training was challenging, as it totally changed my priorities and outlook on life. Rather than studying or goofing off at night, I played with and read stories to my son, and took him to soccer practice or swim lessons.

I found that I used my time better at work, so that I wouldn't have to bring work home with me as much. I

Christine and daughter, McKenna, May 2010, at McKenna's preschool graduation, Montgomery, Alabama.

also really looked forward to coming home every day to be with my family. Being a stepmom wasn't easy, but I still embrace it and do the best that I can.

My husband had finished his undergraduate degree and started working on his master's, when he decided to take a break and become a police officer. It soon became very challenging for us to coordinate our schedules with daycare because we both worked long days and odd hours. Overall, we were able to make do with help from our friends and support from the squadron.

Near the end of my three-year tour, I became pregnant. I was the second woman pilot in the squadron to become pregnant in six months. It was still very unique for there to be more than one or two women aviators in a squadron, so it was even more rare to see a couple of us pregnant. Since the F-15E is an ejection-seat aircraft, pregnant aircrew are prohibited from flying. Although I couldn't fly during my pregnancy, I was able to take on a lot of squadron jobs that other aircrew didn't want or

have time for, like the supervisor of flying and teaching classes. My squadron considered this a huge asset! Again, I was blessed with wonderful and supportive squadron leadership.

Due to the pregnancy, my next assignment was a non-flying staff job. So, a month prior to giving birth, we packed up the family and moved across the country to Nellis AFB in Nevada. Our daughter, McKenna, was born in July 2006—the most amazing, life-changing experience ever. The instant, unconditional love I felt for her was overwhelming. To have a child of my own was a dream come true. I took two months off for maternity leave, and feel very fortunate to have had that time at home with her. I wouldn't have traded it for anything!

I seriously considered leaving the Air Force once I started having kids. My mom stayed home with my brother and me until we left for college—it was what I knew. But, even though I felt very uneasy and sad to return to my job, I realized that I was a happier person working. I also REALLY wanted to fly the F-15E again. Thankfully, McKenna liked spending time with other kids at daycare. Before she turned two, I deployed to Iraq for four months. Being away from my family was extremely difficult, but, fortunately, we talked via a webcam two to three times a week. During this deployment, we received news that I had been selected to attend the Air Command and Staff College, which meant I would be in school for a year. Since that gave me a year of not flying, we decided to have another child. Very soon after returning from Iraq, I became pregnant with our third child.

We moved to Montgomery, Alabama, six weeks prior to my due date. Shortly after my school started, I gave birth to our second daughter, Kayla. She is a wonderful, happy and laid-back baby and spoiled like crazy by her big brother and sister. Thankfully, the instructors and staff were very flexible with my school schedule during my six weeks of maternity leave. Being a full-time student was a nice benefit since it was my primary job, but very challenging, nonetheless, with three kids and a husband who also worked. My next assignment is back to flying F-15Es at Mountain Home AFB, Idaho, and I can't wait to get in the air again.

I am part of a great support network for other women fighter aviators called the Chick Fighter Pilot Association. It started with a group of gals at Luke AFB who wanted to share ideas and lend support for each other. Women only make up 1 to 2 percent of fighter aircrew, so it's a very

Mom to Mom:

The thing that surprised me the most about being a mom is how much you can love another human being so unconditionally. In that first moment after giving birth, you fall in love, and your life automatically becomes re-prioritized. When I had my second daughter, I could almost feel my heart getting bigger to hold that same love for her.

small group. Each base has its own "chapter," and, once each year, we have a big reunion in Las Vegas.

My family is my priority and my bedrock. They help me to be a better pilot and military officer. My husband, Steve, is very supportive, and also very proud of me. It helps that he is a strong, confident man. Moving frequently makes it hard for Steve to pursue his own career. He just finished up his master's in aeronautical science and hopes to work in the aviation industry wherever we go next.

I don't look forward to being away from my family for any period of time, but I know that going back to a flying tour will mean frequent deployments for months at a time—a fact of life in our military today.

I would love for my kids to develop a love of aviation as they grow up. I enjoy speaking at my son's school and bringing the kids out to the flight line. I hope to give my kids some flying lessons when they get older to help build their confidence, and to encourage them to pursue their goals. I want them to know that if they put their mind to it and work hard, they can do anything.

I am so proud to be a mom. It is the coolest thing I've ever done.

Rank:	Air Force Major
Years Served:	13
Current Military Status:	Active Duty
Number of Children:	3

Melissa (Hyland) May

F-16 *Fighting Falcon*

GROWING UP AS AN ONLY CHILD IN UTAH, I WAS USED TO BEING A "MINORITY," AND IT NEVER FAZED ME. I WAS THE CAPTAIN OF MY SWIM team, the founder of an environmental club in my high school, and active on a local snowboarding team, but I didn't know what I wanted to be when I grew up.

One day, my Aunt Linda, who was an airline flight attendant, told me that if she had a daughter, she'd encourage her to become a pilot. She said it was very rare to see a female airline pilot, but she was always so impressed whenever she flew with one. That seemed like a cool job to me!

I looked into different aviation schools, and the Air Force Academy was one of the places known for aviation. I didn't know a thing about the military, but it sounded like a fun place to go—I would be able to crawl around in the mud, get helicopter rides, fly gliders, learn to pilot a single-engine airplane, and jump out of airplanes. I could also swim on the intercollegiate team, and the best part about it was that it didn't cost a thing. Wow!

Months later, I applied to the academy. My dad, who was initially not excited about his only daughter joining the military, actually became my biggest supporter during the application process. The more he learned about the academy and the potential of flying, the more excited he became.

Two weeks after high school graduation, I was off to basic cadet training. Both of my parents were wonderfully supportive during my time at the academy and have encouraged me throughout my Air Force career.

After four years at the academy, I finally made it to pilot training at Laughlin AFB, Texas. I knew that I wanted to fly, and I wanted the opportunity to choose fighters.

That meant I had to be at the top of my class. I don't think I've ever worked so hard! I absolutely loved flying, and pilot training was a blast. In June 1999, I graduated first in my class, and picked the F-16 as my aircraft.

Flying fighters has been the most exciting, rewarding, and gratifying job in the entire world. The camaraderie in a fighter squadron can't be beat. Everywhere I've gone, the other pilots and their spouses have been my family. I've made lifelong friends in the Air Force whom I would literally trust with my life. In most locations, I was the only girl in my squadron, so all of my friends were guys.

I met my husband, Mike, at the Air Force Academy. He is also an F-16 pilot, and we've been fortunate to be stationed together for most of our careers. Besides a stint in Korea where we were at different bases, we've lived together in Japan, Arizona, and now Colorado. Mike is awesome, even though he has to deal with his wife also being a fighter pilot. One pilot ego in the family is bad enough, but with two, it's insane.

When we were stationed in Japan, his squadron deployed to support Operation *Southern Watch*. They were gone for three months; then my squadron replaced them. Two months into our deployment, the war was kicked off by Operation *Iraqi Freedom*, and I flew combat missions into Baghdad and beyond. The standing joke between us is that they sent the "B" team home (his squadron) and brought in the "A" team. Mike's a good sport about it.

We moved to Luke AFB, Arizona, in 2005 and I found myself with five other female instructor pilots—it was absolutely awesome. It was also extremely unusual, since less than 1 percent of Air Force fighter pilots are women. We all just clicked, because we had so much in common. None of us had really ever been stationed with

Melissa and her husband, Mike, with their two children in front of an F-16, 2011, Aviano, Italy.

other girls before. We joked about how we should start a club, and that's how the Chick Fighter Pilot Association was formed. There's nothing official about it, but it has created a venue for women across the world to mentor and support one another. The bonds I have with my fellow female fighter pilots will last a lifetime. They truly are great friends.

After twelve years in the Air Force flying F-16s, I didn't ever think my life could get any better. I have been an instructor pilot, fought in a war, seen places all over the world, and was married to the man of my dreams. When I turned thirty-four years old, Mike and I decided to have a baby. We were stationed at Luke AFB and I was still in a fighter squadron. I was nervous about telling the guys in my squadron, because I wouldn't be able to fly for my last month. The nerves were unwarranted, because

everyone was extremely supportive and happy for me. During that last month, I was entertained with pictures of F-16s with a "baby on board" sign hung in the squadron. If I had stayed longer, they were going to give my unborn child a fighter-pilot call sign. The other benefit to having been pregnant in a fighter squadron is that my son has already pulled 9 g's, since I flew one or two sorties before I found out I was pregnant.

I was wrong about my life not getting any better. Flying fighters is a wonderful job, but becoming a mom is truly more than I could ask for. My son was born on his due date. Mike and I pride ourselves that he was "On Time, On Target." What else would you expect from the son of two fighter pilots? Of course, fighter pilots always have a wingman, so our son now has a little sister who is two years younger and is just as feisty!

Mike and I love every single moment of being parents. It's kind of amazing—and entertaining—to see the reactions of people when they hear I am a fighter pilot and a mom. My life is full and complete. I feel like I really do have it all.

Everyone assumes our children will grow up, join the military, and follow in our footsteps. If they want to do that, we'll certainly encourage it, but they will have to choose for themselves what their passions are. We hope to give them as many opportunities as possible to do what they want. Even though they're at a young age, we can already see that they are both extremely strong-willed and stubborn. Those two characteristics alone make a pretty good fighter pilot! Only time will tell.

Hopefully, my husband and I can finish out our careers as Air Force leaders and F-16 pilots. Having kids puts a new perspective on deployments and military aviation, but I'm convinced we'll be able to not just do it all, but we'll be able to do it all successfully.

If anyone ever asked me for advice about flying fighter aircraft for a living, I would tell them without a doubt that this is the best job in the world. Don't ever pass up an opportunity because you're afraid of the unknown, and don't ever let someone tell you that you shouldn't do something. This job is not for everyone, but you'll never know unless you try.

Flying fighters and being in the Air Force has disciplined me and taught me how to deal with stressful situations. Motherhood is teaching me patience. Both give me strength and love and make me who I am today.

Mom to Mom:

Being a mom is the best thing that has ever happened to me.

The sky is the limit...perhaps.

Rank:	Air Force Lieutenant Colonel
Years Served:	15
Current Military Status:	Active Duty
Number of Children:	2

Lida Dais Dahnke Munz

UH-1N *Huey*

I BEGAN MY LIFE ON A FARM IN NEBRASKA, AND STILL FEEL STRONG TIES TO FARMING AND THE LAND. EVEN THOUGH I ONLY STAYED THERE FOR a few years, I gained great respect for the American farmer.

My family moved several times while I was growing up—finally staying put in Loma Linda, California—and my parents instilled in me a strong sense of duty, service, and patriotism. Joining the military seemed like a logical choice.

After graduating from high school, I attended the University of Southern California on an Air Force ROTC scholarship, intending to be an architect in the Air Force. Then, while I was at college, I enjoyed a few flights in different Air Force aircraft, finally getting a ride in a UH-1N *Huey* helicopter. I knew instantly that was what I wanted to fly.

I already liked the idea of being able to do a mission that was positive, like the rescue mission, and I was thrilled to find that flying helicopters was so much fun. Flying low, you get a sense of speed and maneuverability, and a scenic view of your environment. I also liked the challenges of learning to fly.

In May 1985, I graduated from college with the professional degree of bachelor of architecture and was commissioned into the Air Force. I then went on to receive my master's degree in international relations, with an emphasis in defense and strategic studies.

I left for Fort Rucker, Alabama, to attend helicopter training, honored to be the seventh woman to fly helicopters in the Air Force. After flight school, I was assigned to Ramstein AB, West Germany, as a VIP helicopter pilot flying the UH-1N helicopter, and was in the 58th Military Airlift Squadron working as a scheduler and aircraft commander.

This was really the only time in my career that I got to do the rescue mission that had been my original flying goal. During this assignment, my crew and I were awarded the Military Airlift Command Aircrew of the Year award for our involvement in rescue flights during the Ramstein air show disaster in 1988.

The Ramstein incident was one of the world's worst air show disasters. It took place in front of an audience of 300,000 on August 28, 1988, at the U.S. air base in Ramstein. Sixty-seven spectators and three pilots were killed, and 346 spectators were seriously injured in the resulting explosion. The disaster was the result of an aircraft collision when the Italian Air Force display team was performing their maneuvers.

American helicopters and ambulances provided the quickest recovery efforts for all the injured people. Within minutes of the accident, we had made several flights with severely burned spectators to the nearby hospital. It was such a confusing time, we never learned if our passengers survived or not, but I hope we did some good that day.

As a whole, flying in Germany was great. The scenery was beautiful, and flying over castles brought together my love for flying and my enjoyment of architecture.

I married my husband, Larry, while I was at flight school. Though we had met in high school, our paths crossed several times. Larry was stationed in New Mexico when we married, and we hadn't figured out yet how to get the Air Force to let us live in the same place. This

Lida's official photo as an Air Force colonel, 2009.

factor turned out to have a large impact on both of our careers. With both of us flying helicopters, we found that it was actually harder to get assignments together, since it was against Air Force regulations to be in the same unit. Thankfully, when I got orders to Germany, Larry also got an assignment flying H–53 helicopters at a nearby base.

My next assignment was to Eglin AFB, Florida, as chief of the Airborne Test Review and Safety Board, and the 40th Test Squadron Helicopter flight commander. I also flew the UH-1N helicopter in support of developmental test missions and I found time to finish a master's degree in business administration from the University of West Florida. My general trend toward education continued to grow.

While I was in testing at Eglin, the United States went to war with Iraq. My squadron supported Operation *Desert Shield/Storm* by flying test missions and working

on new munitions programs. We accelerated many test programs to ensure that Air Force personnel overseas had the best equipment and munitions possible.

We waited until our tour at Eglin to start a family. My daughter, Elise, and son, Bryce, were both born while I was still flying. I was one of the first Air Force women to fly helicopters while pregnant, and found no adverse effects when flying during the early months of my pregnancy. I was watched closely to make sure all went well, and felt good about adding a positive step to opportunities for women in flying.

It became harder and harder for Larry and me to get orders together, and it became evident that we both couldn't remain on active duty and raise a family the way we wanted to. Although we thoroughly enjoyed our active-duty time, all the terrific missions we flew, and the great assignments, we decided to get out of the active-duty Air Force and join the Air Force Reserve in 1994. We were both assigned to Air Force Special Operations Command at Hurlburt Field, adjacent to Eglin AFB. This command focuses on the covert insertion and extraction of the military's special operations forces behind enemy lines. I was thrilled to be involved in this mission area. Reserve jobs are typically part-time, mostly on weekends, but I have worked full-time in the Reserves over the past several years. Larry and I both have deployed with the active-duty units we support and, most recently, I deployed for three months to Southwest Asia, supporting special operations, and then for five months as the first commander of Africa Command's 404th Air Expeditionary Group, supporting conventional and special operations on that continent.

We have since had two more kids, our son, Karlyle, and daughter, Siena. In between my reserve job and raising my kids, I also finished a doctorate in education from the University of West Florida. This degree has also been handy in childrearing, working on my children's educational needs, and also provides me the opportunity to teach architecture history at a local college, Northwest Florida State College.

The Air Force Reserve provides me the flexibility to be both a good parent and military member. I look forward to the rest of my time as a mother, wife, and Air Force officer. I am also very grateful for all the support

Mom to Mom:

If you do it right, being a mom is the most confusing, challenging, difficult, frustrating experience in the world. If you do it well, being a mom can also be the most simple, sensible, rewarding, and enlightening experience. The hard work you put into your children at a young age to give them strong values pays off exponentially as they grow into worthy contributors to our world.

and cooperation that my husband, Larry, has given me in continuing an Air Force career, and working with me to raise really great kids.

The most important thing I have learned as a military officer and pilot is that we do nothing in life on our own. We need to work together to be successful. The military is effective due to its emphasis on strong teamwork and integration of differing forces and capabilities. I think that this applies to everything we do, from family life, to community service, to efficient business relations, to conducting military operations.

I would like my children to appreciate the great freedoms and opportunities that we have in this country. I hope they can all do what will make them happy in their lives. Whatever they do, I know they will do it well. They have always been supportive of what I have done, even when it meant I had to be far away for several months at a time. They are full of energy and promise, and they make me proud.

. . . .

Take the high road and do the right thing.

. . . .

Rank:	Air Force Colonel
Years Served:	25
Current Military Status:	Air Force Reserve
Number of Children:	4

Bonnie (Cox) Paquin

C-130 *Hercules*

AT THE AGE OF FIFTEEN, I ALREADY DREAMED OF FLYING AIRPLANES. AS THE DAUGHTER OF A BAPTIST PREACHER WITH THREE OTHER children, extra money for flight lessons was not something I thought I could ask for. I joined my high school's Air Force JROTC program, and took orientation rides in a helicopter, an Air Force C-130, a sailplane, and a Cessna 172. Instantly, my dream expanded to include attending the Air Force Academy, and I will never forget the day I received my appointment.

I was at school and saw my dad in the hallway. Something was different...He wasn't supposed to be there. He came to personally deliver a letter to me from the Air Force Academy. With my dad beside me, I opened the letter. I had been accepted!

Less than two months after arriving at the Air Force Academy, I doubted my decision to be there, as I was very homesick for family. But I didn't quit, didn't give up, and I looked toward that goal of reaching the sky!

The academy helped me realize what I was capable of, both physically and emotionally. Tossing my hat in the air on graduation day with the rest of my class was truly a proud moment for me. It had been a long road to get there, a long road to survive.

Pilot training took me to Vance AFB, Oklahoma—another big challenge, since flying airplanes wasn't as easy as it looked. The environment was foreign to me, it took me a long time to get comfortable being in control of an airplane, and I wondered if I had chosen the right path. My graduation from flight school in June 1997 was probably the most rewarding moment of my career.

For my first assignment at Little Rock AFB, Arkansas, I flew the C-130 for almost four years, responsible for supervising a small crew while flying worldwide tactical airdrop, passenger and cargo airlift, presidential support, and combat-support missions. In those four years, I deployed to Germany, Saudi Arabia, Kuwait, and Kenya.

During flight training, I had started dating a Navy pilot, Chuck Paquin, who was also going through flight school. I realized what a wonderful man I had found the day he took me out on my first-ever ride on his brand new motorcycle, and he let me sit on it by myself. I had never been on a motorcycle before, and as I jumped off the bike, it fell over. I was mortified, but he didn't blink an eye. He picked up the bike, checked out the fresh scratch I'd just put on his new bike, and said, "It's no big deal." I knew then it was a big deal, and I felt awful, but more importantly, I knew that if I'd found a man who could be that patient and understanding, I needed to keep him in my life.

Keep him I did, and I thank the Lord he still has patience after eight years of marriage and a bunch more "scratches" I've made along the way.

In 1997, Chuck graduated from pilot training a few months after I did, and left for his first assignment at NAS Whidbey Island, Washington. Between his deployments in the EA-6B *Prowler* and mine in the C-130, we managed a long-distance dating relationship for more than two years, and married in December 1999. Even as we walked down the aisle, we weren't sure if, when, or how we were going to live together, due to the different assignments we might receive from the Air Force and Navy.

In the spring of 2002, after two years of a long-distance married relationship, we finally received assignments to two different bases in Mississippi—Columbus AFB and NAS Meridian. We bought an eighty-year-old house in a small town between the two. Despite initial

Southwest Airline pilot, Bonnie, with her sons, Sawyer (6 months) and Wade (5 years), July 2008, Anacortes, Washington.

struggles of learning how to actually live together, we made the old house our home. Within six months of finally living together, we learned we were expecting a baby!

I returned to flying just eight weeks after our son, Wade, came into the world. Returning to work was very difficult. I didn't think Wade would be okay without me. I suffered a lot of guilt about going to work and spending many hours away from him each day. Also, I was constantly worried about not making it home each night from flying, due to weather or aircraft maintenance. Flying became very stressful for me.

As Wade turned a year old, our Mississippi assignments that had kept our family together neared an end. I had served my commitment to the Air Force, and I decided to leave the military in order to keep our family together.

Chuck's next set of orders were to Lemoore, California, and shortly after we arrived, he deployed for a six-month cruise on an aircraft carrier. While I enjoyed extra time at home with my family, I found myself looking toward the sky, longing to be back at work, and longing to fly.

I realized that I was a mom, wife, AND a pilot. Without flying, I was missing a whole piece of me. While Chuck was gone on the cruise, I began working on civilian flying qualifications, and eventually was hired by Southwest Airlines. I finished first officer training in the B-737, and began flying for Southwest in the fall of 2006.

We recently moved our family again—the fourth time in five years—and also had our second child, a son, Sawyer. I am currently on maternity leave from Southwest, and in a few months I will return to flying.

My husband is also preparing to deploy overseas on another aircraft carrier for six months. Thankfully, my mother is coming to help care for my children during my husband's absence, so I can return to flying. My oldest son, Wade, is sad to see him go, and our new baby may not know the difference, but his father will have missed most of the first year of his life. Wade said he wanted to fly his daddy's airplane. I told him Daddy's airplane, the EA-6B *Prowler*, wouldn't be flying when he was old enough to fly, since it is being replaced by a different airplane in a few years. I laughed when he said, "Well, I guess I can just fly your 'girl' airplane, then." So, I'm preparing Wade for my own absence, when I return to fly my girl airplane—the Boeing 737—and wonder if all those men I fly with know it's a "girl" airplane.

The greatest military challenge for me was not a single event, battle, or fearful moment, but an overall uphill struggle that I constantly fought as a woman in the military. As a woman, you're constantly judged and almost held to a different standard. You have to work to overcome the fact that some men don't want you there, and many folks believe you might be there just because you're a woman...because of a quota that was filled. You don't get the benefit of the doubt. You have to work harder to prove that you have achieved a certain position or rank based on merit. For some reason, men start out with the God-given right to be there. With women, "we're not quite sure about that yet; we'll have to wait and check and see if women really deserve to be there."

> ## Mom to Mom:
> The thing that surprised me the most about being a mom is the very different kind of love, and overwhelming amount of love, that you can have for another human being—only a mother can understand.

Sometimes, I felt like I had to work twice as hard to be considered half as good

I'd like to say I wish I'd known how hard it would be to have a family while continuing military service and flying airplanes, but if someone had told me along my way, I wouldn't have listened. I wanted to fly airplanes, and nothing was going to stop me! So to those women who want to fly, go for it! You'll just figure it out along the way. It's a challenge, a lot of work, and sometimes a sacrifice, but then, aren't some of life's most wonderful things made out of these?

I want to be an example to my children of what having a dream and making it happen is about. Whether it is aviation or something completely unrelated, I want them to find something that they want, something that really makes them happy, and go for it. While they search, their father and I will do our best to instill the moral foundation that will help them to make the best choices along that journey.

> "To most people, the sky is the limit. To those who love aviation, the sky is home."
> —Anonymous

Rank:	Air Force Captain
Years Served:	9
Current Military Status:	Separated
Number of Children:	2

Sharon (Cleary) Preszler

EC-135 *Stratolifter*, C-21 *Learjet*, F-16 *Fighting Falcon*

M Y LOVE OF FLYING STARTED WHEN I WAS FIVE YEARS OLD. I FLEW TO ENGLAND WITH MY MOM AND SISTER TO VISIT FAMILY. THRILLED BY flying, I told my mom I wanted to be a stewardess when I grew up. My mom was forward-thinking for her time and suggested that I might become a pilot instead. I didn't know what a pilot was, but once she explained it, I knew that was what I would be.

During a summer break from college, I attended Air Force training at Reese AFB in Texas where I got my first flight in a jet, the T-37 *Tweet*. I loved the aerobatics and spins, and I knew then that I *needed* to fly jets.

In 1986, I graduated from college. At the time, aviation slots were very limited for women. Instead of a pilot slot, I got a navigator slot. A navigator is one of the aircrew, and operates communications and navigation gear. I attended navigator training, and selected the EC-135 aircraft at Offutt AFB, Nebraska. Although I enjoyed being a navigator, in my heart I still wanted to be a pilot. So, I got my private pilot's license and applied for Air Force pilot training. I was accepted, graduated in 1992, and flew the C-21 *Learjet* at Andrews AFB, Maryland.

I had been in my C-21 squadron for nine months when the combat exclusion law was repealed. Unbelievably, I was selected to be the first active-duty woman to fly the F-16 *Fighting Falcon*, known to Air Force pilots as the *Viper*. INCREDIBLE!

Six months later, when I started F-16 training, women flying fighters was still very controversial. There were definitely male pilots in the squadron who didn't want me there, but others were willing to give me a chance. My first instructor pilot and my flight commander were

awesome; they did their best to make me feel comfortable and allow me to focus on flying.

The leadership, however, was concerned about their first woman F-16 pilot. My first week in the squadron, my squadron commander called me into his office and told me he had to report weekly to the four-star general on my progress. The high level of scrutiny I was under compounded my stress. Scrutiny or not, I loved the F-16. I still remember the engine transitioning through all five stages of afterburner on my first takeoff. Sitting under that bubble canopy, you can see everything and feel like you can do almost anything.

After training, I transitioned to my first operational F-16 squadron, the 22nd Fighter Squadron, the Stingers, in Germany. I was a little unsure what kind of reception I would get. My husband, James, and I showed up at the squadron where our sponsors warmly welcomed us, and a number of people were willing to give me a chance. After a few months, I felt at home in the Stingers, and this truly was my best Air Force experience.

Squadron flying was simply amazing—flying at 500 feet over the German countryside, dogfighting with F-4s. I traveled a lot, participating in exercises as well as combat operations over Iraq during Operation *Northern Watch*.

In 1997, I left Germany and went back to the 61st Fighter Squadron at Luke AFB in Arizona as an instructor pilot. Even though I was the only woman instructor in nine squadrons, I didn't feel extra pressure. I had become more comfortable in the F-16 and with my role as one of the few women fighter pilots.

In 1999, during my tour with the Top Dogs at Luke, my aircraft had a complete electrical failure that had

Family photo in front of 79th Fighter Squadron jet, December 2005.

never before happened in the F-16. I was able to land the plane, but the brakes malfunctioned due to the loss of electrical power, and the jet didn't slow down.

As I sped down the runway without brakes, I realized the arresting hook wasn't working either. With the end of the runway and a concrete drainage ditch swiftly approaching, I pulled the ejection handle and ejected about 100 feet into the air.

I got about half a swing in the parachute and hit the ground pretty hard. I looked up to see the jet accelerate, jump the perimeter fence, and finally stop in a farmer's field. Though bruised, I walked away with only a cracked tailbone and was up flying eleven days later.

Despite the accident, the tour at Luke was another great assignment. I enjoyed being a mentor to women pilots going through training, and demonstrating to male students that women were part of the fighter community they were joining.

My high school sweetheart, James, and I had married while I was in college. He has been incredibly supportive—I couldn't have asked for a better partner to walk with me on this journey. James and I moved twelve times during my Air Force career. Along the way, he managed to find new jobs, and get his college degree and private pilot's license.

In 2000, I transferred to Leavenworth, Kansas, to attend staff college. James and I decided that after sixteen years of marriage, it was finally time to have a child. This was a great opportunity, since I wouldn't be flying for the next few years. I became pregnant just before we left Leavenworth for Colorado Springs and another non-flying job—North American Aerospace Defense Command (NORAD), a very interesting but extremely busy job, especially after September 11, 2001. Our son, Collin, was born in December 2001.

In 2004, we moved to Shaw AFB, North Carolina, and I returned to the F-16. Soon after we arrived at Shaw, Collin was diagnosed with acute lymphocytic leukemia. I had never been so scared in my life as when the doctor told me.

Collin was in and out of the hospital constantly over the next three years, for treatment that included regular spinal taps and chemotherapy. We were happy when the chemo slowed down to once a month! Through it all, we received great support from our family, friends, and especially our Air Force family. Collin has now received a clean bill of health. Despite all he has been through, he is a wonderful boy—healthy, funny, smart, caring, very empathetic, and happy.

I retired from the Air Force in 2006, and decided to fly for Southwest Airlines, which I dearly love. I am based out of Phoenix, and work about fourteen days each month. I can schedule my trips around Collin's schedule, which allows me to be more involved in his day-to-day activities.

I have wonderful memories of the Air Force—great friends and amazing flying, especially in the F-16. The military taught me discipline and gave me the confidence to handle crises. All that training came in handy when Collin became ill.

Hopefully, Collin has learned from our example to live his life "half full" versus "half empty." We hope to teach him the skills to be a happy person, live his life to the fullest, and try his best at anything he tackles.

There were lots of times when Collin was sick that we were scared. The treatments were painful, and the medicine made him feel "yucky." We tried to teach him about being brave. For us, being brave is doing what you need to do even when you are scared. I would be lying if I said I was never scared flying the F-16, but being a fighter pilot was something I wanted to do, and I wasn't going to let anything hold me back. Hopefully, Collin will find something he enjoys as much, and have the courage to pursue it.

Mom to Mom:

The most rewarding thing about being a mom is watching your helpless baby grow into a happy, independent, and thoughtful person, and knowing that you helped him become who he is.

Bravery is overcoming your fears.

164

Lori (Edinger) Rasmussen

RC-135 *Rivet Joint*

IN A SMALL TOWN IN DELAWARE, I GREW UP IN A PRETTY TYPICAL CATHOLIC FAMILY, WHERE EDUCATION AND CHARACTER WERE EMPHASIZED on a daily basis. My mother was a stay-at-home mom and worked tirelessly to make sure all of her children were well-behaved and respectful. My father was a chemist who drove into us the importance of hard work and determination.

When the time came to apply to college, I really wanted to go to the University of Colorado, but the expense of out-of-state tuition forced me to research other ways to fund my dream.

I first started to think about the military merely as a means of paying for college. Never one to turn from a challenge, I announced to my parents that I was going to apply to the U.S. Air Force Academy. They were shocked at first, but incredibly supportive.

I was initially rejected from the academy, but just two weeks before my high school graduation, while I was waiting tables at a local restaurant, my father came in and sat at my table holding a large envelope. I knew right then that my life would be forever changed. I ripped open the envelope—I had been accepted to the academy and would be heading to basic training within a month! From that day forward, I NEVER hesitated a moment, and I never looked back.

At the academy, I learned more about myself than I ever thought possible. My attraction toward aviation rose out of the flying history imbued in us cadets. You couldn't turn a corner without seeing a memorial or statue of the men and women who sacrificed all for the good of aviation. I don't think it was necessarily a love of flying that led me to apply to flight school, but rather a love of doing the Air Force's primary mission, and the desire to lead others. I also met my best friend, Reid, at the academy, who, many years later, became my husband.

After graduation, I headed to flight school at Laughlin AFB in Del Rio, Texas. Flight school was one of the toughest years of my life. I had no prior flying experience, and the strict environment of flight school took a while for me to adjust to. I was one of those students to whom flying did not come naturally, but I possess fierce determination and never give up. I earned my wings, and an assignment to fly the RC-135 reconnaissance aircraft in Omaha, Nebraska.

RC-135s turned out to be a great assignment. I blossomed as a pilot, and I loved the mission. I deployed to numerous places, including Japan, Saudi Arabia, Turkey, Crete, England, and Wales.

During all of this, my relationship with Reid continued to grow. A few months after I arrived in Omaha, Reid proposed. He, however, was stationed in Fayetteville, North Carolina, at Pope AFB, where he flew the A-10. We got together about once a month, and married in March 1999, but we weren't actually stationed together until three years later.

Reid and I managed to get an assignment together as flight instructors at Columbus AFB, Mississippi. I was assigned the T-37 trainer, and Reid was assigned the T-38. At first, I was not thrilled with this assignment, but it would become one of the most memorable experiences of my life.

When I learned I was pregnant, I had to stop flying, since Air Force regulations prohibited me from flying an ejection-seat aircraft. It amazed me how quickly

Lori with her boys, Foster and Emmett, 2010, Montgomery, Alabama.

flying took a back seat to impending parenthood. Up until this time, flying was the primary focus of my life. To shift gears so dramatically was a shock, but something I took as a huge blessing. Our son, Foster, was born in October 2003, and instantly became the joy of our lives. I really didn't know what to expect when I became a parent, but Reid and I had been a team for so long already, and our approach to parenting was no different.

I returned to flying status seven weeks after Foster was born. I wasn't sure how easily I would regain my flying skills after being out of the cockpit for nearly a year.

Luckily, it came back quickly, and I was soon flying with students again.

My commander at the time, Lieutenant Colonel William Milloniq, gave me an incredible opportunity to be a flight commander. I was extremely concerned about pulling my weight among my fellow instructors. Not only was I the only female, and in command of a flight (a unit) of eight instructors and fourteen students, but I was also the only mom.

On average, I worked twelve to thirteen hours a day. By the time my term as flight commander was over ten months later, Reid and I were exhausted, and I knew I needed a break. Despite this, it truly was the best job I ever had.

In 2004, the Air Force was trying to cut back on personnel, and an opportunity for an early out presented itself to me. For the good of our family, Reid and I thought I should take it. Two pilots on active duty were just too much. I decided to take a reserve non-flying job with the Pennsylvania Air National Guard, working primarily part-time and on weekends.

After his one-year tour to Korea, and another five-month deployment to Afghanistan in 2006, Reid decided that he, too, needed a break from deploying and constantly being away from our family. So, he also decided to join the Pennsylvania Guard; however, he would serve in a full-time active-duty position but in a non-flying role.

I know it was a very hard decision for Reid to take a non-flying job, but like everything else he does in his life, he put our family first, and did what was best for our children. Just before we moved to Pennsylvania, the Guard unit also offered me a full-time non-flying job, as well. Although I am not flying, I am thankful to still be part of the Air Force team.

My Air Force career has been studded with highlights. My time as an RC-135 aircraft commander is definitely something I will never forget. However, being selected as a flight commander during my flight instructor tour has been by far my most rewarding experience. That job allowed me to impact other officers' lives, and really affected how their aviation careers began.

My time in the military has reinforced in me to stay strong and not give up when times get tough. I remember going through basic training and flight school and being exhausted every day. Little did I know that learning how to operate on such little sleep would help me in my flying career, and even more so in my life as a parent.

Reid and I now have another addition to our family—our son, Emmett, born in March 2006. My children are my life, and I am so grateful to be blessed with both of them!

I hope to raise them to be good people who are kind, compassionate, and who understand the importance of hard work. I want to teach them the value of family, and to have self-confidence in everything they do. I also want them to be thankful for everything they have, including this wonderful country we live in.

I know that by giving them love, discipline, and a listening ear, they will develop into men of character and integrity.

Mom to Mom:

The thing I love most about being Mom is understanding my own pure capacity for complete and total love. I have never felt so vulnerable, or as loved, as I do as a mother! My heart is completely outside me and lives in my wonderful two little boys!

I am proud of being a pilot, but I will always be more proud of being a mom.

Rank:	Air Force Major
Years Served:	13
Current Military Status:	Air National Guard (Active Duty)
Number of Children:	2

Louise (Sabelström) Reeves

KC-135R *Stratotanker*

I WAS BORN IN 1963 IN SAN FRANCISCO, CALIFORNIA. MY PARENTS, SWEDISH IMMIGRANTS, TAUGHT MY BROTHERS AND ME TO SPEAK Swedish fluently. We loved going to Sweden during the summers to visit relatives, and those long flights sparked my interest in aviation.

Initially, I wanted to be a flight attendant. However, after seeing the character, Colonel Steve Austin, on the TV show—*The Six Million Dollar Man*—fly a T-38, I thought it would be incredible to fly. When I saw that his love interest on the show, Farrah Fawcett, also flew the T-38, my plans for the future changed—I dreamed to become an Air Force pilot, fly the T-38, maybe even become an astronaut.

I attended the University of Colorado, joining the Air Force ROTC program. Since I had no military background, it was all new to me, and I had my doubts about staying in ROTC. Additionally, getting a pilot slot as a female was incredibly difficult in the early 1980s.

After my freshman year, though, I was awarded a three-year Air Force scholarship. That, along with my parents' encouragement, kept alive my dream of becoming an Air Force pilot. I graduated with an aerospace engineering degree and a commission as a second lieutenant, but not with a pilot slot or what I considered a desirable first assignment.

Assigned to the 544th Strategic Intelligence Wing at Strategic Air Command in Omaha, Nebraska, I found the job very frustrating and unsatisfying. The only fun part was going over to Europe once a year for a NATO exercise.

I met my husband, Sam, during my first exercise. I'd been a second lieutenant three months, and he had been in the Air Force for twelve years, flying B-52s and RC-135s as an electronic warfare officer. Sam supported

my dream to attend pilot training from the beginning, and I still have the framed T-38 trainer picture he gave me. He had written on the mat, "Go for it!"

I had started flying lessons in college and, as I prepared to apply for Air Force pilot training, I resumed flying lessons. Finally, after applying for pilot training three times, I was selected—two weeks after marrying Sam. Off I went to Texas alone.

Overall, I enjoyed flight training and was the only woman in my class of mostly Air Force Academy graduates—a good group of guys. I think having had some active-duty experience made the training much less stressful. My aircraft choices upon graduation were limited if I wanted to get a joint-spouse assignment with Sam. I chose the KC-135R tanker aircraft at Griffiss AFB in Rome, New York, and Sam went back to the B-52 there for his final Air Force assignment.

Shortly after I arrived at my squadron in 1990, Operation *Desert Shield* kicked off, so I deployed to Muscat, Oman. I spent more than four months living in a tent, and flew a refueling mission the first night of *Desert Storm*. It was a great experience, and I thoroughly enjoyed being there. Fortunately, Sam didn't deploy, which was extremely helpful since his fourteen-year-old daughter lived with us. That first Gulf War changed tanker operations, in ways that resulted in more frequent deployments.

Over my next four years flying tankers at Griffiss, and then four years of the same at Grand Forks AFB, North Dakota, I truly got to see much of the world—Oman, United Arab Emirates, Saudi Arabia, Turkey, the Azores, Greece, Spain, England, Japan, Alaska, France, and Panama. I loved the flying and the travel! I always took the opportunity to see and experience each country. The

Louise providing a "How To Become a Pilot" presentation to her son Hunter's kindergarten class, March 2005.

shopping was awesome, too, and I had a big cargo plane to bring home all my unique purchases.

Sam retired after our tour at Griffiss, and next I received orders to an air-refueling squadron and then an operational support squadron in Grand Forks, North Dakota. We had our son, Grayson, while there. Although the operational support squadron job was a flying job, I had the flexibility to take shorter trips away from home.

Sam and I had decided that when he retired, he would stay home with our children instead of pursuing a second career. He was a great stay-at-home dad, and had lots of experience since he had three daughters before we married. That made going back to work and traveling easier for me.

After my tour at Grand Forks, I needed a staff job to get promoted. I worked in Air Force test and evaluation for the next seven years, first in Albuquerque, New Mexico, and then at Edwards AFB, California. While at Albuquerque, I had my second son, Hunter. The test job allowed me the flexibility to travel, but also the option to stay home if I wished. Although this was a staff job, I still flew the KC-135, flying developmental test missions with test pilots, and was in charge of around-the-world operational tests for a major avionics upgrade. It was probably the most rewarding job I had in the Air Force. I was gone for occasional one-month stints during different test events, but the kids were three and five years old by then. I consider myself very lucky that the timing of upgrades, deployments, and children ended up working out so well. I nursed both boys for months, taught both of them to speak Swedish fluently, ski expertly, and swim. On the professional side, I did not achieve the rank of lieutenant colonel, but that was a sacrifice I was willing to make to ensure enough time with my family.

169

In 2005, I retired from the Air Force, and we moved to New Mexico. I now fly for AirTran Airways in Atlanta, Georgia, as a first officer on the 737-700 and love it. The commute from New Mexico to Atlanta hasn't been too bad. I bid three- to four-day trips that start in the afternoon on the first day and finish early enough to commute home the day my trip ends. I actually have more time with my family than if I had a nine-to-five desk job.

I will likely delay upgrading to captain, because I don't want to lose the quality of life that I have right now with my family. There are too many soccer games, baseball games, and school events to attend. I like the variety of the lifestyle, the travel, the airplanes, and, of course, the landings. I feel very fortunate that I have a husband and sons who support my job and make it work for me.

I think military flying is the way to go! Although military pilots have to deal with deployments, there are incredible opportunities to travel the world, fly modern equipment, and perform interesting missions. Aviation, and certainly military aviation, requires flexibility and will often take you out of your cultural comfort zone, but you adapt, and, hopefully, enjoy the experience along the way.

Mom to Mom:

The most rewarding thing about being a mom is seeing the result of all of your efforts in creating intelligent, responsible, capable people.

My boys don't think it unusual for their mom to fly. It's all they know. They don't know that few women fly, and they don't think of flying as a gender-specific career, which is fine with me. I don't really think about it that way either. I just do what I enjoy.

I hope to encourage my sons to follow their dreams and not to give up, even when it might be difficult, not after a first, or even a second, defeat. It took me three or four attempts to become both an Air Force pilot and an engineering graduate. I didn't *ever* envision quitting or failing. My dream for my boys is happiness and success in all their endeavors in life!

Don't let initial setbacks keep you from pursuing your dream!

Rank:	Air Force Major
Years Served:	20
Current Military Status:	Retired
Number of Children:	2

Heather Sharp-Schlichting

C-130 *Hercules*

M Y PARENTS TOLD ME I COULD DO *ANYTHING* THAT I SET MY MIND TO. BECAUSE OF THEIR CONFIDENCE IN ME, I NEVER REALLY THOUGHT of becoming a "female" pilot. I just wanted to be a pilot.

I grew up on a ranch in California where my dad was a veterinarian and my mom rode in rodeos competitively. Riding horses almost every day as a child gave me a lot of confidence, and competing in rodeos increased my sense of courage and adventure. In events like team roping, men competed equally with women, so I did not have any sense of gender inequality.

I learned from my mom's example how to be feminine and capable at the same time. When my parents coached my younger brother and me before rodeos, they said, "Someone is going to win; it might as well be you. Get out there and try your hardest." That later translated into, "Someone is going to be a 747 pilot; it might as well be you."

A defining moment came during a high school career day. I told the counselor that I liked to travel and maybe I should be a flight attendant. She asked me, "Why aren't you considering being a pilot?" With that, I came home and told my parents that I was going to be a pilot.

Later that week, I helped my dad issue veterinary health certificates to a load of rodeo stock headed to Japan on a Flying Tigers 747. After we loaded the animals on the cargo deck, I headed up the stairs to the cockpit to ask the pilots what it was like to fly. I still remember the copilot saying, "This job is a piece of cake—pull back, the houses get smaller; push forward, the houses get bigger. Any idiot can do it; just look at our captain here!" They were having a great time teasing each other getting

ready to fly an 800,000-pound airplane to Tokyo. I was hooked.

I came down the ramp and told my dad, "I am going to fly that thing."

At seventeen, I began taking flying lessons, and by the time I graduated from high school in 1985, I had my private pilot's license. I studied economics at Cal Poly in San Luis Obispo, and, during my free time, I got all of my flight ratings, worked as a flight instructor, and did some charter work. Right out of college, I went to work for Ameriflight, a night freight company, flying to remote stations in California and Nevada.

In 1991, I was hired by American Eagle. Two years later, I was living in a crash pad in Queens, New York, with twenty-seven other broke pilots near JFK airport. This was not the glamorous career I had dreamed of.

Fate again would put me in the right place at the right time, and I was introduced to the Nashville Air National Guard. I applied, and started Air Force pilot training in 1994 in Columbus, Mississippi, the only woman in my class. After graduating, I went to C-130 training in Little Rock, Arkansas, where I graduated number one in my class.

I believe God played a hand when I met my husband in 1995, when I mistakenly sat at the wrong table at an event. Jack was a farmer from Illinois. Up to that point, I had focused on my career. Long ago, my dad had told me that who you marry is the most important decision you will ever make. It affects your happiness, health, wealth, family, kids, and every facet of your life. He was right. I knew that I should spend some time and figure out what my values were and what was important to me. So, like

Heather and her sons, Grant (5 years old) and Ryan (2 years old), 2004, on an A320 flight Heather was co-piloting.

all good pilots, I made a checklist and prioritized it. Good father, responsible, sense of humor, honest, and hard worker topped my list.

Jack proposed during a training exercise at the Guard base in Nashville. The entire base knew about the proposal except for me. I was the tail end of a six-ship formation. When we taxied into parking, I saw a fifty-foot banner that read, "Heather, will you marry me?" and, then, in small letters, "*Jack,*" just in case I didn't know who was asking.

About the same time, I was hired by Northwest Airlines as a 747 flight engineer based in Anchorage, Alaska. Jack was eager to move there and experience the last frontier. In addition to flying for Northwest, I continued flying with the Air National Guard in Anchorage.

I flew C-130s with the Tennessee and Alaska Air National Guard for six years. I loved the C-130's versatility and variety of missions. Each day was different, from medical-evacuation flights out of 3000-foot dirt strips in Alaska, to airdrops of supplies and troops over Columbia or Croatia.

I filed my paperwork to get out of the Guard one week prior to 9/11, when my first son, Grant, was two and I was pregnant with my son, Ryan. Being away from home to fly with the airlines and the Guard was proving to be too much. Little kids need their mom to be home more than five days a month. One career or the other would have been okay, but not both at the same time.

We decided that my husband, Jack, would be a stay-at-home dad. He is a wonderful husband and father, and has a terrific sense of humor and laughs when friends call him "the pilot's wife." We have six horses and a black lab, and the boys hardly miss me when I am away, because they are having so much fun.

Because my husband is a Mr. Mom, we get to take the kids with us on long layovers, and they have traveled quite a bit. When Ryan was about two, I was copilot on the A320 and went back to the cabin to check on them before takeoff. I told them I had to go up to the cockpit and go to work. When I made the announcement to welcome the passengers aboard, Ryan was in the back yelling, "Hey, MOM, I want to sit up there with YOU!!"

I love the variety and flexibility of my airline job, and we take advantage of the perks of free airline travel. I asked my oldest son what he wanted to do for his birthday. In true five-year-old logic, he said that he wanted to see the Loch Ness Monster. "All right! We are on our way to Scotland, buddy." Now how many moms get to do that for their kids?

I would be proud to see my kids fly in the military, if that is what they choose to do. I want them to see the world, experience different cultures, and appreciate what we have here at home in the United States.

I want to pass down a legacy of integrity and personal responsibility to them. I also want them to be self-reliant and leaders, but also enjoy the feeling of camaraderie that comes from working with a team of dedicated people.

Most of all, I want them to know that they can do anything they dream of doing.

Mom to Mom:

Being a mom is by far the best experience of my life. There are no words to express how much I love my kids.

Follow your dreams; you really can do anything you set your mind to.

Rank:	Air Force Captain
Years Served:	8
Current Military Status:	Separated
Number of Children:	2

Monica (Holzhauer) Sylla

KC-135R *Stratotanker*

I GREW UP IN NEW JERSEY, A SHY KID AND ALSO AN ATHLETE. I LIKED THINGS THAT WERE ORGANIZED AND PREDICTABLE. NOT SURprisingly, I was attracted to the military and its uniformity and discipline.

When I told my mom I wanted to join the Army, she quickly recommended West Point. Somehow, I ended up at the U.S. Air Force Academy and majored in math and German.

Of all the pilots I know, I am one of very few who did not yearn to be a pilot. However, it was highly frowned upon for a qualified candidate to turn down a slot to pilot training, and you'd end up as a cop or a missileer; so I decided to be a pilot.

I have great memories of learning to fly a T-41 while at the academy with my friend, Lisa. We'd roll down the hallway on our dorm room chairs, pretending to hold yokes on takeoff roll, screaming, "Right rudder! Right rudder!"

I also vividly remember my first solo in the T-41. During my takeoff roll, a voice came over the radio saying, "T-41 status is now stop-launch." In my head I said, "#$%&!; I'm going!" So I went.

Pilot training was challenging and stressful—I felt clueless! Who was "departure" and where was he? I remember standing up for emergency procedures practice. If you blew it, you were grounded for the day. I had to describe the sequence of an ejection into a forest. After I said I would remove my oxygen mask and discard it, the instructor said, "And it comes back and hits you in the face." Not realizing it would still be attached to my harness, I said, "Sir, I will regret that later," which earned a round of laughter. Clueless, but I wasn't grounded.

I met my future husband, Bill, at the academy the summer before my senior year. While I was a rule-enforcing cadet squadron commander, he was a rule-breaking unranked firstie (senior) who was actually having fun as a cadet. I've learned a lot about rules since then. Bill and I were in the same pilot training class at Williams AFB, Arizona, during which we ended up getting married by a justice of the peace in 1991 in an effort to remain stationed together. We were married in the church a year later, which is the anniversary we actually celebrate.

Shortly before we graduated in 1991, we were told the Air Force had trained too many pilots for the available number of aircraft. Some pilots were given aircraft slots, and others were put into a "bank," possibly waiting up to three years to get an aircraft slot. Bill chose a "banked" KC-135R slot and expected to be called back to fly in about two years. I chose to fly the KC-135R tanker at Griffiss AFB in New York and joined the 509th Air Refueling Squadron as a copilot. During that time period, Bill earned his master's degree in physics and also worked at a laboratory.

Once, while stationed at Griffiss, we made a no-notice deployment to Spain to support Operation *Restore Hope* in Somalia. I spent a month in Riyadh, Saudi Arabia, which turned me into what my husband called "an angry woman." I did not enjoy being treated as a second-class citizen. I also flew in southern France, supporting efforts in Bosnia-Herzegovina and Kosovo. The flying there was pleasant, and so were the beaches and wineries.

Bill was called back to fly after two years and once he completed training, we got joint orders to Mildenhall, England. Mildenhall was the only tanker base in Europe, so when anything happened in the European theater,

Monica and husband, Bill, with children Lydia, Evelyn, and Tom in August 2008 at Tom's 7th birthday party.

we were the first to get called. Sometimes we would get home on a Friday night, just to find a message on the machine telling us we were on standby for the next mission.

We found out we were expecting our first daughter, Lydia, during this tour. As soon as I found out I was pregnant, I stopped flying and didn't get behind the yoke again until after maternity leave. When I came off maternity leave a year later, I had no trouble getting back up to speed flying.

Our next set of orders was to Grand Forks, North Dakota, and this would be a non-flying job for me. I remember my last flight before we left England. Only *I* knew it was likely to be my fini (final) flight in the Air Force. I still remember that day like it was yesterday—it was a refueling flight on a clear day with a pleasant crew. The refueling was uneventful, the Swiss Air Force provided

a friendly interception, and my landing was satisfying. I haven't flown since, but reflect often on what a fine farewell I had that day.

Shortly after arriving in Grand Forks, we found out that we were expecting our second child. Bill was assigned to a flying squadron and deployed almost immediately. The experience there for me was difficult—Lydia was one year old, I was pregnant and working full-time, and my husband was gone for eighty-six days in the middle of the Grand Forks winter.

Our second daughter, Evelyn, was born in 1999. Bill and I had decided that we were done moving, and both chose to get out of the Air Force. We agreed to move to Portsmouth, New Hampshire. Years before, we both had been in Portsmouth for aircraft simulator training and thought, "This is the place for us."

Bill got a full-time job with the New Hampshire Air National Guard. I am now a stay-at-home mom, and describe my job as keeping house, doing laundry, cooking, gardening, mowing the lawn, shoveling snow, and, most importantly, nurturing our children. In 2001, less than two years after moving to New Hampshire, our son, Thomas, was born.

I enjoyed the military immensely, although it was difficult after my first child, Lydia, was born, when I had to be separated from her due to my flying duties. I had an overwhelming maternal desire and wanted to be a mom more than I ever wanted to fly a plane. Twice I requested an early separation, and it was denied both times, because there was a shortage of pilots in my age group. A fellow pilot I met offered to me that if I could make it through the academy and pilot training, then I could do anything for two years. He was right, and his words have come in handy on many occasions throughout my life.

The military is a great place for camaraderie, and offers wonderful adventures and amazing experiences. The flying is fun, but sometimes can be very challenging and downright scary.

Many fellow officers and aviators were wonderful mentors. One pilot, for whom I had the most respect, once said we were very much alike. What a compliment that was, until he followed with, "People think we are really smart, but it's only because we keep all of our stupid thoughts to ourselves."

The military taught me that the people who work for you will eventually reflect you. I really learned this lesson at the Air Force Academy when I was a squadron commander. Amazingly, it also holds true in my role as a mother and as a Girl Scout leader.

I hope that my children will treat others the way they want to be treated, and use their talents to make the world a better place.

Mom to Mom:

Being a mom is unconditional love.

Very little can compare to the peace found on a clear night, stars competing for your attention, as you sit in your own private muffled silence, drilling holes in the sky over an empty sea.

Rank:	Air Force Captain
Years Served:	10
Current Military Status:	Separated
Number of Children:	3

Sheila (Connolly) Thompson

C/LC-130E/H *Hercules*

BY THE THIRD GRADE, I WAS SPENDING HOURS IN THE LIBRARY, READING ANYTHING MILITARY-RELATED. I HAD A RED, WHITE, AND BLUE bedroom; wrote the White House in sixth grade to express my nuclear bomb concerns; and even asked my mom for Army men along with Barbie dolls. My mom says she didn't know what to make of me!

I put myself through college at Ohio State University. During my sophomore year, I took time off to join the Air Force Reserve, and came back a trained high-frequency ground radio operator, bearing two stripes and full of determination to become an officer.

On the flight line at Rickenbacker Air National Guard Base, Ohio, stood the most beautiful airplane—I fell in love with the mighty C-130 *Hercules* and longed to fly it one day, but couldn't at the time due to the combat exclusion law. One of the first friends I met at Rickenbacker, Steve Thompson, was a C-130 pilot.

In 1990, during my senior year of college, I found out the Rickenbacker Reserve Flying Squadron was interviewing women aviators to fly their C-130s in a support role. I had been praying about whether to apply for a C-130 pilot or navigator slot and I felt that God was very clear, encouraging me to apply for the navigator position. However, the other pilots in the flying squadron said becoming a pilot was the way to go and I also thought about the possibility of an airline career down the road. So, I ignored God's voice and applied for the pilot slot and, in the meantime, I earned my private pilot's license and waited for word on my application.

I waited and waited to hear something. Finally, when I couldn't take the suspense any longer, I called the military base where I had sent my application and asked what I could do to make my packet stronger for the next board (I assumed I had not been selected). The clerk answering the phone said, "Didn't anyone call you? You made it!" I shouted for joy, elated I was selected for pilot training!

Soon after, I left for Air Force undergraduate pilot training, and felt a huge amount of pressure to excel, although most of it was self-induced. I did not handle the pressure well. I remember flying with the commander of the training program, and he said I had the hands of a pilot, but not the confidence. I ended up leaving pilot training and returned home to my unit without my wings.

A lot of soul-searching followed, and I was definitely disappointed in myself, but I decided I would always look back with regret if I did not pursue another aviation career available to me—navigator.

Thankfully, in 1995, I was given a second chance, this time to attend Air Force undergraduate navigator training. One of my proudest military moments, one year later, was passing my final C-130 training check ride and receiving my navigator wings. I returned home to Ohio and started flying with the 910th Airlift Wing, a reserve squadron in Youngstown.

I became a "reserve bum," meaning I would fly anytime, anywhere, for as long as the unit had the funding. The unit became my extended family, and I loved the camaraderie. The C-130's varied missions, from the tropics to hostile arenas, challenged and amazed me. I flew all over the world, and loved my job so much that I would have done it for free!

By now, I was dating my C-130 pilot friend, Steve Thompson. After becoming engaged, I left my beloved unit and moved east, because Steve transferred to a flying unit in New York. I joined the 109th Airlift Wing in

Sheila and her daughter, Dani, 2009, at the Old Rhinebeck Aerodrome, New York, during a Girls With Wings event.

Schenectady, New York—an adventure in C-130s I had not imagined. Not only did I maintain my airdrop and low-level qualifications, this new unit added yet another dimension to the C-130's ability—landing on skis! The squadron performed regular Air Force missions, but also had the dedicated mission of supporting the National Science Foundation in Antarctica.

Flying in Antarctica was wild! One minute the visibility was unlimited, and the next was a complete whiteout (called a Herbie). During one portion of the season, the roads were so bad that we had to be taken by helicopter to and from our C-130 instead of being bused each day. Another time, our aircraft had to delay takeoff due to penguins on the skiway!

Although we worked six days a week and racked up flight hours, we also experienced many sights—we spent the night at the South Pole, hiked into a 140-foot

crevasse, explored ice caves, and watched seals and orcas. The continent, rich in history and adventure, caused me to reflect on the enormity of God.

Steve and I married in 2000. Five months later, we were expecting our first child. During my pregnancy, immediately after the terrorist attack on September 11, 2001, Steve was activated with his unit. He returned home shortly before our son, Deven, was born prematurely.

Many months later, after my son's health stabilized, I returned to flying. I thought I could "have my cake and eat it too" and did not expect the inner turmoil and incredible guilt I felt from wanting to fly and from being away from my son. We had no family in the area and scrambled for babysitting. I did a lot of soul searching, reminding myself that I had deeply wanted this child, that I had to deliver him a month early or he would have died and then he had quit breathing hours after being born and had to be revived. I prayed and thought about the path I wanted to pursue in my own life and the legacy I wanted to pass down to my little guy. I decided to take a break from flying, adjust to being a mom, and not take time with my son for granted. I thought it would be easier to go back to flying once he was older. Soon after, I took a non-flying, part-time job as an operations officer at another unit, typically working on weekends.

I had my second child, Daniela, who was also premature and again I struggled to balance multiple home and work priorities. A life reality check came when my husband, Steve, and I had to fill out a family care plan required by our military base, declaring who would legally care for our kids in the event we deployed at the same time. In the end, we decided that, to provide more balance to our family, I would transfer to an inactive reserve status after I completed twenty years.

I love being a stay-at-home mom but it is the hardest job I've ever had. It is difficult for me at times when my husband is off flying all over the world, eating great meals, and getting good nights of sleep, and I am home changing diapers, getting spat up on, and not getting enough sleep. Even so, I wouldn't change places with my husband for anything. God opened a door for me to spend lots of quality time with my kids. I realize they grow up fast and that we only have them for a season.

The biggest thing I have learned from my Air Force experience is something a former military instructor said: "In the military, you can never let yourself have a bad day." He went on to explain to not give up if something goes wrong, but to press on because your teammates are counting on you. I want to pass that on to my children, too—even if there are bumps on the road, press on and persevere.

Mom to Mom:

The most rewarding thing about being a mom is the unexpected hugs, the genuine smiles, the hearty laughs, the adorable artwork, the sleeping innocence—feeling complete.

My advice to any woman wanting to fly is to go for it! If you also want to be a mom, be honest with yourself about your priorities. If you want to be a mom and fly at the same time, get a good support system.

One person who has motivated me along my military journey is Dr. Martin Luther King, Jr. I love Dr. King's street sweeper quote, "If a man is called to be a street sweeper, he should sweep streets even as Michelangelo painted, or Beethoven composed music, or Shakespeare wrote poetry. He should sweep streets so well that all the hosts of heaven and earth will pause to say, here lived a great street sweeper who did his job well." I have tried to keep that in mind, from being a ground radio operator on a small reserve base to navigating a cargo plane over Antarctica at 28,000 feet.

I hope to return to flying in some capacity very soon, but if not, I have been truly blessed with two (now healthy) children, a great career, family, and wonderful friends. I am very thankful that, although I didn't listen to God the first time around when selecting to attend pilot or navigator training, God gave me a second chance to fly in the mighty *Hercules* as a navigator—his first choice for me! God is amazing and I can't wait to see what the next adventure will be.

In the military, you can never let yourself have a bad day.

Rank:	Air Force Major
Years Served:	20
Current Military Status:	Air Force Reserve
Number of Children:	2

Marjorie (Clark) Varuska

C-141B *Starlifter*, T-41 *Mescalero*, C-12 *Huron*

I READ AMELIA EARHART'S BIOGRAPHY WHEN I WAS TEN, AND REALIZED THAT WOMEN DO FLY, SOME FOR THE SHEER ADVENTURE OF IT. WALKING home from school, I saw contrails in the sky and wondered where the airplanes were going and who was flying them.

My dad noticed my interest in flying, and asked a colleague of his, a private pilot, to take me up in a small plane. I remember everything—the beautiful sunny day, the preflight and checklist, a very short takeoff roll, and flying above our home in Gainesville, Florida. I wanted to be a pilot, and if I couldn't, I would do something related to flying.

When I was in high school, my dad came across a newspaper article that said women could apply to the U.S. Air Force Academy for the first time. I was leery of joining the military, having grown up in a liberal university town during the Vietnam era, but the chance of getting to fly overcame my reluctance. We sent for the literature and application.

One day in the spring of 1976, I received a telegram from Representative Don Fuqua nominating me for an academy appointment. I entered the academy in June, in the very first academy class with women. I was eighteen, unfamiliar with the military, and naïve about what it meant to be in the first class of women, but I was motivated by the promise of learning to fly.

I credit two people in particular for helping me through those four years—my first roommate, Kathy Bishop, and my brother, Steve. Kathy and I hit it off from the start, although our backgrounds were very different. She was an Air Force brat whose experiences helped me acclimate to the academy and the military quickly. She

is still one of my very best friends. I am also grateful to my brother, Steve, who "toughened me up" in our formative years, which made the transition to a mostly all-male school relatively easy. I actually enjoyed the disciplined way of life, all the "spit and polish," but found the core science academics tough. I graduated in 1980 as a second lieutenant with a degree in geography and an undergraduate pilot training slot to Laughlin AFB in Del Rio, Texas.

Flight school was a year of hard work, lots of fun, and building of close camaraderie with other student pilots. Toward the end of UPT, we filled out our "dream sheets," a form that listed our choices for airplanes and bases. At that time, women could not fly combat aircraft—fighter, attack, reconnaissance, or bombers—which definitely narrowed my choices. But the plane I really wanted to fly was the C-141 *Starlifter*, a four-engine jet transport that flew all over the world conducting real-time missions, during times of peace and conflict. The C-141 always was in the middle of anything happening. Thankfully, I was selected to fly the *Starlifter* at Charleston AFB, South Carolina, stopping first at Altus AFB in Oklahoma to attend C-141 training.

Flying the C-141 was always an adventure and, because of its diverse array of missions, took me to Europe, Africa, Central America, the Middle East, the Far East, and several remote locations hours away from any continent. I flew in many joint exercises, and in support of military operations in Grenada and Beirut.

During my training at Altus, I first met my husband, BJ, who was going through C-141 flight engineer training, also on his way to Charleston AFB. We both ended up in the 20th Military Airlift Squadron and started dating a few months later. Normally, officer and enlisted personnel are

Margie, now a Southwest Airlines captain, is pictured with daughter, Jenny, a Southwest flight attendant.

not allowed to fraternize, but BJ was exceptionally well liked by the squadron commanders, and they knew he was on his way to earning his commission as an officer. We were married in 1984, with many of our squadron mates there to help us celebrate the day.

BJ spent several years in a reserve squadron in Charleston as an officer candidate, while still performing flight engineer duties in the C-141. He had earned a pilot slot, but, most unfortunately, could not pass the physical due to some high-frequency hearing loss from his days working the flight line. He finished his college degree, received a commission as an Air Force second lieutenant, and decided to pursue a career in the intelligence field, a choice that should have dovetailed nicely with my job as a pilot.

This wasn't the case, however, and our next assignments, our first as husband and wife, with daughter Jenny on the way, were to be apart. We felt this was no way to

start our marriage or our family, so BJ resigned his commission to keep us together and provide a stable home life for our family. He has been an extraordinary father, involved in every aspect of our children's lives, and they are better for it.

We had been at Charleston for almost six years when the Air Force Academy asked if I was interested in returning to teach geography and to instruct in the T-41. I jumped at the opportunity!

The academy sponsored my master of arts degree in geography at the University of Wyoming, followed by a four-year tour at the Air Force Academy in Colorado Springs, Colorado. This was a dream job—not only did I teach my favorite geography subjects, I also taught in the cadet flying program and got to come home every night! It was during this time that we decided to have our second child, Mary Rose.

For my next assignment, I opted for a road less traveled, and interviewed for a military attaché position. My flying and geography background helped get me the job of air attaché to the Cote d'Ivoire (Ivory Coast). Training for this position involved intense study of the French language, C-12 transition, security assistance, the Marine Corp's High Risk Personnel Course, and a three-month attaché course covering security measures, protocol and etiquette, area studies, and more. BJ was encouraged to attend the concurrent spouse training, since these assignments involve the entire family. We arrived in Abidjan, Cote d'Ivoire, in June 1995, and enjoyed a one-of-a-kind assignment.

After our two-year stint in Africa, we returned to the States and lived at Bolling AFB, Washington, D.C., where I was part of the Joint Military Attaché School faculty—the same school that trained me as an attaché candidate just a couple of years before. Three years later, in 2000, I decided to retire from the Air Force after twenty amazing years of flying, teaching, and varied other duties, and left at the top of my game.

I was very fortunate to be hired by Southwest Airlines soon after my retirement. Now I enjoy flying B737s for an excellent company with extraordinary people. We live in Cape Canaveral, Florida—our permanent home after so many years as transients.

I have never regretted my decision to retire from the Air Force, although sometimes I long for the camaraderie and purposefulness of the military. It taught me to expect the best from myself as I chart my own way, and to not be afraid of failing. I learned to be confident in my abilities, but also humble, as sometimes I need to swallow my pride, admit I was wrong, and then learn from the experience.

Mom to Mom:
Being a mom is the most important thing I have done in my life.

As much as I enjoyed my Air Force career, being a mom is the most important thing I've done in my life; it fulfills part of me that nothing else does. The thing that surprised me the most about being a mom is how fast the time has gone. One day the kids were in diapers, and now I'm changing my grandkids' diapers.

Our daughters are now grown and pursuing their own dreams, although neither are involved in piloting airplanes. But not to worry—we now have two grandkids who might get bitten by the flying bug!

I hope to pass down to my grandchildren a passion for pursuing their dreams, and to enjoy life wherever it takes them.

"Some people see things as they are and ask, 'Why?' But I dream things that never were and ask 'Why not?'"

—George Bernard Shaw (paraphrased)

Rank:	Air Force Lieutenant Colonel
Years Served:	20
Current Military Status:	Retired
Number of Children:	2

Shannon Yenchesky

KC-135R *Stratotanker*

'M NOT YOUR TYPICAL PILOT PROTÉGÉ. I WAS BORN IN 1968 WHILE MY FATHER, A CAREER AIR FORCE OFFICER, WAS IN VIETNAM. MY MATERNAL grandfather was a career Marine Corps aviator who flew in World War II. As part of a military family, I was constantly exposed to the many facets of military life, but, despite my family background, I was not particularly interested in joining the military, or becoming a pilot, as I approached graduation from high school.

Throughout my childhood, my parents placed tremendous emphasis on education, and tried to point me and my older sister toward career and professional opportunities opening to women in the 1980s. High on my parents' list were the Air Force Academy and Air Force ROTC. My older sister ultimately won a four-year Air Force ROTC scholarship. I followed a year later with an appointment to the Air Force Academy.

During my senior year at the academy, I got the aviation bug! I enrolled in a flight introduction course to help me better understand the flying component of the Air Force. By the end of the second week, I realized the opportunity in front of me was a once-in-a-lifetime adventure. Piloting wasn't just a macho sport. It was as much a mental challenge as a physical one.

Three months before graduation, I changed my career plans from bioenvironmental engineering to aviation. Six months later, I found myself in undergraduate pilot training at Williams AFB in Phoenix, Arizona, experiencing the thrill of my life.

Shortly after beginning flight training, I met my future husband, Dan, a fellow student. We knew that we had little chance of getting stationed at the same location once we completed flight training unless we were married. Therefore, we shortened our courtship, and, the day after graduation from pilot training, we exchanged wedding vows.

Both Dan and I chose to fly the KC-135R tanker aircraft. Our first flying assignment as "Baby-Copilots" landed us at McConnell AFB in Wichita, Kansas. We were assigned to the same squadron but different flights. This allowed us to go on overseas deployments to the same location. Toward the end of our first tour at McConnell, we decided to start a family.

Nine months after our first child was born, we managed to get a joint assignment to Mildenhall in England. England and continental Europe are challenging, exciting places to fly. Each country has different rules and procedures, the language can sometimes become a barrier, and most missions are operational. Flying the KC-135R during this tour was like running on a treadmill—the mission never stopped! We were constantly responding to some worldwide event.

Many times, I handed off my daughter at base operations to my husband after he landed, so that I could begin my mission planning and go fly. One minute I'm speaking in code to the airspace manager, a few hours later I'm making pancakes for my baby! To this day, I still miss the fast-paced rhythm of European flying.

While in England, I upgraded to instructor pilot, and spent two years as the squadron flight safety officer. These were my two favorite jobs in aviation, and therefore my best two years in the Air Force! I also enjoyed being a mom, and wanted more children. Happily, we welcomed our second daughter into our family. Once we decided to have children, though, our lives became

Family photo under the wing of a KC-135R at the 128th Air Refueling Wing in Milwaukee, Wisconsin, in May 2005. The base hosted a military display in conjunction with Armed Forces Week. Pictured are Shannon and husband, Dan, with daughters Laura (8), Heather (5), and Gretchen (2).

extremely complicated with trying to coordinate our careers. We decided to prepare to get out of the Air Force.

I earned my air transport pilot and flight engineer ratings, and sent applications to the airlines. United Airlines hired me, and my husband was offered a part-time pilot job in the Wisconsin Air National Guard. Our plan was for him to stay home with the children while I was on the road with United. In July 2001, we separated from active duty.

During the next few months, we witnessed several life-changing events: first, the attack on the World Trade Center towers on 9/11, then my husband's unit was activated, and then United Airlines went bankrupt. It might sound like our lives took a turn for the worse. In fact, just the opposite occurred. My husband desperately wanted to participate in any operations to fight the

terrorists. I wanted stability for our young children, and with my husband deployed, I needed to be home. We both got our wishes.

To keep my aviation skills current, I applied for a pilot instructor position with FlightSafety Services Corporation, who held the government contract for all KC-135 academic and simulator training. The company had a site near our home in Wisconsin, and a part-time position was available. By late October 2001, I was offered a job, and, a short time later, we had our third daughter.

The saying, paraphrased from the Rolling Stones, "you don't always get what you want, but you get what you need," certainly applied to my family. After a year of activation, my husband was offered a full-time job with the Air National Guard unit.

The military is his passion. Although I don't share the same zeal, I haven't left it completely. I now serve in the Air Force Reserve, as an admissions liaison officer for the Air Force Academy. I also continue my interest in aviation as a simulator instructor. It's hectic being a soccer mom, room parent, and professional instructor pilot, but I'm thankful to be available for my children. I'm also thankful to my exceptional husband of nineteen years, who has supported me in every aspect of my career.

The biggest lesson I've learned from the military is how to work with others. I was always self-motivated, and quite capable of completing most tasks on my own. However, at the Air Force Academy, and later as an aircraft commander, I learned how to work with others toward a mutual goal, and how to motivate those with different attitudes. It's definitely a life lesson that I utilize almost every day!

I've also learned the importance of doing a job well. My grandmother made a cross-stitch for me that read, "Give the world the best you have, and the best will come back to you." I have always tried to live by that credo. I don't expect my children to follow in my footsteps—I would love it if they did!—but they need to follow their own passion. All I ask of them is to do their best. Right now, that means doing their best in school. If they have a solid foundation in several areas, I believe they will come out ahead of folks who might excel in only one thing.

Mom to Mom:

The thing that surprised me the most about being a mom is how we will manage to pull off this miracle of raising our children without a checklist or instruction manual. I've read lots of guidebooks, highlighted all the appropriate text, and flagged important pages, but none of the text seems to apply to my bright-eyed girls. I'm nervous about passing the flight check at the end, but, like previous flights, have to put past mistakes behind me and focus on the next maneuver!

Plus, they would have gained the confidence that they truly can do, and be, whatever they dream.

When I entered the Air Force, I had every intention of making it a career, with husband and children. I truly enjoyed the experiences and challenges. But after several years of military service, I came to the conclusion you can have it all, but you can't do it all well.

If I didn't have children, I would still be in the active-duty Air Force. But I began to understand how my children would have to make several sacrifices in order for me to maintain my career path. Long separations, numerous moves to different locations, and the constant changes in school systems weighed in my decision. I also saw how I had very little time left over for my husband, or even myself. So leaving was an easy choice, one that I don't regret. Now I'm on a different adventure!

"Give the world the best you have, and the best will come back to you."

—Madeline Bridges

Rank:	Air Force Lieutenant Colonel
Years Served:	20
Current Military Status:	Air Force Reserve
Number of Children:	3

Katharine (Combs) Yingst

T-38 *Talon*, C-130 *Hercules*, T-37 *Tweet*, T-6 *Texan II*

AS AN OFFICER IN THE ARMY, MY DAD TOOK MY FAMILY TO LIVE ALL OVER THE UNITED STATES, AND WE ALSO SPENT THREE YEARS IN GERMANY. Shortly after our arrival in Germany, we met an elegant German woman whom I adopted as my grandmother—I called her Oma. She became a central figure in my life, and in the life of my family. Even after we returned to the U.S., we often visited her in Germany, and she visited us wherever we were stationed.

Once I grew older, I started traveling to Germany by myself during the summer, for extended visits to Oma's house. These early trips fueled my love of airplanes and airports, and my desire to be able to go to Germany often. When I was thirteen, I told my mom I might like to be a flight attendant. My mom said, "Why not be the pilot?" She asked if I had ever heard of the Air Force Academy, and she helped me get some information about it.

I worked very hard throughout junior high and high school, achieving straight As. My father cleverly convinced me the academy would accept no less, and I graduated first in my high school class. I entered the academy in 1986, graduated in 1990, then off to pilot training at Williams AFB, Arizona. I earned my wings in 1991, and transferred to my first flying assignment as a T-38 instructor pilot at Columbus AFB, Mississippi.

I loved teaching students how to fly. My favorite part was when the light bulbs began to flicker, and I could see the students starting to grasp a difficult concept we were discussing. The T-38 is a wonderful airplane, and getting my top choice assignment from pilot training was a dream come true.

I married my husband, Andrew, in 1993. I saw him for the first time when he walked into a Christmas party.

I knew I had to meet him, and asked my guy-friend, with whom he arrived, who he was. My friend said, "That's my new roommate." He introduced us, and the rest, as they say, is history.

From the beginning, we tried to avoid separations. Andrew was a T-37 instructor pilot at Columbus when we met—also an instructor pilot. For our next assignment, we had the potential to fly a variety of aircraft—fighters, tankers, bombers, or cargo. For Andrew, the selection was wide open. For me, combat aircraft were just beginning to open to women, so the choices were somewhat limited. We both thought the C-130 aircraft sounded the most interesting, and therefore chose C-130s and flew out of Little Rock, Arkansas.

As we approached the end of our Little Rock tour, our first son, William, was born. Andrew and I realized that continuing to be assigned together would be difficult. Rather than risk separating our family, we opted to leave the active-duty Air Force and transition to the Air Force Reserve.

We both were hired by one of the pilot training squadrons back at Columbus, to be flight instructors for the T-37 trainer aircraft, and, in 2007, we both transitioned to the T-6 trainer. I would work part-time for the squadron, and Andrew actually got a full-time reserve position. Since we had spent so much time at Columbus as instructors, moving back to Columbus felt a bit like going home.

The transition from full-time, active-duty Air Force pilot to part-time reservist was not without difficulty for me, although I have always known it was the right choice for my family, and for my peace of mind. I wanted to be there with my son, to be there in the middle of the night when he was sick, to watch him take his first steps, watch

Katharine and husband Andrew with daughter Allison (then age 6) and son William (then age 8), November, 2007, at Columbus AFB, Mississippi, in front of a T-6 *Texan II*, which Katharine and Andrew both were flying as instructor pilots.

him learn to read, learn to swim, and watch him grow. Reserve duty allows me to do all of these things with my children, and yet I feel I can still pursue my other life in aviation. A few years after we transferred to the reserves, our daughter, Allison, was born.

I have loved flying and airplanes since my first flight to Germany when I was three years old. Being on the flight line at dawn still gives me a rush, and the sheer beauty of flight is indescribable. And yet, watching my small children sleeping is fulfilling on a completely different level. I've found that reserve duty allows me a unique balance. Additionally, it fulfills my needs as a quiet patriot. Being a citizen-soldier means I can continue to contribute and provide a unique service to my country.

There have been many people who have inspired me throughout my career. Two women in my squadron at Little Rock, who had babies before I did, taught me it was possible to work and breastfeed—they carried breast pumps in discreet black bags onto the airplanes, and I'm sure most people just assumed they were part of our required publications bags that we carried.

A memorable moment that stands out is when my girlfriend Lori, another woman pilot, had her final flight in the T-37, just before separating from active duty. At the post-flight party, Lori gave a little speech. Her son was about one year old at the time, and her husband was about to leave for a remote tour in Korea. Her decision to leave active duty, although necessary and family-driven, was not easy for her. Through her tears, Lori said, "And to my girlfriends, you *ROCK*." We all knew what she meant—four of us in that room had babies while trying to continue our flying jobs. Lori knew firsthand how hard it is to juggle schedules, childcare, late-night feedings, breast pumps, and high-pressure workloads over twelve-hour days. Only another mom really knows.

Another influence was a male friend at Columbus, also a reservist with a busy life, a civilian job, three kids, and a wife who had her own business. I asked him one day (when I was especially frazzled and he looked unflappable, as always) how he could juggle it all and still make it work. With a smile he said, "Well, sometimes the juggling just doesn't work." At that moment, I realized that it doesn't always have to be perfect—in fact, frequently it can't be. You can't always make everything nice and neat and tidy when you're working and raising a family. For a trying-to-reform perfectionist with a Type-A personality, this was indeed a revelation!

Recently, a guest speaker at our reserve unit said that if everyone is upset with you—your spouse, kids, civilian employer, and your reserve unit—then you're probably doing it right. It's tough to balance a demanding job with family and home life, even if the job is part-time. But it's well worth it.

For my children—I want them to have happy and stable childhoods, make their own decisions, and chart their own paths in life. I try to follow a saying from my dad, "Do your own thinking." I try to instill this in my children, as well. I am their biggest fan, and I have tried to teach them that I will support them in their endeavors, but I want them to decide for themselves what they believe and what they want to be.

Mom to Mom:

Being a mom is a dream come true.

Appreciate freedom, appreciate being American, and remember to always call your mom.

Rank:	Air Force Lieutenant Colonel
Years Served:	19
Current Military Status:	Air Force Reserve
Number of Children:	2

marine corps

Sarah (Deal) Burrow

CH-53 *Super Stallion*

AVIATION FASCINATED ME AS A CHILD—I OFTEN RODE MY BIKE TO A FIELD NEAR OUR HOME TO WATCH PEOPLE FLY THEIR REMOTE-controlled airplanes. My fascination with aviation grew. At Kent State University in Ohio, I pursued a degree in aerospace flight technology.

During college, I earned a commercial license to fly single- and multi-engine aircraft, and joined the Kent State precision flight team. We didn't win many events, but we enjoyed great experiences and close camaraderie. I still keep in touch with several team members.

Equally fascinated with the military, by my third year of college I interviewed with the Army, took the aviation flight test, and planned to join the Army Reserve. My family, however, convinced me it wasn't a good idea, so I stopped pursuing it.

The following year, I worked on the airport line crew at the Kent State airport. There, Marine Corps recruiters took prospective Marine Corps officer candidates on orientation flights. The recruiters tried to convince me I would make the perfect candidate, but I just figured they were trying to make their quota.

Even so, do you think I would pass up a chance to fly? Nope; I went up with them...and I loved it. I began to spend time with them and the officer candidates. Seeing their motivation and discipline, and the incredible challenges the Marine Corps offered, I decided the Marine Corps was for me.

Because the Marine Corps prohibited women from flying, the selection officer hesitated to sign me up. He made me promise I would consider all the other services before I decided to join the Marine Corps. I did, and

spoke with Army, Navy, and Air Force recruiters. One by one, I crossed each off my list for different reasons, and I became determined to join the Marine Corps.

In May 1992, I graduated from college and received my commission as a second lieutenant. At the time, the combat exclusion law prevented me from flying for the Marine Corps as it only flew aircraft in a combat role; therefore, I decided to become an air traffic controller. However, during the training, the combat exclusion law was repealed and I immediately submitted an application for flight school.

The day I graduated from air traffic control school, I learned that I was selected to be the first woman Marine to attend naval aviation flight training in Pensacola, Florida. Indescribably elated, I started a few months later. During flight school, when the time came to select the aircraft that I would fly, the decision was a no-brainer—helicopters! I was thrilled to receive an assignment to fly the CH-53E helicopter, based in southern California.

Being the first woman aviator in the Marine Corps, as well as in my Marine CH-53E squadron, was challenging and lonely. Some fellow Marines avoided me, some treated me badly, and others acted as if I were one of the guys, which I definitely preferred. Everyone wanted to give me advice, but the best advice I received was from a former platoon commander: "Make sure you know who your friends are."

During my flight training, I met my future husband, Phil, at McGuire's Pub in Pensacola, a popular hangout for naval aviators. Phil had flown his F-14 *Tomcat* in from Norfolk for the night. We started dating and became best friends. About the time I arrived to fly the CH-53 at my

Sarah and her family, 2007, San Diego, California.

squadron in California, Phil left the Navy and became a United Airlines pilot based in Los Angeles.

In 1997, Phil and I married after my first of two deployments to Okinawa, and, looking back, it was easy to juggle our schedules, because we didn't have kids. We now have three boys—nine-year-old twins, Troy and Brandon, and four-year-old Eric.

My last active-duty deployment in 2004 was really tough. My twins were only fifteen months old, and I stayed in Al Jaber AFB in Kuwait for six months. Beforehand, while training and preparing for the deployment, I was gone from home off and on for five months. Phil did great, and, thankfully, my sisters, who lived nearby, helped a lot. His Navy Reserve unit was very supportive and didn't activate him while I was in Kuwait, though he deployed shortly after I returned home.

Being gone for so long was difficult. I felt more like my boys' aunt instead of their mom, as I saw pictures of

them growing and wearing clothes and playing with toys I had not gotten for them. Even more difficult was when I returned home from deployment and my boys cried every time I tried to hold them. I decided to leave the active-duty Marine Corps because I didn't want to be separated for such long periods from my family—a difficult decision, but the right one. I am now a stay-at-home mom, but I still fly the CH-53Es for the Marine Corps Reserve.

Initially, I joined a reserve squadron at Edwards AFB in California, but we moved our family to Michigan to be closer to my family and to live in a small town. I commuted for a few months to Edwards, but when the squadron decommissioned, I joined a squadron in Philadelphia. Within the year, my new squadron deployed to Afghanistan. Two months before deploying, I left home to join the squadron in Philadelphia to start the pre-deployment process. I tried to fly home on the weekends, but, honestly, it was difficult juggling the squadron's operational tempo and my trips home.

We left for Camp Bastion, a British military base in Afghanistan, in April 2009. We flew an assortment of missions, primarily supporting Operation *Enduring Freedom* and the International Security Assistance Force. My squadron had ten CH-53 helicopters and we would fly six- or seven-hour missions each day, hauling troops and equipment, inserting troops at locations within Afghanistan, supporting both NATO and Afghani military tactical missions. We even supported the Afghani national elections.

When I had left home for Afghanistan, I was confident this deployment would be different from the one back in 2004, because my boys were a bit older and more self-sufficient. Boy, was I wrong! This yearlong deployment was much harder than I had anticipated, both personally and professionally. It was painful knowing that I was missing so many of my boys' milestones—Troy's first baseball game, Brandon's Taekwondo tournaments, and my youngest son, Eric, reaching so many milestones, some of which I had missed with the twins.

When I returned home in November 2009, I expected life to go back to normal. However, I have been surprised how much of an emotional adjustment it has been. Out of the blue, I feel like I overreact to a situation, or respond more emotionally than usual. I also have had a very difficult time sleeping through the night. Other squadron mates have mentioned they are experiencing similar reactions. I hope not to deploy again anytime soon. I recently left the squadron and plan on taking some time off to reconnect with my family and explore my future military career options.

Mom to Mom:

The thing that has surprised me the most about being a mom is that I have to repeat myself to my kids...and sometimes several times. As humorous as it sounds, I envisioned giving my kids some guidance, or asking them to do something, and, just like an order I give to Marines who work for me, I expected my boys to respond quickly and without complaining. I've learned a thing or two along the way about the difference between raising kids and leading Marines, and mostly I've learned those things from my three boys.

The highlight of my military career started with the announcement that women could fly in combat, and that the Marine Corps would start training women to fly. Graduating from flight training, receiving those coveted wings of gold, and achieving the status as the first female aviator in the Marine Corps stand tall on my list of highlights.

Recently, I was promoted to lieutenant colonel, an achievement I had not dreamed of, especially when I joined as an air traffic controller. Initially, I assumed the Marine Corps would be a short four-year stop on my way to an aviation career with the airlines. Along my career's journey, I forged great friendships, from college through my years in the military, but nothing beats a good, strong family. A wonderful family and true friends are the keys to a happy life.

I want all three of our boys to be best friends forever, and to know that family will always be there for them. I also want them to know that it doesn't matter if you are a boy or a girl—you can do anything you put your mind to.

If someone says you can't do something, then they have just challenged you to prove that they are wrong.

Rank:	Marine Corps Lieutenant Colonel
Years Served:	19
Current Military Status:	Marine Corps Reserve
Number of Children:	3

Keri (Berman) May

F/A-18D *Hornet*

BORN IN PHILADELPHIA AND RAISED IN TEXAS, I HAD ABSOLUTELY NO MILITARY INFLUENCE IN MY LIFE. JOINING THE MARINE CORPS WAS THE farthest thing from my mind as I entered my senior year of high school. Then I attended a job fair, met the local Marine Corps recruiter, viewed a motivational video, and I was sold! I would've shipped off to boot camp the next day if he'd have let me.

The staff sergeant had other plans for me, however, and he walked me through the ROTC scholarship application process. Thanks to his diligence and dedication, the Marine Corps awarded me a scholarship, and I spent the next four years at the University of Colorado.

As much as I enjoyed my ROTC experience, I never saw myself as a career Marine. After my commissioning in 1994, I went to the Marine Corps officer basic course, fully expecting to serve my four-year commitment and then leave the Corps.

While I was there, I befriended a handful of Marines who all had guaranteed flight slots, and they talked me into taking the flight qualification test. I didn't know anything about flying, and I felt that eight years after flight school was a longer commitment than I wanted to make. I took the test anyway, and as fate would have it, I passed. I accepted a naval flight officer position and left for Pensacola, wondering what a naval flight officer does.

What got me through flight training was not my lifelong dream of flying, but my lifelong fear of failure. I found the competition thrilling and motivating. From the swim training and the obstacle course through the preflight indoctrination and ground school, I took one day at a time and studied like crazy.

I wanted to ace each test and memorize every word in all of the publications. I believed every bit of the hype—that each day could be my last if I performed poorly—and I had not come that far to fail. Once I had my first familiarization flight, I was hooked. I loved flying and immediately felt fortunate to be going through the training. I'll never say flight school was easy or that I did extremely well, but it was hands down the most exciting time of my life. The vast majority of my instructor pilots were professional, dedicated, and highly qualified.

I earned my wings in 1997 and headed out to El Toro, California, to start training as a weapons and sensors officer in the F/A-18D *Hornet.* The F/A-18D training squadron was much like flight school, a canned environment where every move was scripted and if you could memorize well, you did well.

In the year I spent in training, I learned the basics of running the onboard radar and other sensors like the forward-looking infrared radar. As a weapons and sensors officer, you're expected to know all of the minute details about the entire inventory of weapons the F/A-18D can deliver/shoot, so I continued to spend most of my "free" time studying. I still felt tremendous pressure to be perfect on every flight, and even though I had a lot of fun flying, I was always stressed.

Once I finished the training and joined an operational squadron, it took me a while to get used to daily life as a fleet Marine. Flights were still structured with specific objectives for completion, but there was much more of a fraternity feel and I felt my stress level decrease.

Shortly after I joined the squadron, we traveled to Las Vegas for a two-week mass exercise. I was completely overwhelmed by the responsibility of flying with a division of four *Hornets* and tens of other aircraft in the same piece of sky. Trying to keep from running into another

Keri on the flight line, 1997, shortly before earning her wings of gold, NAS Pensacola, Florida.

airplane or the ground was difficult enough, not to mention running the radar, ensuring our six o'clock position was clear, and talking on the radio to ten different organizations and aircraft at the same time. I felt woefully underprepared for life in a real squadron.

My learning curve was steep, but, thankfully, after our next detachment, I felt things were starting to click. I thoroughly enjoyed my two deployments to Japan and the time in between with my squadron. We experienced hard times, though, when our squadron suffered two major flight tragedies and lost two Marines. As the squadron's aviation safety officer, I was intimately involved in the investigation of one of the accidents.

After a time, I realized that flying in the *Hornet* was not what I wanted to do with the rest of my life. When my applications to change my Marine Corps career path

didn't pan out, I decided I would separate from the service after my next tour.

My husband, John, was also an active-duty Marine when we married, and in order to be stationed together, we both took assignments in the Washington, D.C., area. I was fortunate to be assigned to the Marine Corps' headquarters in the safety division, where I spent a lot of time trying to answer my burning questions regarding human error in aviation.

This was a busy three years for us as we decided to use this non-flying tour to start our family. Our two daughters, Kathleen and Carolyn, were born. Just after I separated from active duty, in June 2005, we moved to Monterey, California, for my husband's final tour as staff member at the Defense Language Institute. In Monterey, I did some consulting for Convergent Performance, LLC, a veteran-owned company specializing in improving human performance in high-risk environments like military aviation.

In January 2008, John retired from the Marine Corps, and we moved into a great little house on the shore of Lake Erie in his hometown of Sandusky, Ohio. Here, John is pursuing his life-long dream of teaching and dabbling in carpentry. I am now an employee of Convergent Performance, LLC, managing a program entitled the Global War on Error®. I love my job, and living near family for the first time since high school is priceless.

Marine Corps life was the epitome of camaraderie. It sounds cliché to write, but they were truly closer to me than brothers or sisters could ever be. I am eternally grateful for the opportunity to be a part of the Marine Corps and to have flown in their aircraft for as long as I did. I do wish some members of my chain of command would have looked more favorably on my choice to leave flying and opened another door to me. If they had, I may have chosen to stay on active duty. Once my children start school, I plan to look into the Marine Corps Reserve for possible opportunities.

I moved around a lot as a child and I learned early on how to fit in with any crowd. This served me well throughout my time in the military and in my civilian life.

Mom to Mom:

The thing that surprised me most about being a mom is how intensely I love my children. So different from the love I feel for the rest of my family, this kind of love is visceral, like a pleasure-pain——it is amazingly fierce and runs so deep. Perhaps it is because I feel entirely responsible for their health, safety, and happiness; but both the joy and the worry that came with being a mother are far greater than in any other aspect of my life!

One thing I learned from my time in the military is diplomacy will get you everywhere. If you take the time to listen actively to your seniors and subordinates and treat them with respect, you will do well.

Our girls are too young to remember Mom or Dad being Marines, but I hope that through my future Marine Corps Reserve activities they'll gain an appreciation for military aviation.

I would like my children to understand how very fortunate we are to be Americans. I want them to travel the world, to know and respect other cultures, and to embrace their freedom.

"You can't always get what you want But if you try sometimes well you might find You get what you need"

—Rolling Stones

Rank:	Marine Corps Major
Years Served:	11
Current Military Status:	Separated
Number of Children:	2

Alexis (Rominger) McCabe

F/A-18A+ *Hornet*

I GREW UP IN AURORA, COLORADO, AS AN ONLY CHILD. MY DAD, AFTER SPENDING FOUR YEARS IN THE NAVY AS AN AIRCRAFT MECHANIC, BECAME one of United Airlines' first male flight attendants in 1972, and flew for them for almost thirty years. My mom worked for the Department of the Army, and then later for the Department of the Interior, as a personnel specialist.

I attended the University of Northern Colorado, and received a bachelor of arts in sociology in 1994. A year prior to graduation, I thought to myself, "Here comes my life, and I'm not ready for it." I decided I would join the military, and talked with my dad about my decision. He was adamant that I would become a military officer and pilot.

I talked to all the military services and was accepted into the Army's warrant officer program to fly helicopters, but they wanted me to start before I finished college. Since I wanted to finish college, I was unsure if the Army was the right choice.

After college graduation in 1994, still unsure if the military was for me, I followed in my dad's footsteps and became a United Airlines flight attendant. I talked to the pilots I worked with, many of whom had been military pilots, and asked them about their experiences. I told them about my desire to join the military and enter flight training. Every pilot I met said that, if given the opportunity, they would do it again. Eventually, I decided to join the Marine Corps, and received a contract that guaranteed me a flight school slot.

So off I went. I graduated from Marine Corps officer candidate school in December 1997, and received my commission as a second lieutenant. Following more training at the Marine Corps basic course in Quantico, Virginia, I arrived in Pensacola, Florida, for flight training at NAS Whiting Field.

After finishing initial flight training, I selected jets, and attended advanced jet training in Meridian, Mississippi. The training at Meridian was a great experience, but stressful! However, I never found it difficult being a woman. My attitude was "there is nothing any guy is going to say to me that is going to offend me." I had a very good group of flight school friends, and that really made the difference. We had the "cooperate to graduate" mentality, and we all made it through.

I had met my future husband, Frank, a former Navy E–2 pilot, when I flew with United Airlines as a flight attendant. Our casual dating became more serious during my time at flight school in Meridian and we married at the local courthouse. It was comical, because neither of us could understand a thing the judge said because of his very thick Southern accent.

In January 2001, I received my wings of gold, and was selected to fly the F/A-18 *Hornet*, a Navy and Marine Corps fighter/attack aircraft. I attended the F/A-18 training squadron at NAS Oceana, Virginia. Before I checked into the training squadron, Frank and I got the unexpected but exciting news that I was pregnant. Haley Katherine was born in August 2001. There was a seven-month delay for Marine Corps pilots to start training, so it actually worked out nicely, and I only started one class later than my original start date.

Typically, Marine Corps *Hornet* squadrons don't fly on and off aircraft carriers but there are a handful that do and, after completing *Hornet* training, I went to one of these "boat squadrons," VMFA-312, Checkerboards, at Marine Corps Air Station (MCAS), Beaufort, South Carolina.

Alexis with her daughter on the flight line in 2003 at MCAS Beaufort, South Carolina. Alexis was preparing to go on a six-month deployment as part of VMFA-312 aboard the aircraft carrier USS *Enterprise*.

I was the second woman *Hornet* pilot in the Marine Corps, but my squadron mates were very open to me being there. Soon after I joined the squadron, we deployed for a six-month cruise on the aircraft carrier USS *Enterprise*, conducting missions in support of Marines and soldiers on the ground in Iraq and Afghanistan.

Flying off the boat (carrier) for me was the tip of the spear. Growing up in the era of the movie *Top Gun,* there was nothing more prestigious than carrier aviation. I soon learned that flying around the boat was one of the most rewarding and challenging experiences I've ever had, especially at night.

I have several career highlights, but a few stand out, particularly standing on the flight deck of the USS *Enterprise* at night, watching the F-14 *Tomcats* and F/A-18 *Hornets* launch into the night, their afterburners lit, to go into Iraq and Afghanistan. When I got to do it myself, that was the epitome of my flying career!

Being one of a few women really was no big deal. Although I was the only woman in my squadron, there were several other women aviators and various other women officers on the carrier. We hung out together on and off the boat and always made a point of doing *girl* things in port. I met some of the greatest women on that deployment and now have lifelong friends.

Flying in Iraq with a great group of fellow aviators, and working for incredible Marine Corps leaders, imbued in me how each military unit's mission is just one piece of a big puzzle; each unit's success depends on another. Overall, deploying on an aircraft carrier was one of the very best things I've done. It was one of my goals. I did it and am now able to look back fondly on that time. It was also one of the experiences that gave me the confidence to pursue future dreams and goals.

Since both Frank and I were flying, we hired a nanny to help us with our daughter, Haley. We had two nannies over the three years, and we definitely could not have survived without these wonderful ladies. I enjoyed deploying with the squadron, but leaving my daughter was emotionally difficult. Haley did great; it was much harder on me than her. Frank managed his flying schedule so he wouldn't be gone for any extended lengths of time, my parents made many trips from their home to stay with Frank and Haley, and we had our nanny. So it worked out.

I went back to Iraq a few years later but this time in a non-flying job with 2nd Marine Aircraft Wing. I was fortunate, though, that I still got some flight time there, and flew with one of the deployed squadrons, the Gators, a reserve Marine Corps *Hornet* squadron. Flying with those guys will always be one of my fondest memories of flying in the Marine Corps.

Following my return from Iraq, I received orders to be an instructor pilot for three years at VT-4 training squadron at NAS Pensacola, where I flew the T-6 *Texan*. After my arrival there, we decided to have another child. Although I was flying, I didn't have to deploy, so this was a perfect opportunity. Our son, Colin Patrick, was born during this tour, in February 2007.

In the summer of 2010, I left the Marine Corps to attend medical school. During my last deployment in Iraq, I had dealt with injured Marines and civilian contractors, and my long-buried goal of becoming a doctor surfaced. I knew it was the next path I had to take.

I have thoroughly enjoyed my time in the military, and, just like all those airline pilots I spoke to years earlier, I would do it all over again. I am thankful for the opportunities, and although my flying career has ended, I look forward to this great new adventure of becoming a doctor.

I have learned that through hard work and perseverance, I can accomplish anything. It has given me a confidence I wouldn't have had otherwise. I've also learned one big difference between men and women, in that men can argue, disagree, ridicule, and say mean things to each other, but in five minutes they will forget it ever

happened. I learned early on to adopt this trait or I would not survive in this environment. It has helped in my own personal life to not take things too seriously or personally.

My daughter, Haley, doesn't think flying is any big deal, since both her parents flew and that's all she knows. She has been able to identify an F/A-18 since she could talk. Colin loves airplanes and anything about flying.

I want to pass on to my children, particularly my daughter, the knowledge that a woman can be successful in anything she chooses to do. She can have career goals and still be feminine, a wife, and a mother. She can choose the path that is right for her. If Haley chooses to have a career and family, that's great; if she chooses to stay home with her family, that is also great—as long as she's happy. For my son, I want him to follow the example of his father. If he chooses to marry, I hope he supports his wife in whatever choice she makes for her life, whether she chooses to stay at home with her family or to embark on a demanding career. I also want both of my children to learn a sense of duty and patriotism, as well as good manners and respect for themselves and others.

> ## Mom to Mom:
> The most rewarding thing about being a mom is coming home to my children. They are always so excited to see me, and always greet with me with big hugs. Regardless of my day, I am instantly renewed. It's so nice to have such great, unconditional love.

"**Twenty years from now you will be more disappointed by the things that you didn't do than by the ones you did do. So throw off the bowlines. Sail away from the safe harbor. Catch the trade winds in your sails. Explore. Dream. Discover.**"

—Mark Twain

Rank:	Marine Corps Major
Years Served:	13
Current Military Status:	Separated
Number of Children:	2

Jen (Hall) Nothelfer

CH-46E *Phrog*

I GREW UP IN HORSE COUNTRY IN WARRENTON, VIRGINIA, WHERE MY PARENTS ALLOWED ME TO TRY JUST ABOUT ANYTHING WITHIN REASON. I competed in soccer, gymnastics, volleyball, field hockey, swimming, and equestrian pursuits. If I had to use a few words to describe myself, they would be competitive, honest, sensitive, and loyal.

Partway through Virginia Intermont College in Bristol, Virginia, on an academic scholarship, I transferred to Marymount University in Arlington, Virginia, and majored in business administration with a concentration in paralegal studies, graduating in May 1993.

While I have always loved aviation, I did not really recognize it until I started working for Atlantic Coast Airlines as a flight attendant. On one flight, I struck up a conversation with a passenger. Jay Bradshaw was a corporate pilot and on his way to pick up an aircraft. We started talking about flying lessons, and he invited me out to Manassas Airport to go flying with him.

The day I went out for a ride, it just happened that they were flying a Cessna 172 to Lancaster, Pennsylvania, to pick up a *Learjet*. Needless to say, as soon as we took off the end of the runway, I was HOOKED! As soon as I got back from the flight, I signed up for flying lessons with Jay as my flight instructor.

Since the lessons were expensive, I searched for ways to fund this endeavor. Around the same time, I started dating a Navy F-14 aviator, and I enjoyed the camaraderie of his squadron parties and the military way of life. The relationship didn't last long, but one good thing did happen—he bet me I couldn't get a flight contract with the military. It took me a few years of trying, but I finally got it!

I was commissioned in the Navy through officer candidate school in October 1995. Due to the approach of Hurricane Opal, the graduation ceremony lasted ten minutes and did not include most families, because the base was closing due to the oncoming storm.

Flight school was amazing. I loved the solo aerobatic flights during primary flight training. It always amazed me that after only a few flights, we were out executing barrel rolls, snap rolls, and loops, with no instructor onboard. It felt like I stole the keys to the car—it was fantastic!

While at officer candidate school, I realized I wanted to be a Marine Corps officer. I was impressed with the Marine Corps drill instructors, and wished I had pursued a Marine Corps flight contract. During the final phase of flight training, I decided to apply for a transition to the Marine Corps. I received my wings of gold in June 1997, and then waited six months for the transition to be approved. Finally, in November 1997, I was commissioned a Marine Corps first lieutenant, the highlight of my military career.

I spent the next six months at the Marine Corps officer course in Quantico, Virginia. While focused on infantry training, it also expanded my professional development as a Marine Corps officer. When asked what helicopter I wanted to fly, I chose the CH-46E *Phrog* for its mission, as well as for the community atmosphere. After reporting to MCAS New River, North Carolina, I spent ten weeks learning to fly the CH-46. In October 1998, I was assigned to HMM-264, the Black Knights.

I loved the tactical flying, and spent time on deployment for training missions, as well as six months of workups (preparations for deployment) for the 26th Marine Expeditionary Unit. I think the most rewarding time in the

Jen and her family celebrate family beach week, April 2010, Emerald Isle, North Carolina.

fleet was flying off the ship wearing night-vision goggles. Hearing the combat Marines cheering and hollering in the back of the aircraft was motivating. That's what flying the CH-46 was all about—getting those guys into the zone the fastest and safest way possible.

I credit my first commanding officer, Colonel Jeff Tomczak, and Sergeant Major Ken Strickland with showing by example how to be a Marine. Colonel Tomczak never looked at me as a female aviator, but as another valued squadron pilot. Having three daughters of his own, he encouraged them to succeed, and he also gave me that same opportunity. I still call him for advice today. Sergeant Major Strickland was always honest and straightforward. I gained strength from his ability to connect with the Marines. He was tough, but that toughness was what I admired most.

My husband, Kirk, and I met in flight school. It was love at first sight. We were engaged after dating only eight weeks, and married the following year. He is also a Marine aviator, and is a naval flight officer in the EA-6B

Prowler. I left active duty in July 2003, just after my twins, Alexis and Bridget, were born. Three years later, our third daughter, Emma, arrived.

Although no longer an active-duty Marine, I still am very active in the Marine Corps Reserve. During one of my reserve drills, I had the amazing opportunity to assist with the opening of the National Museum of the Marine Corps. The opening ceremony was scheduled the same day as the Marine Corps birthday—November 10, 2006. The colonel of my reserve unit asked me to escort the family of deceased Corporal Jason Dunham during the opening ceremony events. It had not been publicly announced, but, during the opening ceremony, the president of the United States would posthumously award Corporal Dunham the Congressional Medal of Honor, an award not bestowed on a United States Marine since the Vietnam War. Corporal Dunham had died when he smothered an enemy grenade with his own body to save fellow Marines.

Initially, I was taken aback that my colonel asked me to be the escort. Although proud to have been chosen, I was unsure what to expect. I didn't know anything about the fallen Marine or his family, other than he had given the ultimate sacrifice—his life. I knew there would be painful emotions but, as a Marine, I thought I could handle it...but I also knew I was human...and I was a mom.... the thought of losing a child was unbearable.

My role for the day was to escort Corporal Dunham's parents, Deb and Dan Dunham, during the opening events and then to meet the president. Deb and Dan were just incredible people—very generous, caring, and so proud of Jason. Ironically, November 10th was Jason's birthday, a bittersweet day, I thought, for his parents to receive this historical award.

In addition to spending time with Corporal Dunham's family, I also had the honor and privilege to meet many of the Marines he had served with in Iraq. I was amazed at their candor and their openness. As I drove home that evening, I cried the entire way, raw with emotion, humbled and numb from the day.

As the months passed, my family and the Dunhams kept in touch. Deb was very nurturing with a calm demeanor and when my husband, Kirk, prepared for deployment, Deb would email me and call to check in with me and my girls.

Reflecting on the experience of that day back in 2006, I am grateful—grateful for Jason's sacrifice, grateful for meeting the Dunhams, and grateful for being a United States Marine. The pride, esprit de corps and camaraderie that I felt that day will be with me for a lifetime. It left an indelible mark and motivates me to be a better human, a better mom, and a better wife.

I know how fortunate I am to live in a country where we are free, thanks to Marines like Jason Dunham, willing to give their life for a fellow Marine. I know I would have liked Jason, for the person he was and for the legacy he leaves for others to aspire to become.

I have learned that the Marine Corps' core values of honor, courage, and commitment provide the foundation for how to live life. Doing the right thing for the right

reason can only amount to a win-win situation. My husband is my source of energy. I have watched Kirk make difficult decisions within the Marine Corps and in life, and he always falls back on those core values. I hope to inspire others, as well as our children, to live life this same way.

Not only do I draw strength from my husband and fellow Marines, I also gain strength from strong women. I am a member of several organizations—Women Marines Association, Women Military Aviators, Whirly Girls, and Women in Aviation, International. I have enjoyed being a member of Women Marines Association the most. I meet some amazing women, and hear endearing stories about their Marine Corps careers. Some were in the Marine Corps during the era of "Free a Man to Fight;" some were intrigued by the esprit de corps and camaraderie; and some fell in love with the Corps by falling in love with their husbands, who happened to be Marines. Whatever their motivation, their dedication and purpose are still evident, sometimes more than forty years later.

These women endured and overcame many of the issues women in typically male-dominated careers are dealing with today. Like me, they are hard-charging, determined, and confident. A group of us remains friends, and I call upon them often when faced with adversity, or just as a sounding board before making a decision.

I want to pass to my daughters that the sky is the limit, and I hope to inspire them to be passionate in whatever they pursue. They can dream big dreams! Kirk and I will be here to support whatever dream they choose to pursue.

Mom to Mom:
The most rewarding thing about being a mom is nurturing three beautiful daughters on how to create an amazing life full of endless possibilities while being true to themselves and their own dreams.

I am a Marine; I can do anything. You (my kids) also can do anything and everything.

Rank:	Marine Corps Major
Years Served:	15
Current Military Status:	Marine Corps Reserve
Number of Children:	3

UNN-Kristin Solberg

CH-53E *Super Stallion*

ALTHOUGH I WAS BORN IN LONG BEACH, CALIFORNIA, MY NORWEGIAN PARENTS MOVED OUR FAMILY BACK TO NORWAY WITHIN A YEAR following my birth. We returned to California for a summer vacation when I was eight years old, and a family friend took my dad, my brother, and me on an unforgettable flight in a Cessna 172, through the mountains and valleys of northern California. At the end of our vacation, I was determined that I would either be an actress or a pilot. During high school, I started flying gliders at a local flying club, and absolutely loved it.

I went back to the United States to attend college at Purdue University in Indiana, and graduated with a bachelor of science in electrical engineering. I planned to return home to Norway after graduating, but I decided to stay in the States a little longer, after receiving a few job offers in the windy city of Chicago.

After working about a year at a computer desk, I decided I needed more excitement. My boyfriend, Jerry, who later became my husband, asked me, "If you could do anything you want, what would it be?" Well, ever since I was eight, I had wanted to fly high and fast. Jerry, at the time an enlisted member in the Marine Corps Reserve, gave me the number to a Marine Corps recruiter, stating, "If you want to fly, you have to do it with the best."

A few months later, I found myself in the Marine Corps' officer candidate school and then the officer basic course. After starting the basic course, I ran into my greatest challenge thus far—I was pregnant. I had to put my plans of flight school on hold. Three months after the birth of my daughter, Helena, I resumed the basic course and then continued on to flight school in Pensacola, Florida, bringing our daughter with me. My husband, who was going to George Washington Law School, remained behind in Washington, D.C. Meeting the demands of flight school while being a single mom was a challenge, but I had a blast nonetheless.

In June 1999, I finally received my wings of gold, and selected the CH-53E helicopter. First stop was to learn how to fly the CH-53 at MCAS New River, Jacksonville, North Carolina, and then I was finally on my way to my first fleet squadron at MCAS Miramar in San Diego, California, in June 2000. I checked into HMH-465, the Warhorses, as the first woman in the squadron. I was totally excited, and had high expectations for the future.

In the spring of 2001, the squadron prepared to deploy to Okinawa. It would be my first deployment with the squadron, and I looked forward to the opportunity to visit new parts of the world, and to finally participate in overseas squadron operations.

Then another immense challenge came my way— I realized I was pregnant again, and the doctors determined the pregnancy was high-risk, preventing me from going on the deployment. I stayed with the squadron long enough to get them embarked and on their way. Four months later, along came Liv Annika, fulfilling Helena's dream of a little sister.

After maternity leave, I returned to flight status, ready to go back to my squadron. Going back, however, proved quite challenging. Although I was extremely happy to fly again, the squadron climate had changed. The guys in the squadron shared a common bond from the deployment, and some of them also thought that I had gotten pregnant to get out of deploying.

About eight months later, I transferred to a new helicopter squadron, and prepared to deploy with the 13th

Kristin and her girls, Maia, Liv-Annika, and Helena, 2007, Miramar Air Show, California.

Marine Expeditionary Unit on the USS *Peleliu* (LHA 5), a Navy amphibious assault ship. In August 2003, we boarded the boat, scheduled for a nine-month deployment.

I thoroughly enjoyed life on the boat. For the first time in years, I found time to work out every day, read books, listen to music, write journals, watch the sunset, and study. The separation from my kids and husband was bittersweet. I missed them tremendously, but at the same time found freedom in having time to myself.

Fate would once again alter my plans. A couple of months into deployment, I faced another challenge, topping the previous two combined. I was pregnant again! Standing military policies prohibited pregnant women from being deployed on naval vessels, and forced me to leave the ship.

Upon returning home, I contacted my original squadron to see if I could rejoin them and deploy with them to Okinawa. The squadron approved the request, and soon after, I joined that squadron and flew with them until my third trimester. I remained in Okinawa until three weeks prior to the birth of my third daughter, Maia.

After Maia's birth, I transferred to wing headquarters in a non-flying job, until I got out of the Marine Corps in August 2006. My Marine Corps aviation career did not exactly unfold as I had planned or foreseen when I started on this journey. After having our third child, I finally reached a point where I had to be honest with myself and admit that giving my all, which required 120 percent at the squadron while fulfilling my family responsibilities of a wife and mother of three at the same time, was simply too much. Something had to give. I decided it was time for me to move on and leave the Marine Corps.

Upon transitioning to the civilian world, I started working for a private government contractor in the unmanned aerial vehicle industry, keeping me close to both aviation and defense. I also finished my MBA from Indiana University, Kelley School of Business.

At the same time, I joined a West Coast reserve squadron and flew a couple of days each month. My time with this squadron was incredible. The three other female pilots and I agreed we were in the best squadron of our careers. Unfortunately, budget cuts and force restructuring left our squadron on the list of units to shut down, along with most other Marine Corps reserve squadrons on the West Coast. The squadron closed down in August 2008.

Life happens in mysterious ways, and I believe nothing happens by chance. I thought I had my path in life figured out and that obstacles were there to keep the journey challenging. However, as I reflect on the timing of different life-changing events that have occurred throughout my journey, the ones that have thrown me off my path or directed me to go a different and unplanned way than what I had envisioned have taught me to swim with the tide rather than against it.

Prior to having kids, it was easy to set my goals and accomplish them, even when challenges abounded. Having children changed everything. My perspective on life and the relative importance of its contents shifted. No longer was charging to accomplish that next goal highest on the list. Instead, my priorities in life centered on providing my children everything they need, along with creating and capturing memorable moments through fleeting times. There are times I catch myself thinking, "I wish I could have...," then I take a look at my children and remember what an incredible gift they are and why raising them is the most important responsibility I could ever be entrusted with.

Mom to Mom:

The most rewarding thing about being a mom is the unconditional love and excitement greeting me at the door at the end of each day; the endless pieces of artwork and letters saying "I love mommy" on them; and the sparkles in their eyes when they talk about Christmas wishes—the look of anything is possible!

I believe in the workings of karma and that what you give to others will return to you. I believe the energy you radiate is magnified and reflected back at you, and that recurring themes provide some necessary life experiences. One needs to have the right attitude to appreciate those life experiences and blessings. I have also recognized the importance of living in the moment and not waiting for some special future event, thereby potentially regretting that an event or situation may not have unfolded the way I had envisioned.

I want my children to grow up to be strong yet compassionate; independent yet team players; self-confident yet humble; to stay true to their personalities, and realize that they can do ANYTHING they want, if they put their minds to it. When things don't go according to plan, or events throw them off their tracks, I want them to trust that it is okay to modify their goals and admit new dreams; the purpose of the distraction may be to enable them to discover another adventure to put in their bags-of-life experience. Thus, when things happen beyond their control and seem to bring them to a stop, they need to look past closed doors and find the open ones.

Live, Love, Laugh

Rank:	Marine Corps Major
Years Served:	14
Current Military Status:	Marine Corps Reserve
Number of Children:	3

Celese (Roberts) Stevens

EA-6B *Prowler*

BOTH OF MY PARENTS SERVED IN THE AIR FORCE. MY MOM SEPARATED WHEN SHE BECAME PREGNANT WITH ME, AND MY DAD STAYED IN for more than thirty years. Our family loved attending air shows, and as a kid I developed an affinity for anything related to flying.

My parents dared us to explore and achieve our dreams. I attended Texas A&M University, was immediately drawn to their Corps of Cadets, and spent the next four years working toward a degree and a commission in the United States Marine Corps. In May 1996, I graduated with a bachelor's degree in industrial distribution—an engineering degree combined with a business degree.

Off I went to the Marine Corps' initial officer training—a six-month school for all newly commissioned officers to learn the basics of being a Marine Corps officer. While in school, I took the flight qualification test and found I was qualified to attend flight school. Since officer billets were assigned during this initial training, I had to compete with approximately two hundred other second lieutenants for the six available naval flight officer slots, and I qualified. As a naval flight officer, I would fly in either the front right seat or the back seat of an aircraft, and assist the pilot by operating the radios, navigation gear, and weapon systems.

I went to NAS Pensacola for flight school, which took about eighteen months to complete. I chose the EA-6B *Prowler* for its mission—supporting and protecting other aircraft and ground troops through the use of electronic warfare.

In January 1999, I earned my wings of gold and left for the *Prowler* training squadron at NAS Whidbey Island, Washington. Naval flight officers who fly in the EA-6B *Prowler* are called electronic countermeasures officers.

After training in Whidbey, I was assigned to MCAS Cherry Point, North Carolina, to start my three-year tour with VMAQ-4, one of the four Marine Corps *Prowler* squadrons there. I was the second female aviator to join the squadron, just months after my good friend, Alicia.

Our commanding officer was an outstanding leader, so the traditionally male work environment functioned in a very professional manner. I felt welcome and was tasked appropriately for my abilities and level of experience.

One month after I arrived, the squadron attended an exercise in Canada called *Maple Flag* where we participated in training missions with aviators from several different countries in preparation for our future deployment. Just a few months later, we flew all of our squadron aircraft over to Iwakuni, Japan, where we would be deployed for six months conducting training missions in the region. The deployment was, of course, a time to bond with squadron mates, but also a great opportunity to work toward my flying qualifications. Seeing different parts of Japan, Korea, Okinawa, Guam, and Iwo Jima while we trained was also a great adventure.

I earned my call sign of "Scrappy" during this deployment. I got into an argument with our squadron flight surgeon at the officers' club in Iwakuni, Japan. By everyone else's account, he was fairly immature. I became the target of his childish advances and did *not* tolerate it. At the time, I would have welcomed a little help from my squadron buddies, but they said I had the situation under control. The following day, there was a top-ten list of call signs for me. "Scrappy" was the one that stuck.

I also experienced an incident during this deployment that changed the course of my military career. We

Family enjoying vacation at Disneyworld following Celeste's husband's six-month deployment, 2009.

had to quickly descend during a flight and I experienced a sinus block. It ultimately resulted in sinus surgery and nerve damage. After almost a year of doctor visits and trials with possible solutions, a military medical board evaluated my flight status. The doctors came to the conclusion that I could no longer fly at the operational level without the pain I was continually experiencing.

I was terribly disappointed and spent the next few years exploring my options. Though the Marine Corps was happy to keep me working in some other capacity, I could really not imagine a career in the Marine Corps that did not involve flying. Over the next few years, I worked with the Marine Corps' EA-6B *Prowler* and EA-18G *Growler* test and acquisition community. The adjustment of not flying truly took years to digest. After all, I had worked so hard to achieve my flying goals. I eventually left the Marine Corps in 2005.

The friendships I made while flying are some of the strongest bonds I have still today, including my husband.

Mike, also a Marine Corps aviator, was a couple of classes ahead of me in flight training, but I didn't get to know him well until I moved to Whidbey Island. He, too, was going through *Prowler* training and on his way to Cherry Point. We became the best of friends despite our opposite deployment schedules, and married in 2004. We now have three kids all under the age of four—Hayden, Kaela, and Ashley.

Mike is still in the Marine Corps and flying *Prowlers* in a squadron at Cherry Point. We've been back here for a year now, and Mike is preparing for his second six-month deployment to Iraq. During his last deployment, our son, Hayden, grew three inches, daughter Kaela grew four inches, and our youngest daughter, Ashley, was born. The wonderful network of Marine Corps friends makes Cherry Point feel like we're home with family, especially during deployments.

I am thrilled to have had the opportunity to be a Marine Corps aviator, and although my career didn't turn out like I had originally planned, I am thrilled to be a stay-at-home mom and view this as the most important job I could have in life. The jobs of aviator and mom are worlds apart, but the military and aviation training I've had—especially leadership and multitasking—has truly prepared me for caring for and teaching my kids every day. Hopefully, I will spend the pre-school years at home teaching my children and enjoying the world through their eyes.

I have so many highlights of my time in the Marine Corps, especially my aviation experiences, such as landing and taking off from the air-craft carrier, the USS *Constellation*. During my time in the training squadron at Whidbey Island, I got the opportunity to participate in carrier qualifications with other student aviators. Knowing that I would not likely get to see the carrier again since the Marine Corps squadrons are land-based, I felt fortunate to have had that experience.

Another awesome experience was taking an EA-6B from our home base in North Carolina and flying it to Iwakuni, Japan, via California, Hawaii, and Wake Island. I'll also cherish the awesome experience of flying in and out of Iwo Jima and remembering how the people there (all men) marveled at the sight of a female aviator.

I revisit these experiences now and then. When I see cloud formations, I can still envision "surfing" the clouds,

Mom to Mom:

The most rewarding thing about being a mom is how God uses your children to teach you the hardest lessons about yourself...if you let them. I am surprised at how much I am willing to sacrifice on my children's behalf, how selfless motherhood can be, and how awesomely rewarding that sacrifice is.

and if I close my eyes, I remember flying low-level flights through the mountains, seeing a rainbow from above, and watching towers of clouds build into thunderstorms.

I want my kids to know how much they are loved, I want them to be proud of me—for the things I have done and will do—and I want them to love and believe in their country. Mike and I hope to teach them to not be afraid to try new things, but if they are, to try anyway, to dream big, and to do what it takes to make their dreams reality.

The years I spent flying are spe-cial memories I hold close to my heart. Overall, flying was an amazing experi-ence...a life somewhere between *The Great Santini* and *Top Gun*. I treasure the experiences, the training and hard work, and will love sharing all the details of flying with my three little blessings!

Happiness comes amidst the attempts to accomplish something bigger than we believe we are capable of accomplishing.

Rank:	Marine Corps Captain
Years Served:	8
Current Military Status:	Separated
Number of Children:	3

coast
guard

Polly (Pieterek) Bartz

HH-65 *Dolphin*

MY PARENTS NEVER NUDGED ME IN ANY DIRECTION, BUT ALWAYS SAID, "DO YOUR BEST." I DIDN'T KNOW WHAT I WANTED TO DO IN college, but I did know I wanted something more than the normal college experience. Though I had no knowledge of the military or its academies, I ended up applying, and getting accepted into, the Coast Guard Academy.

I met my future husband, Chris, during my sophomore year at the academy. We married a year after graduating, and were fortunate to both get orders to St. Petersburg, Florida, on two different ships.

I was assigned to the Coast Guard Cutter *Decisive*, patrolling the Gulf of Mexico and the Caribbean, as a deck watch officer. As much as I enjoyed my two-year tour, something was still missing from the equation of what I really wanted to do as a career.

Because of the prominent law-enforcement mission in the areas where the *Decisive* patrolled, the ship always had a helicopter onboard. With the opportunity to talk to the many pilots who deployed with us, I quickly learned that pilots love their jobs. After one year on the ship, I decided to apply to flight school. Chris applied to flight school at the same time, and fortunately, we both were accepted and started pilot training together, in 1992.

I had very little aviation exposure growing up, so after getting accepted to flight school, I signed up for a couple of private flight lessons. Afterward, I wasn't sure if I could make it through the fast-paced program of pilot training.

The first part of flight school was mostly classroom instruction and physical training. Once I began learning to fly the T-34 *Mentor*, I was instantly overwhelmed. However, I never once considered dropping out. The benefits of working extremely hard and sticking to it made me realize I could set and achieve high goals.

After T-34 training, Chris and I both chose to fly helicopters (helos), because that is where the action is in the Coast Guard. At our first Coast Guard air station in Oregon, we flew the HH-65 *Dolphin* helo, primarily in support of search-and-rescue operations. The flying was amazing, and so was the camaraderie at the air station. Chris also flew with the polar operations division in support of science missions, flying off Coast Guard polar icebreakers in Antarctica.

My next tour, as an instructor pilot at the Coast Guard aviation training center in Mobile, Alabama, has been one of my career favorites. Although initially hesitant to accept orders to the training center, I found this assignment to be one of the most rewarding of my career.

In 2002, we headed to the Midwest to an air station in Detroit. I flew the HH-65 again, conducting search-and-rescue and law-enforcement operations. The Great Lakes provide the unique opportunity for ice rescues—when people on the ice fall through, or are set adrift on an ice floe. I also deployed for two months aboard a 270-foot Coast Guard cutter off the coast of South America, flying missions in support of law-enforcement operations.

After Detroit, it was time for both Chris and me to do staff tours, so we asked for Washington, D.C., because we wanted the experience of working in the nation's capital. It was the first tour since attending flight school where we

Polly, with three future Coast Guard pilots—her daughters, Bridget, Claire, and Audrey, 2005, Air Station Detroit.

did not fly. We enjoyed our time in D.C., but soon found ourselves up for orders again, and transitioning to life in the South, in New Orleans, Louisiana. Chris became the executive officer at the Coast Guard air station, and I command a personnel support unit. Although I'm still flying a desk, being in command has been fantastic, and an incredible honor.

Thankfully, Chris and I have managed to be stationed together for all of our different tours so far. We had our first daughter, Audrey, at the end of our flying tour in Oregon, in 1998, and then second daughter, Claire, came along three years later. We knew that we wanted to have another child during our third flying tour in Detroit, but we had to plan it around deployments.

Shortly after arriving in Detroit, I volunteered to go on a deployment so that I could get it out of the way as soon as possible, and then had our third daughter, Bridget, before leaving Detroit. Our daughters' ages were purposefully planned to be three years apart, in the hopes of making the balancing of career and family easier. For us, it proved successful, because, as the older

child became less dependent, we brought another child into the family.

The work and family balance was certainly easier when the kids were younger, because there are many more activities to squeeze into the already tight schedule as the kids get older. Chris and I share all the family and household roles and responsibilities— from laundry to dishes to paying bills. I don't think we could do it any other way, unless we bring in full-time outside help. Of course, we've always had an extensive list of friends to call on when a plan didn't go as anticipated.

I chose the military for my career because of its structured way of doing things, and because I love the continuous challenge of change. After twenty years, I have enjoyed almost every minute of it—flying, raising three daughters, and having a wonderful and understanding husband who is also enjoying a successful Coast Guard career. At work, we have carefully tried to avoid the perception that we wanted or received any special treatment because of our marital status.

Our oldest daughter, Audrey, is very independent, confident, and inquisitive. She has started to ask questions about flying a helicopter and being in the Coast Guard. We purposefully have not pushed her or our other daughters in any certain direction with what they may want to do with their lives. I want to expose them to as much as possible, and then let them make the decision themselves. Our second daughter, Claire, loves animals and dreams of becoming a veterinarian, and our youngest, Bridget, is the jokester in the family.

The same thing that my parents passed down to me, I want to pass down to my girls—always do your best. If you come up against an obstacle, find a way to get to the other side. There is always a way; you just have to look hard enough to find it.

Mom to Mom:

The thing that surprised me the most about being a mom is facing the occasional complicated and challenging situations concerning kids. But every day brings rewards.

The highlight of my career has been doing it all!

Rank:	Coast Guard Commander
Years Served:	20
Current Military Status:	Active Duty
Number of Children:	3

Elizabeth (Francis) Booker

H-65 *Dolphin*

WHEN I WAS SIX, I DECIDED I WANTED TO BE AN ASTRONAUT. I QUICKLY REALIZED THAT, IN ORDER TO BECOME AN ASTRONAUT PILOT, I first had to become a jet pilot.

This passion for flying stuck with me throughout my childhood, and my parents—two college administrators—were very supportive. They even planned my birthday parties at Johnson Space Center and paid for flying lessons.

During my first two years of high school, I attended an aviation magnet school, started aviation ground school, and also joined the Navy Junior ROTC program. I was the girl who had posters of the F-14 *Tomcat* and SR-71 *Blackbird* on my walls instead of rock stars.

Despite my desire to fly, I didn't have a passion for school. Impatient and frustrated when my family moved to Georgia and I had to attend a non-aviation high school, I dropped out and earned my GED. After foundering at the local junior college, I enlisted in the Coast Guard. Unbeknownst to me, my grandmother had been a member the SPARS, the Women's Reserve of the U.S. Coast Guard, during World War II.

After only a few months of working on the deck of a Coast Guard ship, I knew that I wanted to go to officer candidate school. The Coast Guard required a few years of enlisted time, some college credits, and promotion to petty officer second class to apply. In the meantime, I trained to navigate ships and, more importantly, my son, Lance, was born in August 1992.

My first few years in the Coast Guard were tough, since my specialty as a navigator required me to be at sea for several weeks at a time, leaving Lance at home. Having Lance made me even more determined to accomplish my goal of becoming an officer, so I could provide a better life for him. In 1996, I was accepted to officer candidate school, and it suddenly dawned on me that, as an officer, I could apply to flight school. There was no stopping me now!

I excelled, driven by the hope of attending flight school and, upon becoming an officer, I was assigned to an air station in Port Angeles, Washington, to manage small boats. I was surrounded and nurtured by a crew of wonderful pilots who took me flying with them, included me in their meetings and parties, and helped me write a winning application to flight school.

When I arrived in Pensacola, Florida, for flight training, I had little knowledge of how long and difficult training would be. My in-brief with the Coast Guard captain included a warning: "This is a marathon. You have to have serious endurance to make it through," and he was right! My incredibly supportive husband, Robert, made sure his schedule was flexible, so he could care for Lance while I focused my energy on learning to fly.

After flying T-34 turboprops at the VT-2 training squadron, affectionately called the Doer Birds, I trained in the TH-57 in the helicopter training squadron—HT-8. When I knelt down for my six-year-old son to pin on my naval aviator wings, I couldn't help but feel tremendous pride in how far I had come from that little girl who had dreamed of flying.

My first assignment out of flight school was to Coast Guard Air Station San Francisco, California, flying the HH-65 *Dolphin*. During my four-year tour, I mastered the art of flying helicopters in the execution of Coast Guard missions. I had a great experience as a junior pilot with my bosses and peers in San Francisco. They were wonderful

Liz with daughter, Brooke, 2005. Brooke liked to dress up just like Mommy.

to my son and treated him like a little brother, including him in lots of their activities.

Some of my favorite operations were hovering over a small boat to lower a basket for a rescue hoist, holding the aircraft in position to drop a rescue swimmer out the door, landing on the backs of Coast Guard cutters underway at sea, and flying around mountains and fog—even under the Golden Gate Bridge on occasion! Absolutely nothing compares to the feeling of successfully delivering a patient to a hospital or a cold and grateful person from water to dry land. Flying around the beautiful California coastline will always be one of my fondest memories.

During our time in San Francisco, Robert was hard at work finishing his bachelor's degree in accounting, generously tailoring his class schedule to be sure he'd be home for Lance before and after school.

During my third year there, I carried an extra passenger for a few months—my daughter, Brooke. I flew

through my second trimester of pregnancy, and the other pilots made sure I was well fed with midmorning snack breaks every day. They even planned a pool to bet on the baby's gender, making me promise not to reveal anything. I was pretty far along when I announced that we had chosen a name. They threw up their hands and said, "NO—don't tell us! We don't want to know if it's a boy or girl yet!" "Okay," I replied, "I'll just tell you that the name we picked has the same letters as our last name." There was a long pause and finally one of the guys said, "Koober?" Ever since then, our daughter, Brooke, has lovingly been referred to as Koober by the pilots who flew with me in San Francisco.

Expecting new orders in 2003, we requested to move to Miami, Florida. I flew the HH-65C helicopter at Coast Guard Air Station Miami, and regularly deployed throughout the Caribbean and out of Key West, Florida, on search-and-rescue, drug and migrant interdiction, and port security missions.

As one of the Coast Guard's largest aviation units, our operations were high tempo and dynamic. My mom was able to help out with Brooke for my first year in Miami and, again, my husband's flexibility and support were the keys to my success in this job. While I spent a couple of weeks flying around the Haitian coastline, Robert was back home putting Lance on the school bus, dropping Brooke at daycare, and managing the house while working as a full-time accountant and finishing up his master's in business administration at the University of Florida.

After all these years, I finally found my passion for school. Working with Haitian and Cuban migrants over the years piqued my interest in U.S. foreign policy and international affairs. I graduated with my bachelor's degree in international relations and political science in June 2006, and the Coast Guard graciously selected me to attend graduate school, on their time and money. In July 2007, I left Miami to attend Harvard University for a master's degree in public administration.

After graduation, I was assigned to the Coast Guard's Officer Personnel Management office in Arlington, Virginia, where I was responsible for staffing the Coast Guard's twenty-seven air stations with 1,200 pilots, selecting flight school candidates, and hiring pilots from other services. Helping to shape the future of Coast Guard aviation was tremendously rewarding. Staff assignments are referred to as "cockpit appreciation tours" for a reason, though, and I couldn't wait to get back out to

Mom to Mom:

The thing that surprised me most about being a mom was how vulnerable it made me. Someone wisely said that having a child is like having a piece of one's heart walking around in the world. Any pilot likes to be in control, but you can't control your children or everything that happens to them in life. You can only guide them and hope for the best—truly a white-knuckle experience!

the fleet to serve as chief pilot—operations officer—and hopefully command an air station some day.

For women who are considering a flying career while nurturing a family, I say, go for it! Nothing is better than fulfilling your dreams while setting an example of success for your children.

I love flying, and am proud to have pursued my dream. From my experiences, I hope my children learn to grab hold of their dreams and ride them as far as they can go.

I have truly enjoyed being a mom and watching these little creatures, woven together with recognizable threads from our families, blossoming into beautiful individuals, while receiving their unconditional love. I think I learned how to truly love from my children.

· ·

"We do not need magic to transform our world; we carry all the power we need inside ourselves already: we have the power to imagine better."

· ·

—J. K. Rowling, Harvard Commencement Speech, June 5, 2008

Rank:	Coast Guard Lieutenant Commander
Years Served:	19
Current Military Status:	Active Duty
Number of Children:	2

Lauren (Felix) Cox

MH-65C *Dolphin*

M Y CLOSEST ASSOCIATION WITH THE MILITARY GROWING UP WAS MY GRANDFATHER, AN AIR FORCE B-24 BOMBER NAVIGATOR AND TAIL gunner, who flew in World War II. Since he died when I was young, my most vivid memory is a picture of him dressed in his uniform at my grandma's house.

My high school basketball coach had attended the Coast Guard Academy for two years, and recommended that I apply. I wanted something different from the typical college experience, so I applied during my last year of high school, and started the academy the summer after graduation.

The Coast Guard Academy's main focus was *going to sea*. The only time aviation was mentioned, literally, was during the graduation flyovers performed by Coast Guard fixed-wing aircraft.

When I graduated in 1999, there was no other option for a first tour but to go to sea. Off I went, to Coast Guard Cutter *Polar Sea,* affectionately called "Polar Roller." Stationed in Seattle, I deployed on *Polar Sea* twice to the South Pole. Two aviation detachments were also onboard the cutter, each consisting of pilots and aircrew with two HH-65A helicopters. Interested in the aviation mission, I qualified as a helicopter control officer and landing signals officer—pretty much as close as I could get to the helicopter without being part of the detachment.

Pilots and flying intrigued me, so I submitted a package for flight school and was accepted. I attended the Navy's flight school in Pensacola, Florida, in 2001. Flight training wasn't as easy as I thought it would be. I actually got airsick on my first three flights, and we were only flying straight and level! But I wanted my dad to be proud of me.

I remember struggling to learn how to land, and my instructor asked me if I was afraid of the ground. Funny question, I thought, so I said no. He said, "Well, you should be." I guess my approaches were a tad bit too low for his liking.

After initial training in the T-34C *Turbo Mentor,* or, as we liked to call it, the "Tormentor," I chose to fly helicopters (helos). When I completed the Navy's TH-57 helo training, one of the most exciting and satisfying days in my life was graduation—my dad pinned on my wings. The Coast Guard assigned me to fly the HH-65A *Dolphin.*

I learned to fly the *Dolphin,* and started my first operational Coast Guard tour as a pilot in North Bend, Oregon. Typical missions were fishery patrols, medical evacuations, search-and-rescue for lost hikers and boaters, and lots of training flights.

After four years at North Bend, I transferred to an air station at Humboldt Bay in McKinleyville, California, in the summer of 2006. Again I flew the HH-65A, primarily flying fisheries enforcement and search and rescue. The flying weather at Humboldt Bay, however, presented more challenges compared to North Bend, and fog was always an issue.

During one duty night, while I was an aircraft commander, my helicopter crew responded to a stricken sailing vessel in forty- to fifty-foot seas fifty miles off the Pacific coast. As we arrived on scene in our HH-65C *Dolphin,* the winds were whipping at forty-five to fifty knots, and the huge waves were knocking the small sailboat from side to side with incredible intensity. I knew the rescue would be difficult, especially at night. We lowered a rescue swimmer Into the water with the helicopter's

Lauren and her oldest daughter, Andreya (4 months old), in 2005 in front of a Coast Guard HH-65A Dolphin at Air Station Group/Air Station North Bend, Oregon.

rescue cable. He swam over to the boat and loaded the stranded boater into the rescue basket. Several months later, my crew was awarded the *Rotor & Wing Magazine*'s Public Service 2007 Above and Beyond the Call Award.

Initially, when I first joined the squadron at Humboldt Bay, I was the only woman. The next woman didn't come until my third year there, and she only stayed six months. Looking back, there are very few times when I felt different because I was either the only female or one of the only female pilots at my unit.

I recently transferred to the *dreaded* desk job—a staff tour. But this job will give my growing family a little stability.

I had met my husband, Andrew, during my North Bend, Oregon, tour. My landlady's friend, Martha, set us up on a blind date. Andrew and I became good friends, and I got to know his eleven-year-old son, AJ, who lived with him. I knew within a few months that he was the one for me—I was smitten! In addition to being very handsome, he is so darn nice, and he also makes me relax

and enjoy the moment. Exactly one year after we met, we were married.

We decided to have our first child as soon as possible; however, I didn't think I'd get pregnant as quickly as I did. I flew up until my third trimester, and finally delivered my daughter, Andreya, one week following her scheduled due date. I took the six weeks of military maternity leave, followed by two weeks of my own personal leave.

It surprised me how quickly my work attitude changed after having my daughter—I no longer lingered at work. I also didn't volunteer for any exciting cross-countries or temporary assignments elsewhere.

Shortly after we had moved to Humboldt Bay, in 2006, I found out I was pregnant again, and this time with twins. I flew until I was five months pregnant, and then took myself off flight status.

My twins were born unexpectedly, one month early—my older twin, Laura, was born in the front seat of our Pontiac Grand Am, and my youngest, Albina, while I was on the gurney being put into the awaiting ambulance.

217

Both birth certificates reflect the place of birth as 500 yards north of mile marker 81 on Highway 101, with my husband and me as the attending physicians. Unbelievably, I had no idea I was in labor!

Returning to work was challenging—at one point, the twins were going to one daycare and my other daughter to another. Sometimes I would have a night flight, and then would have to try and arrange night care, because Andrew worked part of the week out of town. There were times I had to cancel flights, or beg someone else to cover for me, because either the kids were sick or their sitter was, or I couldn't get someone to watch the kids for that night flight. Even so, I always wanted a big family, and we are now expecting our fifth child.

I love to fly, and I love to save lives. If you've never experienced the adrenaline rush of waking up at two a.m. to the sound of the search-and-rescue alarm—there's nothing like it. The love of flying sometimes comes in second to the feeling of satisfaction of doing good and being able to say, "I did that."

I have loved my career as a Coast Guard pilot, but I love being a mom even more. Maybe I will fly again, maybe I won't, but I will still be a mom!

Mom to Mom:

The thing that surprised me the most about being a mom is how a child stops and smells the roses, and gets excited over the simplest thing. As a mom, you see the world through your children's eyes and watch as simple pleasures light up their faces.

I want my girls to always follow their dreams, and to not let anyone tell them they can't do something because they are girls. Young kids have such ambition and excitement about what they want to do when they grow up. In their eyes, their future is limitless. I never want to see that change.

I want my daughters to grow up to be strong, independent women who know their self-worth, and know their mom and dad will always love them for who they are.

**Yesterday is history.
Tomorrow is a mystery.
Today is a gift.
That's why it's called the present.**

—Alice Morse Earle

Rank:	Coast Guard Lieutenant Commander
Years Served:	11
Current Military Status:	Active Duty
Number of Children:	5

Kristy (Horvath) Kiernan

HU-25 *Falcon Jet*

I WAS BORN IN AUSTRALIA TO IMMIGRANT PARENTS, REFUGEES FROM THE FAILED ANTI-COMMUNIST HUNGARIAN REVOLUTION OF 1956. IN 1973, MY father was offered the chance to complete his medical residency in California, and we set off for America, our land of opportunity. In 1979, my father transferred to the Bronx Veteran's Administration Hospital, and we started our new lives in New York.

On a rainy day, I picked up a favorite childhood book, *Charlie Brown's Super Book of Questions and Answers.* One question jumped out: "What is a cosmonaut?" The answer read, "A cosmonaut is a Russian astronaut. The word *astronaut* comes from Greek words meaning *sailor among the stars.*" I was captivated by the romance of the phrase, and I was certain I had found my calling.

My interest in space soon expanded to include all of aviation. A few years later, when my older sister sent me a pamphlet about Brown University's flying club, I knew I had found the right college.

I took my first flying lesson on September 28, 1987, and I loved it even more than I expected. As I prepared to graduate from college, I believed my road to the National Aeronautics and Space Administration (NASA) lay in the military. Only test pilot school graduates could become astronaut pilots, and only the military sent people to test pilot school. But I also knew I would not be comfortable with some of the missions I might be asked to perform. However, when I found out about Coast Guard aviation, I knew I'd found the perfect fit.

Three months after graduating from college, I found myself at Coast Guard officer candidate school in Yorktown, Virginia, thoroughly unprepared for military life. After seventeen weeks of school, which I enjoyed much more in retrospect than at the time, I was commissioned a Coast Guard ensign.

Flight school in Pensacola, Florida, was a dream come true. I couldn't believe my good fortune. I was with the best of the best, and I could not have been happier. There were few women in flight school, so we all knew each other and looked out for one another.

After flight school, I was fortunate enough to get my first choice, the Coast Guard's *Falcon,* a jet based out of Coast Guard Air Station Miami, the world's busiest air-sea rescue unit. It was an incredible first tour, and I flew primarily search-and-rescue and law-enforcement missions.

My next set of orders was to Mobile, Alabama, where I flew a variety of missions, including search-and-rescue, fisheries conservation, and environmental protection. While the location was less glamorous, the search-and-rescue mission was quite rewarding. One night, we were called out to look for two teenage brothers who had failed to return home from a fishing trip. Their dad was monitoring our radio calls from the marina, and you could hear the agony in his voice whenever he made a transmission. We were already on our second bag of gas, the weather was bad and getting worse, and still none of our assets had found anything.

Around two in the morning, we were on the last leg of our last search area, and suddenly I saw a pinprick of red light in the otherwise complete darkness. The boys had seen the lights from our aircraft and lit off a handheld flare. The relief in their dad's voice when we told him that his sons were coming home was something I will never forget.

Kristy and her family Christmas-tree shopping, December 2008.

The *Falcon 20* is the most beautiful airplane ever built, and flying a *Falcon* on search and rescue was the most wonderful experience I will probably ever have. Every single time I climbed into that airplane and settled into that familiar seat, I felt like I was coming home. The airplane was an extension of me, and when I walked away from it after a flight, if no one was looking, I'd give it a kiss goodnight.

Although I loved being operational and flying in support of Coast Guard missions, I also wanted the challenge of being an instructor pilot, and I received just such an assignment. I loved the opportunity to become a technical expert on the *Falcon* as well as the challenge of teaching students fresh out of flight school. I spent two wonderful years there, writing course materials and teaching student aviators.

One day, near the end of my first flying tour in Miami, I stopped into a Subway sandwich shop near the air station to pick up lunch. As I was leaving, a young man held the door for me and said, "Excuse me, are you a naval aviator?" I explained I was a Coast Guard aviator, and we had a lovely, though brief, conversation. I told him my name and where I worked, and the next day, he called my office. I was typically never there, as I was usually flying or deployed, but that day I picked up the phone, and we talked for longer than you should when you are technically at work.

Pete, I discovered, served in the Navy as a supply officer, and had recently left active duty and moved to Miami for an accounting job. He was funny, kind, adventurous, and smart. In short, everything I had been looking for, and more. We dated for a year, and then married just before I transferred to Mobile.

When we decided to have children, we wanted to have one parent at home. Because I absolutely loved my job, we decided Pete would stay home for at least the first two years, while I stayed on active duty. Our daughter, Abigail, was born in July 2000, and, in October, I went back to work with a surprisingly heavy heart. When we decided to add another child to our family, I knew it was time to make a hard decision. I had always loved my job and, ironically, just as I was contemplating my future, the Coast Guard solicited applicants for two absolute dream jobs—a NASA internship, and, unbelievably, test pilot school. My childhood dream was within my grasp.

But my life had changed, and with it my priorities. I gave it a great deal of thought and prayer, but my decision was never really in doubt. I left active duty after the birth of our second daughter, Claire, in 2002, and I have always been grateful that *I* got to choose my future. It was as if God put me at the crossroads and said, "You decide." I did, and if I ever come to regret my decision, I will always take comfort in knowing it was I who made the choice.

Not long after Claire was born, we decided our family was not quite complete, so we began the process of adopting a child from China. The adoption process was long and difficult, but by the summer of 2007, we were finally getting close.

Mom to Mom:

Almost everything about being a mom surprised me. I was surprised by how much work it was, surprised by how hard it was, very surprised by how humbling it is. But I think what surprised me most is how much I enjoyed it. I'm not really a kid person, so I was quite surprised by how much I love it. I was also surprised by how much it changed me as a person. Being a mom is by FAR the most challenging thing I've ever done. Having children has been the greatest adventure of my life, and, to quote Albus Dumbledore, "Between you and me, that's saying something."

Just a few months before we hoped to leave for China, we found out I was pregnant. Pete and my dad went to China in October 2007 and brought back our beautiful daughter, Anna. Three months later, I delivered our son, Andrew. Our family is now, without a doubt, more than complete!

Although I love being home with our children, I miss aviation and its constant challenges. Fortunately, I was accepted into the inaugural class of Embry-Riddle Aeronautical University's Ph.D. in Aviation program. I hope to earn my Ph.D. just as our youngest child starts school, and then return full time to aviation, my first love.

I hope, through my example, my children learn to follow their dreams, wherever that may lead them. But, most of all, my hope for all of them is that they always stay close to God and try to do His will. There is no greater blessing I could ask for, for them or for us.

> **"God didn't tell us how it would end; he just told us what to do."**
>
> —C.S. Lewis (Paraphrased from *The Silver Chair*)

Rank:	Coast Guard Lieutenant Commander
Years Served:	12
Current Military Status:	Separated
Number of Children:	4

Susan (Ator) Maitre

C-130 *Hercules*

M Y CHILDHOOD, THOUGH REMARKABLE FOR ITS SIMPLICITY, WAS UNREMARKABLE IN TERMS OF MEMORIES AND INFLUENCES. THE MIDDLE child between two brothers, I was raised in the same Baltimore neighborhood for seventeen years. For college, I had two options—apply somewhere I had a good chance of getting a scholarship, or choose a private or Ivy League school and then spend the next ten years repaying tuition debt. I chose conservatively, winning a four-year scholarship to the University of Maryland.

Five years and two undergraduate degrees later, I was bored with job prospects and looking for adventure. I stumbled upon the Coast Guard. Despite, and perhaps because of, my mother's insistence that I couldn't join the military—I "didn't know how to follow rules"—I applied and was accepted to the Coast Guard's officer candidate school.

Four months later, I was commissioned an ensign, and was extremely fortunate to get a pilot slot right out of officer candidate school. Overall, I really enjoyed flight training, but it was *very* challenging, and I worked hard to learn the basic skills needed to take off, control, and land the aircraft.

Upon completion of flight school in 1997, I reported to C-130 training, and then to my first Coast Guard air station in Hawaii. The unit's primary mission was search-and-rescue and law-enforcement, with a commission to protect 14.2 million square miles of open ocean, atolls, and island nations.

Saving lives and getting to travel made flying fantastic and extremely rewarding. I remember my first launch as a new aircraft commander. We were requested to fly to Acapulco, Mexico, in support of hurricane relief. After accomplishing our mission, our aircraft broke down, and we ended up performing a double prop change in Acapulco. As the only crewmember who spoke Spanish, navigating foreign clearances and airfield equipment shortages to support our mission was logistically challenging for me. But two weeks in a resort town also kept the crew in high spirits, mitigating the long, hot workdays.

After this tour in Hawaii ended in 2001, I coordinated orders to co-locate with my husband, Ben, whom I had been married to for two years. I got orders to NAS Whiting Field, Florida, as an instructor pilot to train new flight students in T-34s at VT-3, the same squadron where I learned to fly several years earlier. My husband was assigned to Hurlburt Field, Florida, but ended up deployed to the Middle East much of the time. During my VT-3 tour, in 2002, I was recognized as instructor pilot of the year.

By now, I felt very satisfied professionally, and decided I was ready for a more personal challenge. I got pregnant in the fall of 2003. With the flight surgeon's consent, I flew until my third trimester. I still remember when I felt my baby's first kick—as formation lead returning home from the practice area. I mentioned it to my student over the radio, but I don't think he appreciated it as much as I did.

We were up for our next set of orders, and, fortunately, Ben received an exchange tour with the Coast Guard to fly C-130s in Clearwater, Florida. I got similar orders, so we essentially worked alongside each other. We moved to Clearwater when I was six months pregnant, and I was grounded for the remainder of my pregnancy.

After having my son, Sam, I took a total of eight weeks off before returning to work. As much as I hated the time away from my new baby, it was a relief when I

Sue, husband Ben, and oldest son Sam (3 months old), 2004, sitting on the throttle quadrant of a C-130, when Ben and Sue were both flying the C-130 during a joint assignment in Clearwater, Florida.

had to stand overnight duty and got the most continuous sleep I'd had in more than two months! To provide some stability at home, we hired a live-in au pair when Sam was three months old. Live-in care was invaluable when our schedules changed hourly.

There were days that were just plain difficult, especially when one of us was deployed and the flight scheduler called, as he did often, to ask us to pick up additional flight duties. Clearwater is a very busy air station with a lot of night flying. I was okay if I could parse together seven or eight hours of sleep in a night. But, with getting up every three hours to feed Sam in addition to flying several times a week all night, sleep deprivation became the norm. I remember waking some mornings and just sitting in the bathroom, crying from exhaustion. But that only lasted a year and a half.

Ben's next set of orders were to the Naval Postgraduate School in Monterey, California. I had just

gotten pregnant with our second child, and there was no Coast Guard job that would allow me to co-locate with Ben to Monterey. Thankfully, I qualified for a temporary separation from the Coast Guard, a program offered to members who have completed their obligated service. The program would allow me to take two years off—transfer to the Coast Guard Reserve—and then return to the active-duty Coast Guard. As much as I loved my career, every part of me felt it was right to take this two-year break, to keep our new family together. I looked forward to departing the rat race to spend a few years with my young children. Shortly before we moved to Monterey, we had our second boy, Max.

After twelve years in the Coast Guard, it was definitely an adjustment to be a full-time mom, and it wasn't at all the break I thought it would be. I worked harder in those two years than I ever had before. But from what I learned of life and parenting, I know I'm a better mom and Coastie.

After Monterey, Ben received orders to Tampa, to MacDill AFB. While I loved my time home with my boys, much of me still longed to return to the challenges of the Coast Guard, to the flying and professional growth.

I returned to the active-duty Coast Guard in August 2008, and requalified to fly search-and-rescue and law-enforcement patrol. Six months later, I upgraded to C-130 aircraft commander, and we're back to juggling deployments, school, and nannies.

My husband was recently promoted, and hopes to eventually become a squadron commander. And, more than ever, I sense I will shoulder the greater burden of career sacrifice as the next assignment cycle rolls around. It's something of a bitter pill. But when folks ask me why I would want to deal with our disparate military flying careers, I just tell them, "I'm living the dream." And I believe it.

My girlfriends and I talk about what it takes to be a mom and a professional and hold it all together. Perfection is unrealistic. Despite this obvious reality, there is considerable pressure to be a fabulous mom, hold the family together, keep a clean house, and maintain a successful career.

Mom to Mom:
Being a mom is not hard, but being the mom my boys deserve is some of the hardest work I've ever done.

Why stay in the military? I can't think of any job I'd want other than the one I have. We do good things. We work with exceptional people. We are challenged daily to improve ourselves. While my husband's career and mine may not neatly align, we both want to stick it out as long as we can, and keep the family together.

We love each other, but our country and duties run a close second. I love being a mom, because it reminds me every day what really matters, and what really doesn't. The bottom line is really very simple: Between the grins and giggles and hugs and kisses, I realize that my husband and I are molding these sweet creatures into remarkable lives of their own.

Aim for the moon! Of course you might not get there but you can grab a few stars along the way.

Rank:	Coast Guard Lieutenant Commander
Years Served:	15
Current Military Status:	Active Duty
Number of Children:	2

Aviatrix Mom Tales

It was very amusing to watch passengers' faces as a very pregnant pilot (me) waddled out to the tarmac (flight line) and climbed into the cockpit.

—*Susan Allen*

As part of a C-9 aircraft crew, I flew German dignitaries across the country. A journalist took particular interest in me because he had never flown with a female pilot. I joked with him that it was my first flight (although it wasn't), and even posed with him for photos. He said he wanted to prove to his mother that girls can pilot airplanes.

—*Susan Allen*

I was flying in the back of the F-14 *Tomcat* over New York City and handling navigation and communications. After I checked in with the local air traffic controller, there was a long pause and the controller asked, "Are you in the F-14?" I jokingly responded, "When I took off, I was in an F-14." The controller said, "But you are a woman." I quipped back, "I know," and from there we had a very comical conversation about a woman flying in an F-14.

—*Barbara Bell*

It's much the same wherever I fly: we land, people watch us exit from the cockpit, and they still have to ask, "You fly helicopters?"

—*Victoria Cain*

When I was flying a mission out of Christchurch, New Zealand, as a C-141 pilot, we took some of the Air Mobility Command leadership with us on a mission. The night before the mission, we had a social at the hotel for the generals to meet the crews. The two-star general came over to the group I was standing with (three guys and me) to chat. We all shook his hand and told him our names, since we were in civvies and wore no patches or nametags. He asked if we were active duty or reserve (we always had crews from both squadrons flying the ice missions). I said, "Keith and I are active duty, and Steve and Joe are reservists." The general then asked what crew positions we were. Keith said, "I'm a nav (navigator) and they're pilots," gesturing to the rest of us.

The general looked right at me and said, "And what do you do?" as if there was no way I could be a pilot or a nav. My buddies just cringed, wondering how I would react. I replied politely, "I'm a pilot, too, sir." To this, the general then asked me, "So, will tomorrow be your first time to Antarctica...?" (I could almost hear him thinking, "...little girl.")

By now, my buddies were trying not to burst out laughing. I looked right at the two-star, raised my eyebrows, and said, "Actually, no, sir. I'll be your aircraft commander tomorrow, and will be instructing these two to certify them for ice missions," gesturing to my two reserve pilot friends.

Needless to say, the man just stared at me for a moment. Then he smiled and said, "Well, I guess I'll see you all tomorrow morning," and walked over to another group of aircrew.

Naturally, my three crewmates thought this was hysterical, and had a good time ribbing me about it afterward. I played along, and told them he was probably just jet-lagged from the long flight from the U.S. to Christchurch!

—*Susan Foy*

During my tour with the Marine Corps, I was the only female aviator, and we had no female aircrew or female officers. When it was time for sexual harassment training (at that time required by the Navy but not being done in the Marines), my commanding officer ordered a stand-down day and made me give the training to the entire squadron. It did not go over very well. Cured me of my fear of public speaking, though, because I can't imagine a tougher subject in front of a tougher crowd.

—*Catherine Gillies*

The Air Force allowed military retirees to travel with us on our international flights, on a space-available basis. The first time I had the opportunity to fly such a mission, I stood by the door while our passengers boarded. One fellow looked at me and said, "I did not realize the KC–135 had a stewardess." I said, "No, sir, I am not your stewardess. I am your captain." He looked at me, shook his head, and said, "Are you sure?" I guess he was convinced by the end of our flight, as he thanked me on our arrival in England.

—*Kelly Hamilton*

When I first began flying, a woman's voice on the radio was not very common. One night while flying, I tried to check in on a very busy Seattle air traffic control frequency. A few minutes went by with no response, so I tried again. This time the controller responded, "Everybody stand by. I want to talk to the lady." This moment in time was later memorialized in an aviation cartoon by Bob Stevens.

—*Kelly Hamilton*

The funniest times for me are when older gentlemen don't believe it when I say I am a fighter pilot and that is my airplane parked out there. They kind of nod their heads and mutter something, and there is no understanding in their eyes. I often think they are saying to themselves, "Crazy lady. Clearly that is her husband's jet. Why does she dress up in a flight suit and pretend to be the pilot?"

—*Jamie Johnson*

When I deployed to Iraq, I took my breast pump with me. (Yes, I wanted to return home a nursing mom, the way I had left.) I was the only female in my crew, and upon landing in Bagram, Afghanistan, I informed everyone that the ground time would have to include a visit to the

"ladies lounge." Unfortunately, that was a long, dark walk through streets made of boulders, looking for an access point in the dead of night.

Finally, I found a trailer where I could plug in my electric pump, only to shut down all the lights immediately upon turning it on. Knowing we had some electrical compatibility issues, I then had to crawl out in the dark, inform civil engineering that I blew out the bathroom for who-knows-how-many soldiers, and then proceed to the men's bathroom, where I was able to finish on battery backup, after literally scaring several male soldiers out of their wits. (Surely this was not a sight they were used to seeing, but... push had come to shove.)

—*Valerie Kester*

During my tour in the Philippines flying the SH–3 *Sea King* helicopter, I flew over to the Manila International Airport to pick up our new arriving executive officer (second in command of a squadron). As the aircraft commander, I was responsible for the helicopter and the personnel on board. Manila has a very macho male culture, and so when we arrived in Manila, the airport personnel refused to speak to me, a woman. My enlisted crew chief had to do all the talking, since they would not address me or answer my questions. I was bemused but figured if that's what it took to locate the new executive officer, then I'd go with it.

—*Lori Lindholm*

Every time I pulled up onto the flight line of a different base, the ground crew was always shocked to see a WOMAN in the front seat of the mighty F-14 *Tomcat*. Even when they watched me scale the side of the plane and hop down, they would still come over and ask, "Did you really fly that fighter?" ...Ummm, yes, we don't just swap out so the RIO can let me taxi.... (The RIO is the radar intercept officer who flies in the backseat, handling the communications, navigation, and weapons.)

—*Carey Lohrenz*

In my first fighter squadron, I was the only girl. We were all going to a squadron holiday party, and everyone was dressed up. I was wearing lipstick, and one of the lieutenants said, "SHOCK, you can't wear lipstick." (SHOCK is my call sign) When I asked him why, he replied, "You have to decide: you're either a girl or a fighter pilot—you can't be both." I got a good laugh out of that one.

—*Melissa May*

I was the first female F-15E Weapon Systems Officer, so there were a lot of unique situations. The first time I deployed to Aviano AB, Italy, with my squadron, we had to stay in "tent city" on base. The guys all stayed in a couple of big tents right next to each other, but the commander there didn't know where to put me (the only female). They wouldn't let me stay with the rest of the squadron, so they found a broom/equipment closet and cleaned it out for me. It was big enough to fit a cot in it with a little bit of room to slide in next to it. They put a lock on the door, and that was where I was supposed to stay!

Later in my career, when there were a few more females in the F-15E, I was in the 336th Fighting Squadron, the Rockets, and one of my woman pilot friends in the squadron was leaving. When you leave a squadron, you typically get to choose who you want to fly with on your "fini" flight. She chose to fly with me and two other females...it was the first "unmanned" F-15E two-ship!

—*Kelley Marcell*

When I deployed with my F-15E *Strike Eagle* squadron to Incirlik AB, Turkey, there was only one bathroom, so we had a sign on the door to flip between "Men" and "Women." Since there were only two women among the thirty or so men, most of the men didn't pay attention to the sign. My female roommate and I were stuck in the stalls quite a few times, waiting for guys to finish using the urinals.

—*Christine Mau*

My daughters told me that when they met Navy people, they asked the girls how it was to be my daughter, since they viewed me as powerful. My girls couldn't understand. They told me that, to them, I was more like June Cleaver, Beaver's mother. When I took them to work with me for "Take Your Daughter to Work Day," my girls said they saw the transformation, which I was unaware of, that I made every day when I put on my uniform. Too bad I couldn't have exercised some of that power over them when they were teenagers!

—*Jane O'Dea*

There were no female heads (bathrooms) in my first squadron hangar. When I pointed out this shortfall to my commanding officer, he told me I could walk to the next hangar where there was one. The heads were marked "Officers" and "Men." I decided that since I was an officer, it was totally appropriate to use the one marked "Officers." After the first time I walked in on a couple of the officers (stalls had no doors), the commanding officer re-designated them "Men" and "Women."

—*Jane O'Dea*

I was a new C-130 copilot assigned to a crew with a female aircraft commander. We deployed to Nairobi, Kenya, and flew support missions for the U.S. Army, which was involved in joint peacekeeping operations in Kenya.

We were taxiing on one of their airfields when the African man marshaling us attempted to position our aircraft too close (according to Air Force regulations, in our opinion) to a light pole nearby. My aircraft commander chose to taxi a little off from the marshaller's instruction, in order to maintain the required safe distance. It was obvious the marshaller wasn't pleased with our decision.

When we emerged from the airplane, a male squadron mate who had just parked his C-130 prior to and adjacent to us, greeted us with a funny story. The African marshaller who parked us noticed there was a female pilot in one of the seats. He said to our male squadron mate, "Do you have woman pilot in that airplane?" Our squadron mate said, "No, there is not one woman pilot in that plane; there are two!" He said the African marshaller threw his hands up in the air and said, "Aha! No wonder they do not follow my instructions!"

—*Bonnie Paquin*

I was a C-130 aircraft commander, deployed overseas. We landed in Morocco for an overnight stay and, as was the normal procedure, I exited the plane to greet the service personnel, and to confirm the gas and other logistical needs. When I reached out to shake one man's hand, he wouldn't take it. I tried again, and he just sort of nodded to me. After he shook the hand of my flight engineer, I realized he wasn't going to shake my hand because I was a woman. Then he kept asking "to speak to the plane captain." I told him I was the plane captain. He said, "No, no, the plane captain...the person in charge of the plane." He didn't believe that I was the aircraft commander. My co-pilot and navigator, who were both men, came out, and we worked together with this man to confirm our aircraft needs, but that man never accepted that I was, in fact, the plane captain.

—*Bonnie Paquin*

An interesting comment from a Southwest Airlines captain I recently flew with: "You know...you're a pretty good pilot, considering you're a mom and all." I thought I might be offended at first, and then I realized what he was saying was, "Wow, you do an amazing job performing the same tasks I do at work...flying this airplane, studying, keeping current in the books, passing check rides, AND THEN you also go home to run a household—cook, clean, do laundry, pay the bills, wash the dishes, wipe dirty bottoms, dry tears away, take kids to school and practice and doctor appointments, and do homework!" So, I decided it was actually a really big compliment.

—*Bonnie Paquin*

As the first woman F-16 pilot in the Air Force, I got a lot of unusual receptions. Anytime we went on a deployment, I was asked the same questions. I would be in my flight suit at *Red Flag* or *Maple Flag*, wearing my squadron patches and nametag with my wings and an F-16 on it, and guys would ask me, "So, what do you do with the squadron? Or, "Are you the new flight surgeon?" It often took a while to convince others that I was a real live F-16 pilot, and that I flew in combat. It was funny, and kind of sad at the same time. I am happy to report that I didn't leave

that stereotyping behind when I left the military. Flying for Southwest, I am often mistaken for a flight attendant when I check in at the hotel—despite my uniform or leather jacket!

—*Sharon Preszler*

I was the only female in my flight, and the designated flight commander of about fifteen fellow pilots and fifteen students. I had just had my first child when I returned to flight status, still nursing. I had to stand up in front of all the guys on my first day back and announce, "This little black briefcase is a breast pump. Are there any questions?" All I got was thirty red-faced men staring back at me with nothing to say. It was hysterical, and so fun to make those grown men blush!

—*Lori Rasmussen*

I was accepted to flight school without knowing that the minimum height requirement was 5'4", which I happened to be. Nearly all of the men could jump into the UH-1 helicopter and only have to make minor adjustments to the rotor pedals. I, on the other hand, had to scoot the heavy metal seat up as far as it would go, which always seemed to take an inordinate amount of time to get ready—exasperating for my fellow male pilot and a bit humiliating for me at the time.

—*Connie Reeves*

We flew to Malaysia to provide training in air combat maneuvering. When we arrived, the Malays were most surprised to see female pilots in our squadron. At the time, I was working on my adversary qualification, and when we went to brief for the flight, I was with our instructor pilot, "Frog." After the brief, the commanding officer of the Malaysian squadron asked to speak with Frog. Frog came in the ready room a few minutes later and told me there was a problem. The Malaysian commander asked if I was actually flying on the event. Frog said yes and the commander said they would have to cancel. "Why?" Frog asked. Well, if a woman were to beat a Malaysian pilot in air combat maneuvering, even though it was just training, it would be highly embarrassing and would cause him to lose face.

We talked about it and came up with a solution. Since they couldn't tell that it was a woman in the plane once I got suited up, I would fly in the front seat of the TA–4J, and Frog would make all the calls as if he were flying. They would never know. I didn't get upset about this. One, because I was relatively new in the squadron, and two, we were there to not only provide good training for these guys, but we also wanted to keep a good relationship with them. And after all, *I* would know, and that was all that mattered.

We went out and had a great time. We won some engagements, and they won some. Training accomplished, we all headed over to the bar for the debrief. Frog debriefed as if he had flown the airplane the whole time. After we finished, one of the pilots asked us, "Okay, who really flew the plane?" I smiled, and Frog said, "I did, of course!" Knowing he was not being truthful, they proceeded to tease the pilot we flew against for the rest of the night, "You were beaten by a woman!" But it was all in good fun; nobody was offended, least of all me.

—Paula Senn

Before the military, I was a twenty–four–year–old copilot on a nineteen–seat commuter aircraft for American Eagle; it was small enough that we did not have any flight attendants. After the flight, I was saying goodbye to the passengers, and a really angry older woman came up and demanded my name, employee number, and my boss's phone number. It had been a really smooth flight, and I had made a better than average landing. Taken aback by her irate demeanor, I asked what was wrong. "You were up there flirting with that pilot the whole time. You never once came back and served us one thing!" I was able to keep a straight face and happily gave her my boss's phone number. I never set her straight or gave a

head's–up to my chief pilot. I heard later that the conversation was pretty entertaining.

—Heather Sharp-Schlichting

During my first deployment, we were flying over the Mediterranean and had to divert into Turkey to get the aircraft fixed. As we taxied up the Turkish military side of the base, we saw numerous Turkish officers there watching us pull up. I said, "I'm surprised to see so many people out here. They must have never seen an American F–14 before." My RIO (radar intercept officer) just chuckled and said, "Just wait till they see YOU get out of the airplane." Sure enough, when they found out that I was the pilot of the aircraft, their jaws dropped.

—Kerry Smith

One of my favorite memories is from being on a C–130 trip to Pope AFB with another female pilot and, coincidently, a female engineer. This was not a big deal to any of us, since we all viewed ourselves and each other as professionals doing our jobs. We were temporarily assigned to work with the Army, dropping airborne troops out of the back of our C–130. The other pilot was, and still is, a dear friend of mine, and, I have to say, she was the best pilot in our squadron and had a tremendous depth of knowledge about the C–130 systems and mission.

Well, she and I walked around to the back of the airplane to talk with the jumpmaster, as is customary. We were both in our flight suits and leather jackets, carrying our checklists (clearly the pilots). The jumpmaster walked up to us and said, rather nervously and with shifty eyes, "Are you the pilots?" I said, in the same nervous but conspiratorial tone, "Yeah, are you the jumpers?"

—Katharine Yingst

Little Flybys

Amusing quotes and insights from the kids

When my son, Kevin, was almost two years old, we flew on a C-9 aircraft to Alaska as passengers, and I was excited to share the Navy flying experience with my husband and son. My husband, Dan, was suitably impressed. My son, on the other hand, was more excited about riding in a taxi and a bus. He wasn't impressed at all with the plane ride. Flash forward to last year. The mother of one of Kevin's first-grade classmates drives a school bus. My son thinks driving a school bus is the coolest job, and he asked me if I could learn to drive a bus, too. When I told his friend's mother about Kevin's request, and that I used to fly airplanes, she thought it was hysterical! Driving a bus is a skill—the hills, snow and ice, screaming kids—that I will leave to the professionals. It takes a special kind of person to handle that job!

—Susan Allen

My children never knew me or their father in any other occupation, so they never looked at my being an aviator as unusual. However, once when I went home to my parents as a young, high-speed fleet aviator, my father was reluctant to let me cut the grass with his Sears riding lawnmower, for fear that I would hurt myself mowing the very gentle bank in the front yard. I simply looked at him and said, "Dad, do you have ANY idea what I do for a living?"

—Karen Baetzel

My son calls me "mommy captain," to my wholehearted delight. He thinks women flyers are a fact of life and that flying and wearing uniforms are simply what we do.

—Barbara Bell

On the way home from a preschool field trip to the local Air National Guard base, my son said, "When I grow up, I'm gonna be a pilot in the Guard, and we can go on trips, and you can call me 'son.'"

—Lisa Berente

"No, Zoli, only girls can fly," said my four-year-old daughter, Courtney, to her three-year-old brother, making him get off the toy airplane ride.

—Lisa Berente

My daughter, Brooke, gets lots of exposure to wonderful role models, since many of my female peers are also my best friends. One day, she was sitting next to me, looking at the pictures while I flipped through a copy of *Aviation for Women*, the magazine published by Women in Aviation, International. She looked at me and asked, "Mommy, is it okay if boys fly helicopters, too?" How's that for a fresh perspective? I'm grateful that I can offer her an environment that nurtures her confidence.

—Liz Booker

Wherever we are, when my daughter sees a *Black Hawk* helicopter, she says, "There is Mommy's *Black Hawk*! There is Mommy's *Black Hawk*!" So, they are all mine; I own the entire fleet!

—Victoria Cain

Whenever my husband or I had to leave on a flying trip, my children asked, "Who's going to be home, you or

Dad? When Dad is home, dinner is *not* like when you are home."

—*Barb Garwood*

My oldest loves career day when I can come to her class and she can show me off to her friends.

—*Catherine Gillies*

I will never forget when my son's daycare provider told me that he asked one of the new kids, "What does your mommy fly?"

—*Kristin Greentree*

When my son was three years old, I was driving him to daycare, and I asked him what he wants to do when he grows up. He said very simply, "I want to fly Mommy's airplane and Daddy's helicopter." I replied, "Wow, Austin, that sounds great. I would love to fly Daddy's helicopter, too. That would be so fun." He quickly responded with, "No, Mommy, girls don't fly helicopters!" I found it quite humorous that a little boy thought girls could only fly fighter jets! I tried to convince him that lots of girls flew helicopters too, but he remained skeptical for a couple of years!

—*Kristin Greentree*

"Mommy, don't leave me! Take me with you when you go flying!"

—*Jamie Johnson*

When my son attended preschool, his class frequently had show and tell. I encouraged him several times to take one of my flight helmets. Finally he said, in an exasperated voice, "Mom, I don't want to take your helmet. I want to take my Transformer watch." Uh, okay....

—*Linda Maloney*

My son says that "flying is women's work, but my mommy will make an exception for me."

—*Jean O'Brien*

"Mommy, for Halloween, I am going to dress like you. I want to wear a pilot costume!"

—*Lori Rasmussen*

When my daughter was in middle school and had friends over, sometimes during discussions I would pop into the living room from the kitchen and say, "When I was a helicopter pilot...," only to be greeted by my daughter saying, "Enough already about helicopters!" Now, however, just like her dad, she finds that talking about my being a helicopter pilot, and one of the first women helicopter pilots, is a reliable conversational icebreaker.

—*Connie Reeves*

My twelve-year-old son had a list of things he wanted to do in his life. Some realistic, some not. One of them was to be a professional baseball player. Knowing how the Minor League can be, I said, "You don't want to just travel around with a bunch of men, do you?" He answered, "Well, that's what you do...travel around with a bunch of men."

—*Louise Reeves*

My son thinks every mom flies. When he meets a new friend, he will say, "My mom flies helicopters. What does your mom fly?"

—*Tami Reynolds*

One day my three-and-a-half-year-old son, Harrison, asked me if I could fly my helicopter to the moon. When I told him, "No, but I can fly to 10,000 feet," he replied, "Wow! Can you see God up there?" I responded, "Every day I see evidence that He's been there!"

—*Shari Scott*

My family was trail riding with friends in a remote area. A four-ship of C-130s was conducting a low-level training mission and flew overhead. One of my friends asked what type of aircraft was flying overhead. Before I could answer, my son piped up and said, "That's the four fans of freedom, baby!"

—*Heather Sharp-Schlichting*

My son, Marshal, nine years old, and I were eating lunch together at his school, and one of his friends said, "So, your daddy is a Southwest Airlines pilot." Marshal responded, "BOTH my parents are Southwest Airlines pilots, and that is pretty cool." I was taken aback by his response, because typically he is a humble little guy with a quiet nature.

—*Tammie Jo Shults*

"Mommy, whose helicopter is faster, yours or Daddy's?!"

—*Jenny Tinjum*

I was dressed in my uniform and leather jacket, traveling with my youngest daughter. She looked at me and said, "Don't you feel really cool?"

—*Margie Varuska*

Glossary

AB	Air Base
AFB	Air Force Base
Boat	Term used by military personnel to describe an aircraft carrier
Boneyard	Storage area for aircraft that are retired from service
COD	Carrier Onboard Delivery. Aircraft that ferry personnel, mail, and high-priority cargo (like replacement parts) on and off a naval ship (typically an aircraft carrier).
Det	Detachment
Dogfighting	Art of maneuvering a combat aircraft to attain a position from which an attack can be made on another aircraft
ECMO	Electronic Countermeasures Officer. NFO assigned to fly in the EA-6B *Prowler* aircraft.
Fini flight	Final flight at a unit or squadron
Firstie	Senior-year student at Air Force Academy
Fleet aviators	Aviator in the fleet, in operational squadron or unit
Herbie	White-out conditions
JROTC	Junior Reserve Officers' Training Corps—high school program
MCAS	Marine Corps Air Station
NAS	Naval Air Station
Nav	Navigator. Aviator responsible for an aircraft's weapon systems employment and tasked with copilot-type duties depending on the type, model and series of aircraft
NFO	Naval Flight Officer. Officer in the Navy or Marine Corps specializing in airborne weapons and sensor systems. NFOs are not pilots, but may perform many copilot functions, such as navigation and communications, depending on the aircraft
NROTC	Naval Reserve Officers' Training Corps—college-based, officer commissioning program
Plebe	First-year student at the Naval Academy
Primary flight training	Navy's initial flight training
RIO	Radar Intercept Officer
ROTC	Reserve Officers' Training Corps—college-based, officer commissioning program
SAR	Search and Rescue
Slick	No weapons or stores carried on the aircraft
Sorties	Flights or missions
Tarmac	Airport runway or flightline

TOPGUN	Popular name for the United States Navy Strike Fighter Tactics Instructor program
TPS	Test Pilot School
Undergraduate pilot training (UPT)	Air Force initial flight training course
VFW	Veterans of Foreign Wars
WASP	Women Airforce Service Pilots
WSO	Weapon Systems Officer/Weapons & Sensors Officer. Aviator directly involved in the air operations and weapon systems of an aircraft. The WSO integrates with the pilot to collectively achieve and maintain crew efficiency, situational awareness, and mission effectiveness.

Photo Credits

Barb Bell's photograph by Christopher W. Wells, Christopher Wells Photography.

Victoria Cain's photograph by Melanie Mauer.

Sarah Burrow's photograph by Kris Nieder, San Diego Family Photography.

Kelly Goggin's photograph by the Department of Defense.

Christine Mau's photograph by Gina Marie, www.photographybyginamarie.com. (Title page photo)

Linda Maloney's photograph by Alisa Albers, Timeless Treasures Photography. (Biography page photo)

Lida Munz's photograph by the Department of Defense.

Jen Nothelfer's photograph by Caroline McGath, The Portrait Cottage.

Lori Rasmussen's photograph by Stacy Schaub, Heart Photography.

Tammie Jo Schults's photograph by one of her squadron plane captains.

Katharine Yingst's photograph by Alexis Rubenstein, Red Stone Photography.

Biography

Linda Maloney

LINDA MALONEY, ONE OF THE FIRST WOMEN IN U.S. HISTORY TO JOIN A COMBAT MILITARY FLYING SQUADRON, IS A RETIRED MILITARY AVIATOR AND officer and a recipient of numerous military awards, including the distinguished Air Medal for combat, awarded for flights flown over Southern Iraq in support of the no-fly zone during her deployment to the Arabian Gulf. Along with her passion to share the stories from *Military Fly Moms*, Linda is a motivational speaker highlighting the importance of passing down a lasting legacy to future generations. She is also actively involved in several mentoring programs in which she encourages young people, especially young women, to reach beyond the boundless ceiling of success. She recently started My Mom Flies, a women/mom-focused company, which encourages and supports moms who are managing family and career priorities while striving to achieve balance and margin in their lives. She currently lives in Rhode Island with her husband, Dan, and two young sons.

18144427R00136

Made in the USA
Charleston, SC
18 March 2013